The Transformation of War

THE
TRANSFORMATION
OF WAR

Martin van Creveld

THE FREE PRESS

New York   London   Toronto   Sydney   Tokyo   Singapore

The Free Press
A Division of Simon & Schuster Inc.
1230 Avenue of the Americas
New York, N.Y. 10020

Printed in the United States of America

printing number

4 5 6 7 8 9 10

Library of Congress Cataloging-in-Publication Data

van Creveld, Martin L.
    The transformation of war / Martin van Creveld.
      p.   cm.
    Includes bibliographical references and index.
    ISBN 0-02-933155-2
    1. Military art and science—History—20th century. 2. Military art and science—History—19th century. 3. War. 4. World politics—1945-   5. World politics—1900–1945. 6. World politics—19th century. 7. Military history, Modern—20th century. 8. Military history, Modern—19th century.   I. Title.
U42.V36   1991
355.02′09′04—dc20   90–47093
                                                CIP

To my children
May they never have to fight

Contents

Introduction:
What, Why, How

The present volume has a purpose; namely, to address some of the most fundamental problems presented by war in all ages: by whom it is fought, what it is all about, how it is fought, what it is fought for, and why it is fought. These questions are by no means new, and indeed merely to list the answers to them that have been given by various people at various times and places would be tantamount to a record of civilization. No doubt many readers will also regard some of these questions as too philosophical, even irrelevant to the "practical" business of waging war. However, it is axiomatic that no human activity can really take place, let alone be carried out successfully, without a thorough understanding of the principles involved. Therefore, finding correct answers to them is vitally important.

The present volume also has a message—namely, that contemporary "strategic" thought about every one of these problems is fundamentally flawed; and, in addition, is rooted in a "Clausewitzian" world-picture that is either obsolete or wrong. We are entering an era, not of peaceful economic competition between trading blocks, but of warfare between ethnic and religious groups. Even as familiar forms of armed conflict are sinking into the dustbin of the past, radically new ones are raising their heads ready to take their place. Already today the military power fielded by the principal developed societies in both "West" and "East" is hardly relevant to the task at hand; in other words, it is more illusion than substance. Unless the societies in question are willing to adjust both thought and action to the rapidly changing new realities, they are likely to reach the point where they will no longer be capable of employing organized violence at all. Once this situation comes about, their continued survival as cohesive political entities will also be put in doubt.

This work aims at providing a new, non-Clausewitzian framework for thinking about war, while at the same time trying to look into its future. Accordingly, its structure is as follows. Chapter I, "Contemporary War," explains why modern military force is largely a myth and why our ideas about war have reached a dead end. Chapter II, "By Whom War Is Fought," discusses the relationship between war, states, and armies, and a variety of other warfighting organizations that are neither armies nor states. Chapter III, "What War Is All About," examines armed conflict from the point of view of the interaction of might with right. Chapter IV, "How War Is Fought," offers both a description and a prescription for the conduct of strategy at all levels. Chapter V, "What War Is Fought For," investigates the various ends for which collective force can be, and has been, used. Chapter VI, "Why War Is fought," constitutes an inquiry into the causes of war on the individual, irrational, level. Chapter VII, "Future War," analyzes the probable forms of future war from all these points of view and offers some ideas on how it will be fought. Finally, there is a brief postscript called "The Shape of Things to Come." Its task is to tie the strands together and outline the likely nature of war ten, twenty-five, or fifty years hence.

A book is written by a single person but reflects the contributions of many minds. Those involved in the present one include Moshe Ben David, Mats Bergquist, Menachem Blondheim, Marianne and Steve Canby, Seth Carus, Oz Fraenkel, Azar Gatt, Steve Glick, Paula and Irving Glick, Eado Hecht, Ora and Gabi Herman, Kay Juniman, Benjamin Kedar, Greta and Stuart Koehl, Mordechai Lewy, Dalia and Edward Luttwak, Ronnie Max, Leslie and Gabriele Pantucci, Yaffa Razin, Stephanie Rosenberg, Joyce Seltzer, Darcy and David Thomas. For inspiration, friendship, hospitality, or all of these, thank you.

Jerusalem, April 1990

The Transformation of War

CHAPTER
I

Contemporary War

The Military Balance

A ghost is stalking the corridors of general staffs and defense departments all over the "developed" world—the fear of military impotence, even irrelevance.

At present, as during the entire period since World War II, perhaps four-fifths of the world's military power is controlled by a handful of industrialized states: the United States, the Soviet Union, and their allies in NATO and the Warsaw Pact. Between them these states spend over four-fifths of all military funds. They also originate, produce, and field a corresponding share of modern, high-tech, military hardware from tanks to aircraft and from Intercontinental Ballistic Missiles (ICBMs) to submarines. The armed forces of these states, particularly those of the two superpowers, have long served the rest as models and, indeed, as standards by which they evaluate themselves.

The principal military states also "own" perhaps 95 percent of all military expertise, if that can be measured by the number of publications on the subject. They have even managed to turn that expertise into a minor export commodity in its own right. Officers belonging to countries which are not great military powers are regularly sent to attend staff and war colleges in Washington, Moscow, London, and Paris, often paying through the nose for the privilege. On the other hand, the principal powers themselves have sent thousands upon thousands of military "experts" to dozens of third-world countries all over Latin America, Africa, and Asia.

1

The above notwithstanding, serious doubt exists concerning the ability of developed states—both such as are currently "liberating" themselves from communist-domination and such as are already "free"—to use armed force as an instrument for attaining meaningful political ends. This situation is not entirely new. In numerous incidents during the last two decades, the inability of developed countries to protect their interests and even their citizens' lives in the face of low-level threats has been demonstrated time and time again. As a result, politicians as well as academics were caught bandying about such phrases as "the decline of power," "the decreasing utility of war," and—in the case of the United States—"the straw giant."

So long as it was only Western society that was becoming "de-bellicized" the phenomenon was greeted with anxiety. The Soviet failure in Afghanistan has turned the scales, however, and now the USSR too is a club member in good standing. In view of these facts, there has been speculation that war itself may not have a future and is about to be replaced by economic competition among the great "trading blocks" now forming in Europe, North America, and the Far East. This volume will argue that such a view is not correct. Large-scale, conventional war—war as understood by today's principal military powers—may indeed be at its last gasp; however, war itself, war as such, is alive and kicking and about to enter a new epoch. To show that this is so and why it is so is the task of the chapter at hand.

Nuclear War

By far the most important armaments of the principal military powers are, of course, nuclear weapons and their delivery vehicles. From the moment the first bomb was dropped on Japan, its power stood revealed for all to see. From that moment, too, the nuclear arms race got under way, and has lasted to the present day.

Though the first two atomic bombs were comparatively primitive devices, each one was a thousand times more powerful than anything previously employed in war. Ten years had not yet passed since Hiroshima before it became possible to build weapons more powerful than all the devices ever used by man in all his wars since the beginning of history. In 1961 the USSR exploded a monster bomb with an esti-mated yield of 58 megatons, i.e., 58 *million* tons of TNT—a figure that resulted from a scientific miscalculation, or so the Soviets later claimed. By that time, research into the development of yet larger weapons had virtually come to a halt, not because it could not be done, but because in Winston Churchill's words, they would only make the rubble bounce.

The United States was the first country to acquire the bomb, and for four years she held a monopoly on it. In September 1949 that monopoly was broken by Stalin's USSR. The testing of hydrogen bombs by the superpowers in 1952 and 1953 represented an important development, though its significance was nowhere as great as that of the first two bombs. Since then the number of countries fielding nuclear arsenals has continued to grow. Britain, France, China, and India have joined the club, each (except, as far as we know, the last) producing first fission and then fusion devices. A number of other countries, though they have not openly tested nuclear weapons, are widely believed to have them in stock or else to be capable of rapidly assembling them. A still larger number of countries could easily produce the bomb if they wanted to but have no intention of doing so; this being perhaps the first time in history when any number of governments have deliberately chosen not to develop weapons that, from the technical and economic point of view, they could acquire easily enough.

The reluctance of so many states to push ahead towards nuclear weapons becomes readily understandable when one examines the political benefits that do or do not ensue from their possession. Developing a nuclear arms program has put a tremendous strain on the technical and financial resources of poor countries such as China, India, and probably Pakistan. All three either already have the bomb or are on the verge of acquiring it, yet none has been able to translate ownership into significant political advantage. Thus, China has not been able to recover the lost province of Formosa, nor even has been able to "punish" neighboring Vietnam, an incomparably smaller military power. The bomb has not noticeably helped India solve either the problem of Tamil separatism in Sri Lanka, or that of Moslem irredentism in Kashmir. Finally, Pakistani officials in informal talks like to justify their nuclear program by their fear of conquest at the hands of India. They point out that, up to now, no nuclear country has been wiped off the map. This is true enough, but ignores the fact that the number of nonnuclear states that *were* wiped off since 1945 has also been very small.

The political benefits conferred on medium powers such as Britain and France by the possession of nuclear weapons are, if anything, smaller still. The bomb has not helped either country to regain or retain something resembling its former great-power status—in Britain, indeed, one reason why the nuclear disarmament movement has lost much of its original impetus is that nobody cares anyhow. The bomb came too late to prevent the loss of their colonial empires; however, had it come earlier, it could have done precious little to slow down, let alone stop, the disintegration of those empires. Today the nuclear arsenals at their disposal almost certainly cannot prevent these countries' remaining overseas possessions from being occupied by a determined aggressor; this is true even in the case of an aggressor who himself does not have nuclear weapons. For decades on end, the rationale that both countries adduced to justify the money they spend on nuclear weapons has been the need to deter a Soviet attack in case the American guarantee fails. This line of reasoning was plausible, except that, if put into effect, it would lead to national suicide that would be certain, swift, and final.

The superpowers themselves undoubtedly have derived a large part of their status from their uniquely powerful nuclear arsenals. Still, even in their case, translating this status into tangible political benefits has proved problematic. This was already evident in June 1945 when Stalin failed to be properly impressed by President Truman's announcement of the bomb during the Potsdam Conference. During the next four years the American nuclear monopoly failed to stop the Soviets from consolidating their East European Empire; Western observers at the time noted how Soviet foreign minister Molotov contrived to act as if the United States did not have the bomb or, alternatively, as if he had it too. The bomb did not save Czechoslovakia from going communist in 1948. Nor could it prevent China from falling to Mao Tze Dong, an event which for decades was regarded as the single greatest defeat ever suffered by the West in its struggle with world Communism.

Since by that time the Soviet Union also had nuclear arms, year by year the likelihood of their being used declined. During the Korean War Douglas MacArthur wanted to use the bomb against China, only to be fired when he went public with his demands. The United States in 1954–58 repeatedly waved nuclear weapons in front of China's nose, to what effect remains unknown. Next it was Khrushchev's turn to rattle intercontinental missiles which, it later turned out, he did not possess. Perhaps the last time when anybody seriously threatened to use nuclear weapons was during the Cuban Missile Crisis of October 1962. Even then, the manner in which President Kennedy handled the crisis— imposing the blockade, offering Khrushchev a way out by proposing to withdraw American missiles from Turkey, etc.—was designed specifically to ensure, as far as was humanly possible, that nuclear weapons would *not* have to be used. The chances of the President actually ordering that the button be pressed were, in the words of National

Security Adviser MacGeorge Bundy, around one in a hundred. Still, one in a hundred was quite sufficient to give the world a fright which has lasted to the present day. It has helped open the way to a number of agreements—some international, and some bilateral among the super-powers—the purpose of each pact being to limit the weapons, their delivery vehicles, or both.

Having effectively neutralized each other, the superpowers' next discovery was that nuclear weapons do not confer great advantages even in their dealings with countries that do not possess them. Since 1945 both the United States and the USSR have seen their influence subject to many fluctuations, especially in the Third World. The United States first "lost," then "won," a whole series of countries from Egypt to Indonesia and from Somalia to Iraq. For the USSR over the decade and a half since 1973 the process has often worked in reverse: it "lost" Chile and temporarily "gained" Ethiopia—assuming that having one of the world's poorest countries as an ally does, in fact, constitute a gain. To list the dozens upon dozens of cases when, often following a domestic coup, some third-world republic switched alliances from West to East or vice versa would be tedious as well as irrelevant. As far as anyone can determine, *none* of these changes was significantly governed or even influenced by the question of which power, the United States or the USSR, possessed the more powerful nuclear arsenal.

The reason why the political impact of nuclear weapons has been so small is, of course, that nobody has yet come up with a convincing idea as to how a nuclear war could be fought without blowing up the world. This has not been for lack of trying. Attempts to devise a "war-fighting doctrine" got under way during the fifties. Had the realities behind them not been so horrible, in retrospect they would make entertaining reading. This was a period when schoolchildren living in major cities or near military bases all over the Western world were put through nuclear-alarm drills, adapted, as one would expect, from World War II. Upon the alarm being sounded they were made to file out of class into the basement, or else dive under their desks, cover their heads with their hands, and close their eyes. Meanwhile, homeowners were told to dig shelters in their gardens. The shelters had to be stocked with provisions that would last for a few days or weeks until the worst of the radiation was over. Luxury shelters were also advertised, sometimes accompanied by pictures that made them look just like the average American living room magically transferred underground and ren-dered radiation-proof. People in danger of being caught in the open were advised to make advanced note of the nearest available shelter. To be on the safe side they were told to wear light-colored clothes, wide-rimmed hats, and sunglasses.

Nor were the proposed countermeasures confined to the time of the actual attack. Serious strategists spent time calculating that, if the superpowers' populations could be evacuated in time and evenly dispersed over their respective continents (one person per so many square meters) most of them would survive the blast of nuclear weapons. If they also had shallow dugouts they might even live through the initial period of radiation; though how one could deal with the problem of nuclear winter—assuming that this is not just a figment of some scientist's imagination—was a different matter altogether. There was much talk of stockpiling food, medical supplies, fuel, and earthmoving equipment for the postnuclear scene. Perhaps wisely, few countries other than Switzerland ever did much to put these ideas into effect, and even many Swiss find it hard to take them seriously. Nevertheless they gave rise to cautious optimism. During the early sixties in particular it was argued that, given proper preparation, the setback to civilization would not be *too* great. True, a superpower subjected to nuclear attack would be devastated and a sizeable portion of its entire population killed. Still, the reasoning went, given determination and a reasonable amount of preparation, the superpower would recover much of its previous viability within no more than ten (or twenty, or fifty) years after the war. Hopefully, by that time the only remaining sign of the nuclear attack having taken place would be an increased rate of cancer and genetic mutation.

While thinkers strategized and teachers drilled, politico-military leaders were busy devising methods of fighting a nuclear war. As might be expected, their first priority was to ensure a modicum of safety for themselves. Over the years billions were invested in early-warning installations, blast- and radiation-proof bunkers, airborne command centers, and communication networks to link them with each other and with the launching bases. The exact state of these preparations has been shrouded in understandable secrecy. Still, to judge by the relatively well-publicized American program, present-day equipment should be able to offer about twenty minutes' warning before the first warheads hit their targets. Should the first attack, however, be carried out by submarines firing their missiles on so-called depressed trajectories, the warning time would be down to perhaps six or seven minutes.

Theoretically, fifteen minutes should be enough for America's president to be whisked aboard a special aircraft that is kept on constant alert at Bohling Air Force Base, just across the Potomac from Washington, D.C. Forty-six other key officials are also tracked around the clock, and preparations for their evacuation are said to have been made. Some 200 more have the *right* to be transported out of the capital, but only in case the aggressor should be kind enough to launch the offensive during business hours. These preparations notwithstanding, the fact is that not even the president's own survival can be guaranteed in the face of a carefully-planned nuclear first strike. Whether, assuming he has survived, he will then be able to get in touch with whatever retaliatory forces have ridden out the attack—especially submarines and missiles in their silos—is also moot.

Given these problems, there have been many attempts to find ways to make the world safe for nuclear war by imposing limits on it. An early suggestion, raised by Dr. Henry Kissinger among others, was that the nuclear powers agree not to use bombs with a yield greater than 150, or 500, or whatever, kilotons (quite sufficient to deal with any target, given that Hiroshima and Nagasaki were devastated by bombs developing 14 and 20 kilotons respectively). Another bright idea was that they agree to use them only against selected targets, such as military forces, bases, or installations. The attempt to ban the most powerful weapons and avoid cities—the most important targets by far—was, of course, commendable. However, it begged the question as to why belligerents who could reach such an agreement should go to war at all, especially one that threatened to terminate the existence of both. Looking back, one can draw some comfort from the fact that these think-tank brainwaves never seem to have been seriously taken up either by the military or by their political masters. Nor have there ever been formal talks between the superpowers aimed at putting them into effect, an even better indication of their purely speculative nature.

How to conduct a war *with* nuclear weapons was not, however, the only problem confronted by military planners. It was equally important to consider ways and means by which conventional forces could operate *in* such a war and still survive, let alone retain their combat power. In the United States at any rate, the introduction of "tactical" nukes during the fifties led to the so-called "pentomic era." Beginning in the mid-fifties, traditional divisions, normally consisting of three brigades or regiments, were carved up into five smaller and hopefully more mobile units. Linked by the small, transistorized communications that were coming into use just then, these new units were supposed to operate in a decentralized and dispersed mode unlike any used in history. They were to leap from one place to the next, opening and closing like some huge accordions. To this end they would require novel types of equipment, beginning with giant cross-country landwalking machines and ending with flying jeeps; some visionaries even painted pictures of tanks with detachable turrets jumping into the air and shooting at each other.

Since the internal combustion engine was perceived as too inefficient and too demanding for such tasks, a substitute had to be developed. With ordinary lines of communication blocked, one scenario envisaged supplies being delivered by cargo-carrying guided missiles dropping in from the stratosphere and sticking their noses into the earth like enormous darts. Organizations, too, were to change. A particularly lugubrious idea was to divide the troops into "radiation classes" according to the dose they had received; depending on the time they could expect to live, each class could then be sent on its appropriate mission. One article in *Military Review* entitled "Atomic Impact on G-1's [personnel] Functions" proposed that the Army's grave registration service be greatly extended.

Serious attempts to design a "nuclear warfighting strategy" again proliferated during the 1970s. They were, if anything, even more harebrained than their predecessors, but insofar as technical means for "limiting" the damage now appeared to be available, they were also more dangerous. At the head of the team was Dr. James Schlesinger, secretary of defense under Richard Nixon and a man deservedly famous for his ability to "articulate strategy." He and lesser luminaries spent rivers of ink designing ways to use the new devices then being deployed, namely the MIRV (Multiple Independent Reentry Vehicles) and cruise missiles. The most important quality which distinguished cruise missiles and MIRV from ordinary ballistic missiles supposedly was their pinpoint accuracy (notwithstanding the fact that experimental devices aimed at test-ranges in the South Pacific sometimes turned up in Northern Canada). The capability of pinpointing hardened targets as small as missile silos permitted the power of the warheads to be reduced by an order of magnitude without any loss of destructive effect, even to the point where it was considered feasible to score a direct hit on the Kremlin.

During this period the weight of strategic opinion was moving away from nuclear stalemate towards so-called "warfighting" doctrines. Small, accurate warheads might be used to give the President "flexible options." They might be used for "nuclear shots across the bow," meaning that one side would serve warning to the other by exploding a nuclear weapon at some place—at sea, for example—where it would do little or no harm. Instead of going to full-scale war, the United States would be able to destroy a military base here, perhaps even a small city there, acting at discretion and constantly monitoring the other side's reaction. The goal to aim for was achieving "escalation dominance," i.e., frightening the enemy into submission. A few self-styled strategists went even further: the United States might "decapitate" the Soviet Union by striking at selected government, party, and KGB command and communication centers. The phraseology was often arcane and has been aptly compared to the theological debates of the Middle Ages. Still, when all is said and done, every one of the above terms was simply a euphemism for using nuclear weapons in ways that would hopefully not bring about the end of the world, at any rate not automatically.

As Schlesinger saw it, the problem was how to use the accurate warheads now available for a "surgical strike" against the USSR. His successors during the Carter Administration were to reverse this line of reasoning; they worried about what would happen if the USSR used *its* MIRVed missiles (the dread SS 18) to "take out" America's own land-based missiles leaving the United States, if not exactly defenseless, forced to rely on its manned bombers and missile-launching submarines for retaliation. For several years many different ideas were proposed to prevent the Soviet Union from leaping through the so-called "window of vulnerability." One was to station American missiles under the sea or else on moving platforms that would crawl over the bottom of lakes. Another was to lead them on giant trucks and shuffle them from one firing position to the next along an underground "racetrack" half as large as the American midwest. A third school proposed digging holes thousands of feet deep. The holes would be sealed, and the missiles inside them provided with special equipment that would enable them to screw their way up to the surface in the aftermath of an attack.

Fortunately for the national debt, none of these proposals was ever adopted. "The best available estimates"—in truth, guesses based on assumptions, every one of which could be challenged—indicated that, even in a "clean" Soviet strike directed against America's missile fields, as many as 20 million people would be killed. This would happen even if none of the two- to three-thousand−odd Soviet warheads used in the attack missed its mark and landed, say, on a major city such as Chicago or Los Angeles. In the face of such vast "collateral damage" the question of retaliation—especially limited retaliation—turned out to be academic. As the 1970s turned into the 1980s, this particular wave of nuclear warfighting doctrines followed its predecessor and died. The cause of death was the same in both cases; namely, choking on one's own absurdities. Some would say, however, that the doctrines in question did not die at all. Under the Reagan Administration they ascended into the starry heavens and were transmogrified into the Strategic Defense Initiative, a greater absurdity still.

Over the last forty-five years it would be difficult to point out even a single case when a state possessing nuclear arms was able to change the status quo by threatening their use, let alone by using them; in other words, their political effect, if any, has been merely to enforce caution and freeze existing borders. The most important reason behind this state of affairs is, of course, that nobody has yet figured out how to wage a nuclear war without risk of global suicide. Truth to say, nuclear weapons are instruments of mass murder. Given that there is no defense, the only thing they are suitable for is an act of butchery that would be beyond history, and quite possibly would put an end to it. They cannot, however, be employed for waging war in any meaningful sense of that term. The chasm separating the apocalyptic implications of nuclear weapons from the puny attempt to "use" them for sensible ends is tremendous, even inconceivable; so much so, in fact, that the most rational response to the oddly matched pair may be that of a young woman, a student of mine, who as we were discussing these things in class broke into uncontrollable, hysterical laughter.

Conventional War

Nuclear weapons were first built to give the military and their political masters unprecedentedly powerful tools for making and winning war. In fact, however, ten years had not passed before they threatened to put an end to war, and indeed some people had foreseen this development much earlier. Nor was the problem confined to nuclear weapons only. By the mid-fifties both superpowers had assembled fission bombs numbering perhaps in the low hundreds and were busily building fusion devices. Under such circumstances, the possibility of a conventional attack being launched against either also appeared increasingly unlikely. With each superpower now in control of the larger part of a hemisphere, conventional attack against either could only be successful if it were launched on a very large scale. So large an attack would surely be answered with nuclear weapons, particularly if it threatened to become successful. During the fifties the American secretary of state, John Foster Dulles, went out of his way to suggest that an attack might be quite small and still elicit such a response. Known as "brinkmanship" and "massive retaliation," this doctrine was designed to make sure, as far as possible, that even small attacks would not be attempted in the first place.

With the superpowers thus virtually immune to attack, conventional as well as nuclear, those whose job it was to think about waging war turned their attention to each power's allies. However, it soon became clear, as British Air Marshal Lord Tedder said, that "the dog that can take care of the cat can also take care of the kittens." In neither West nor East was there anybody who could come up with a way to attack a superpower's close allies without running the risk of Armageddon. For about a decade and a half, from the 1948 Berlin blockade to the last West Berlin crisis in 1963, the superpowers maneuvered like two dogs testing each other's resolve. Though there were some very tense moments, the testing ultimately did not work, and both sides ended up conceding defeat. This situation was literally poured in concrete when one side erected the Berlin Wall and the other tacitly accepted it.

The de facto division of Europe into two zones of influence, not to say domination, closed the doors of the most important single theater in which conventional warfare might still be waged; a fact that the recent demolition of the wall has merely confirmed. In 1953 the end of the Korean War created a similar situation on the other side of the globe, and this time too it was soon cemented by permanent fortified lines. Basically this left only two places where large scale conventional fighting could still take place—one along the Indo-Pakistani border, and the other in the Middle East. If only because they could not manufacture all their own arms, the states of those regions were also tied to the superpowers' apron-strings. However, thanks partly to racial circumstances and partly to geographical ones, they were not considered close allies. India, Pakistan, Israel, Egypt, Syria, and the rest were able to fight the superpowers' wars by proxy, as it were. Incidentally, they also served as laboratories where new weapons were tried out and new doctrines put to the test.

Thus the effect of nuclear weapons, unforeseen and perhaps unforeseeable, has been to push conventional war into the nooks and crannies of the international system; or, to mix a metaphor, into the faults between the main tectonic plates, each dominated by the superpowers. The faults tended to be located in what an earlier generation had called the "rimlands." The rimlands are a broad belt of territory stretching from west to east and dividing Asia into two regions, northern and southern. Something resembling conventional war occasionally broke out in other regions, such as the Horn of Africa; however, the lack of a modern infrastructure and the consequent inability to field major weapon systems meant that those conflicts were minor in scope compared to the ones taking place in the rimlands, Whatever their size, the danger always existed that the tail, comprising some third-rate or even fourth-rate country, would end up by wagging the superpower dog. This was brought home during the October 1973 War when President Nixon put America's forces on nuclear alert to stop an alleged Soviet threat to Israel. The threat, if one existed, was successfully averted. However, it seems to have left both Washington and Moscow disinclined to repeat the experiment.

As the small nations—e.g., Israel and her neighbors—fought each other, the superpowers stood on the sidelines. For the most part they watched, though not without taking good care to bring the fighting to an end as soon as their own welfare appeared to be even remotely threatened. Many members of their military establishments probably envied the combatants (the Israelis in particular) who, thanks to their very diminutiveness, were still able to play the game of war. Those establishments themselves had expended immense intellectual capital and millions of dollars finding ways whereby a superpower could engage in large-scale conventional warfare in a nuclear world. The U.S. Army in the late fifties carried out a series of field tests with nuclear weapons, with the result that decades later the American Government was being sued for wilfully exposing its troops—and civilians—to the effects of radiation. According to the best available information, the Soviets in 1954 held a test in which numerous Red Army troops were killed, after which their "nuclear" exercises were apparently confined to igniting masses of ordinary fuel and carefully driving around them. None of these experiments offered convincing proof that conventional forces could survive, let alone fight, on the nuclear battlefield. Nor, truth to say, is it easy to imagine a way in which such an experiment could have been designed.

In retrospect, the dilemma facing the planners was simple. If conventional forces (in the form of the "Pentomic" Army) were to stand the slightest chance of surviving a nuclear war they would have to disperse and hide. If hide and disperse they did, discarding much of their heavy equipment in the process, they would no longer be capable of waging conventional war. Thus the effect of nuclear weapons, tactical ones in particular, was to threaten the continued existence of conventional forces, especially ground forces. Yet if fighting was to take place at all, the only forces that could engage in it without threatening to blow up the world were conventional ones. It was left to the Kennedy Administration, guided by Secretary of Defense Robert McNamara and Chief of the Joint General Staffs General Maxwell Taylor, to try and square the circle. Their solution, if that is indeed the word to use, consisted of plunging all out for conventional war, nuclear weapons be damned. A new strategic doctrine known as "flexible response" articulated this approach and was officially adopted by NATO in 1967. Henceforward preparations for conventional war in Europe and elsewhere were to proceed *as if* the threat of nuclear escalation did not exist.

The purpose of flexible response, namely safeguarding the continued existence of conventional forces, was achieved. The doctrine led to massive investments as successive generations of surface ships, submarines, tanks, armored personnel carriers, artillery tubes, fighter bombers, and attack helicopters were phased out while others, newer and much more expensive, took their place. Each such change gave rise to a flood of studies, both classified and public, struggling to understand the implications of the new weapons and to work out esoteric doctrines for their use. Year after year NATO forces stationed in West Germany went on their maneuvers, carefully trying to prevent their massive machines from damaging civilian property whose owners would have to be compensated later on. The catch was that, given the alleged Soviet superiority in conventional forces, and the West German refusal to fortify their borders, most Western analysts believed a determined Soviet attack could only be stopped by using "tactical" nuclear weapons. As early as 1955, a series of war games played on behalf of the Supreme Allied Commander, Europe (SACEUR) had shown that employing such weapons would cause so much devastation in West Germany that there would be little left to defend. Nevertheless, NATO—but particularly the Americans who, after all, were preparing to fight on other people's soil—forged ahead. Thus it came to pass that, during the last quarter century, much of the Western effort aimed at preparing a defense against the USSR has amounted to a gigantic exercise in make-believe.

Whether, at any point in time, the planners in Moscow and Washington really believed in the illusion of a protracted, large-scale, conventional war in Europe is difficult to say. In the Soviet Union before Gorbachev, a tradition of secrecy and deception (*maskirovka*) has long meant that a doctrine is incredible *because* it is the officially proclaimed one. Americans are not secretive, but they regard the invention of military doctrines as both an industry and a pastime: as a result, so many conflicting doctrines have been put forward by so many people representing so many interests that it is often difficult to take them seriously at all. A clue to the true Soviet position may be found in the fact that, for all their occasionally bellicose rhetoric, they have not conducted even *one* conventional war during the entire period since 1945. The United States on its part fought just two such wars, one in 1950–1953 and another against Iraq in 1991; and already there is talk of this being "the last scream of the American Eagle".

One factor affecting conventional war as waged by both the super-powers and, increasingly, by other countries, is that nuclear weapons make their dampening effect felt in such wars even when nobody threatens their use. As a result, the United States for one has only been able to employ its conventional armed forces in cases where its vital interests were *not* at stake. The war fought in Korea, a small appendix of Asia several thousands of miles away, provides an excellent case in point. The American Chiefs of Staff recognized this even at that time, empha-sizing the fact that the really significant areas were Japan and Philip-pines. The same also applied to Lebanon (1958), Vietnam (1964–72), the Dominican Republic (1965), Cambodia (1972–75), Lebanon (1983), and the Gulf Crisis (1991). In all these cases, except (perhaps) the last, so microscopic were the stakes for which GIs were supposed to die that they could hardly even be explained to the American people. On occasions such as the Mayaguez Affair (1975) and Grenada (1983), so puny were the opponents against which American forces pitted them-selves that hostilities took on a comic-opera character.

Nor was the United States the only one to suffer from this problem. The USSR deployed naval forces to cover the Cuban landing in Angola in 1976, helped the Ethiopians defeat the Somalis in 1979, and sent some advisers to Central America during the eighties; all of these were marginal issues, however, far removed from the center of Soviet power. Though Mao at one time spoke of nuclear weapons as a "paper tiger," China's own frantic efforts to acquire the bomb prove otherwise. Be this as it may, after China developed a nuclear arsenal and a second-strike missile force to deliver it, the clashes along the Sino-Soviet border—clashes that at one time threatened to escalate into a major war—came to an end. Since then China's single largest military effort has consisted of its fifteen-mile drive into Vietnamese territory in 1979. Attempting to teach Vietnam a "lesson," the Chinese ended up by learning one them-selves. During the last decade the country's revolutionary rhetoric has declined, as has its involvement in actual war. The Chinese supplied weapons and perhaps advisers to countries such as Iran and Saudi Arabia as well as to guerrilla organizations in Cambodia and Af-ghanistan. They have done little else.

Among the former colonial powers, France since its defeat in Algeria has been fairly active in Africa. However, it did not have the occasion to employ forces larger than a regiment, nor in all probability would French public opinion have condoned such an involvement had it been attempted. After the unhappy experience of Suez in 1956 Britain's' career as a conventional power appeared to be over, a fact acknowledged by the switch from conscript to professional forces and subsequent cut-backs in their strength. When, much to the government's surprise, Britain did go to war over the Falklands in 1982, this was only made possible by the fact that few people knew where the Falklands were. The Islands' climate makes them suitable only for sheep. They are thinly populated, devoid of natural resources except seaweed, and separated from the nearest mainland by hundreds of miles of salt water. Against the background provided by the energy-crisis, Britain's apparent determination caused some people to postulate the presence of undersea oil reserves nearby. Although—or perhaps because—no such reserves have ever been announced, the Islands presented the ideal stage on which to fight a splendid little war from which nobody, not even the belligerents, stood much to gain or lose. Now that the war against Iraq is over, both countries plan to go ahead and reduce their forces.

The nuclear threat apparently affected even the countries around Israel, where hatred and death-defying fanaticism are rife. If internationally published sources can be credited, Israel, with French aid, started developing the bomb during the late fifties. The same sources present Nasser's 1967 adventure and the closing of the Straits of Tiran as a last-moment attempt to prevent it from being produced, much as President Kennedy applied pressure to the Soviets over Cuba. Apparently the first device became operational in 1969; nor did the possibility that Israel *might* already have the bomb escape Arab notice at the time. This may well have been one reason why the October 1973 War was as limited as it was. Though the Arabs had missile delivery systems, Israeli home territory was scarcely attacked at all, and the few Syrian missiles that fell on *kibbutzim* in the north seem to have been intended for a nearby military airfield. Neither the Egyptians nor the Syrians tried to advance very far beyond their respective armistice lines in the Sinai and on the Golan Heights; even so, rumor, taken up by *Time* magazine, has it that on the fourth day the Israeli Government came within a hair of losing its head and ordering the bomb to be used.

Whether or not this incident actually took place, the report must have attracted the Arabs' attention. The same applies to subsequent information concerning Israel's nuclear capabilities which was leaked by government circles in Jerusalem or else disclosed against its will and spread by the world media. While it is impossible to be certain about the role played by the nuclear factor vis-à-vis other considerations, the plain fact is that there have been no more large-scale conventional wars in the Middle East since 1973. Israel, to be sure, did invade Lebanon in 1982. Prime Minister Menahem Begin, whose military knowledge was amateurish at best, was told by his advisers that "Operation Peace for Galilee" would be a small one. It was supposed to penetrate no more than twenty-five miles into Lebanon, avoid entanglement with the Syrians, last perhaps three days, and keep casualties to a few dozen. Had he known it would turn into a war, he would never have ordered it; once he realized it *had* turned into a war he underwent a nervous collapse and resigned.

A final case in point, demonstrating the very limited role still left to conventional war in the nuclear age, is provided by the Gulf Crisis. The region had long been considered one of the most important in the world; fears of what would happen if armed conflict broke out had been voiced for a decade and a half before the Iraq invasion, giving birth to at least one best-seller (Paul Erdmann's *The Crash of 1979*). As things turned out these fears proved greatly exaggerated. Heading a coalition of thirty states, the United States took forty days and a very small number of casualties to defeat an opponent with one fifteenth of its own population and (perhaps) one seventieth of its own GNP. As the Crisis unfolded, the price of oil continued the downward movement that had started in the spring of 1981; proof, if proof were needed, that even the loss of the oil of Iraq and Kuwait together was no longer critical to the world economy.

In retrospect, one may wonder what might have happened if Iraq, instead of fighting a conventional war, had possessed a credible nuclear deterrent. In that case, obviously a great deal would have depended on the meaning of "credible"; however, it might not be altogether misguided to suggest that, had he only been able to field a hundred invulnerable, nuclear-tipped, missiles capable of reaching targets in the United States President Bush would not have ordered the war against him to be fought. Then, perhaps, a smaller force would have done as well. Twenty missiles capable of reaching London—and, of course, Rome, and Paris as well—surely would have sufficed to prevent the B52s taking off from British airfields on their way to bomb Iraq. Finally, had Iraq only been able to arm ten out of the hundreds of Scud missiles which it did possess with nuclear weapons then surely the Saudis would have thought twice before allowing their country to be used as a basis for invasion; or, if they had not, then in spite of the unexpectedly successful performance of the Patriot anti-missile system Riyadh might no longer have existed.

As the twentieth century is drawing to an end, it may still be too early to celebrate or lament, depending on one's point of view the demise of conventional war among regular, state-controlled, armed forces. Some facts do stand out, however. Since 1945 no superpower has engaged another in conventional hostilities, and indeed in almost all cases even the threat of launching such hostilities against a superpower has bordered on the ludicrous. The superpowers' non-nuclear allies have also been virtually immune to conventional war, except when launched by the side which claimed to offer them "protection" (e.g., the Soviets in East Germany, Hungary, and Czechoslovakia). Korea forty years ago was the last example of a superpower engaging in large-scale conventional warfare against a non-nuclear country. The number of cases when nuclear countries other than the superpowers fought conventional wars may also be counted on the fingers of one hand. Though Britain had acquired nuclear weapons in 1952, four years before she went to war over Suez, their existence proved irrelevant. Perhaps the only other two instances are the 1973 Arab-Israeli War and the 1982 Falkland Islands War.

Countries not in possession of nuclear arsenals have, it is true, engaged each other in conventional war more frequently. The most important clashes took place in the Middle East (1948–49, 1956, 1967, 1973, 1982, and 1980–88), between China and Taiwan (1954, 1958), India and China (1962), and along the Indo-Pakistani border (1947–49, 1965, 1971). However, during the 1970s nuclear weapons seem to have been introduced into these regions, sometimes openly and sometimes not. Whether or not this is the reason since then the incidence of conventional war has undergone a marked decline. Egypt and Israel have signed a peace treaty. As of the time of writing Israel and Jordan are unofficially at peace, and even Syria's Assad has been dropping occasional peaceful hints. China has declared its intention of using only peaceful means to achieve reunification with Taiwan, a country that has nuclear potential if not a bomb in the basement. Though the Indians still dispute their border with China, another war between the two countries does not appear in the cards so long as both retain their nuclear arsenals and, as important, their national cohesion. Meanwhile India and Pakistan remain at loggerheads over Kashmir. They are unlikely to fight another war, however, and in January 1989 they agreed to refrain from bombing each other's nuclear installations in case they do.

Similar conclusions emerge if one looks, not at how many conventional wars there have been and by whom they were fought, but at the way they ended. Out of several dozen such conflicts, very few have led to internationally-recognized territorial changes. One exception to the rule was the 1948–49 war in the Middle East which led to the establishment of Israel; even so, Jordan's annexation of the West Bank as a result of the same war was not recognized by the international community at large or even by its fellow Arab countries. Another was the Indo-Pakistani War of 1971 which, though it led to the establishment of Bangla Desh, did not result in the drawing of new frontiers. Depending on whether one considers South Vietnam, for example, to have been an independent county, there may have been one or two other cases, but on the whole the trend is clear. "Employing armed force for acquiring territory" has, after all, been declared unacceptable by formal, written, international law. The signs are that, faced by actual nuclear weapons or by the ability to build them quickly, states have grown wary not merely of territorial expansion but of conventional war itself. There is, of course, no way to predict the future, but all things considered the Iran-Iraq War may well have been among the last the world will see.

Low-Intensity War

Nuclear forces constitute the ultimate defense of every country that has them. So immense is their power that they make conventional weapons look like a bad joke. Therefore, during the decades since 1945 conventional forces ought to have declined both in size and expense. To some extent, this is what happened: U.S. armed forces today number just over 2 million, down from almost 12 million in 1945 and 3 million in 1960. Although the Soviets have always put greater emphasis on conventional war, during the same period their forces have been cut by three quarters, and the decline is continuing. Still, the process has not been nearly as rapid as might have been expected. In all countries combined, the number of soldiers who are in any way involved with operating nuclear weapons is probably less than 100,000. Meanwhile the count of all men and women wearing uniform worldwide is perhaps 15 to 20 million. Though conventional war may be withering away, conventional forces and their weapons systems are alive and well.

The key point to understand is that nuclear weapons are, economically speaking, a relative bargain. For example, in World War II the Western Allies devoted perhaps 35 percent of their total military expenditure to the construction of strategic air forces numbering thousands upon thousands of heavy bombers. Such an effort, involving the coordinated action of millions of people, naturally took time; it was not before January 1942 that the British were able to mount the first thousand-aircraft raid and cause serious damage. Once created, the forces had to

fight their way through the opposition represented by the Luftwaffe—
with the result that the British Bomber Command suffered proportionally heavier casualties than any other arm of service. Two and a half
years of intensive operations as well as several million tons of bombs
dropped before Germany was finally brought to her knees. Even so, the
outcome of the air war was ambiguous. Its cost effectiveness compared
to other forms of war has been questioned, and indeed to this day
historians are arguing among themselves whether it was the bombing
that did bring Germany to her knees.

Were the same job to be carried out with the aid of modern nuclear
weapons, there would be no room for argument and, indeed, precious
little left to argue about. There would be no need to create a large
industrial and logistic infrastructure, build up strong forces, or to fight
one's way through opposition of any kind. A single Trident-II type
submarine, its crew numbering fewer than 100 men, could take up
station somewhere below the ocean surface at a distance of up to 5,000
miles from its target. Depending on the range selected, in fifteen or
thirty minutes it could rain down devastation on such a scale that the
country almost certainly would never recover. Having dropped several
warheads on every German town, the captain would still have enough
missiles to spare to inflict a similar fate on another country of equivalent size.

Thus, the number of platforms needed to wage nuclear war—if
that is the name for a unilateral massacre against which there is no
defense—is smaller by perhaps two orders of magnitude than that
required for conventional war. The same applies to the number of
personnel necessary to operate them, with the result that the sheer size
of an armed force no longer represents a significant factor either
economically or militarily. Whichever way one looks at it, there is no
doubt that, compared to conventional forces nuclear ones are dirt
cheap. This is true absolutely, and much more so in terms of relative
destructive power.

Officially, the principal reason why military powers for many years
devoted so much effort preparing for conventional conflict in a nuclear
age was the imperative desire to prevent a nuclear war from breaking
out. This line of reasoning, embodied in the doctrine of "flexible
response," was formally adopted by NATO as the cornerstone of its
entire strategy. The doctrine has gone somewhat as follows. Unless they
have conventional forces at their disposal, decision makers in Western
(and Eastern) capitals could find themselves unable to respond to a
crisis, however small. Alternatively even quite a small crisis might force

them to resort to nuclear weapons, a less attractive possibility still. For a quarter century the declared rationale of maintaining strong conventional forces was to prevent this awful dilemma from arising. In case it did arise, starting the war with conventional forces would hopefully buy time for negotiation; this was known as raising the nuclear threshold.

Whether, in view of what has been said about the utility of both nuclear and conventional war in the present age, "flexible response" has made sense remains for the reader to decide. Be this as it may, the upkeep of conventional forces and the hardware that they require is currently taking up around 80 percent of NATO's military budget, and an even greater share of its military manpower. The same probably applies, to the countries forming the Warsaw Pact, and also to other nuclear powers such as China and India, both of which maintain armed forces numbering in the millions. One would expect forces on which so many resources have been lavished to represent fearsome warfighting machines capable of quickly overcoming any opposition. Nothing, however, is farther from the truth. For all the countless billions that have been and still are being expended on them, the plain fact is that conventional military organizations of the principal powers are hardly even relevant to the predominant form of contemporary war.

To support this claim, consider the record. Since 1945 there have been perhaps 160 armed conflicts around the world, more if we include struggles like that of the French against Corsican separatists and the Spanish against the Basques. Of those, perhaps three quarters have been of the so-called "low-intensity" variety (the term itself first appeared during the 1980s, but it aptly describes many previous wars as well). The principal characteristics of low-intensity conflict (LIC) are as follows: First, they tend to unfold in "less developed" parts of the world; the small-scale armed conflicts which do take place in "developed" countries are usually known under a variety of other names, such as "terrorism,""police work," or—in the case of Northern Ireland– "troubles." Second, very rarely do they involve regular armies on both sides, though often it is a question of regulars on one side fighting guerrillas, terrorists, and even civilians, including women and children, on the other. Third, most LICs do not rely primarily on the high-technology collective weapons that are the pride and joy of any modern armed force. Excluded from them are the aircraft and the tanks, the missiles and the heavy artillery, as well as many other devices so complicated as to be known only by their acronyms.

Besides being numerically predominant, LICs have also been far more bloody than any other kind of war fought since 1945. The clashes between Hindus and Muslims in 1947–49 may have claimed 1 million lives or more. Up to 3 million people are said to have perished during the Nigerian Civil War from 1966 to 1969. Well over 1 million died in the thirty-year Vietnamese conflict, and perhaps another 1 million died in the rest of Indochina including Cambodia and Laos. A million probably died in Algeria, another 1 million in Afghanistan, where there have also been some 5 million refugees. The conflicts which took place in Central and South America were much smaller, yet they have certainly involved hundreds of thousands of deaths. I have yet to mention the wars which took place and are still taking place in the Philippines, Tibet, Thailand, Sri Lanka, Kurdistan, Sudan, Ethiopia, Uganda, Western Sahara, Angola, and half a dozen other countries. The total number of those who died has been put at 20 million or more.

Since, in every case, the majority of victims were villagers who did not belong to any formal organization, the above figures are highly uncertain. Still, they are much larger than those generated by any post–1945 conventional conflict. To this rule there have been only two exceptions: the Korean War, where the majority of casualties were probably civilians, and the eight-year Iran-Iraq War. For the rest, the following example may give an idea of the orders of magnitude involved. Fifteen years of civil war in Lebanon, a country with a population of approximately 2.5 million, are said to have claimed over 100,000 dead. By contrast Israel—a country justly famous for the number and scale of the wars it has fought—had lost a total of some 14,000 killed in the four decades of its existence. Out of those 14,000, between 2,500 and 3,000 lost their lives as a result of the October 1973 War, which at that time was the largest and most modern conventional conflict fought anywhere in the world since 1945. The campaigns of 1956 and 1967 cost 170 and 750 dead respectively; by this standard they were mere skirmishes scarcely even meriting the appellation of "war." Fully 6,000, or 43 percent, of Israel's casualties, fell during the "War of Liberation" in 1948–49. From the point of view of the forces engaged and the weapons used, that war in many ways was itself a "low intensity conflict."

Assuming that politics is what wars are all about, then LICs have been politically by far the most significant form of war waged since 1945. Out of several dozen "conventional" conflicts waged since 1945, almost the only one which resulted in the establishment of new frontiers was the 1948 one between Israel and its neighbors, and even then the outcome was not an international border but merely an armistice line. During the same period the consequences of LICs, numerically about three times as strong, have been momentous. From South Africa to Laos, all over the Third World, LIC has been perhaps the dominant instrument for bringing about political change. Without a single conventional war being waged, colonial empires that between them used to control approximately one half of the globe, were sent down to defeat through LIC's known as "wars of national liberation." In the process, some of the strongest military powers on earth have suffered humiliation, helping put an end to the entire notion of the white man's inherent superiority.

Perhaps the best indication of the political importance of LIC is that its results, unlike those of conventional wars, have usually been recognized by the international community. Often, indeed, recognition preceded victory rather than following it, shedding an interesting light on the interaction of right with might in the modern world. Considered from this point of view—"by their fruits thou shalt know them"—the term LIC itself is grossly misconceived. The same applies to related terms such as "terrorism," "insurgency," "brushfire war," or "guerrilla war." Truth to say, what we are dealing with here is neither low-intensity nor some bastard offspring of war. Rather, it is WARRE in the elemental, Hobbesian sense of the word, by far the most important form of armed conflict in our time.

This much granted, how well have the world's most important armed forces fared in this type of war? For some two decades after 1945 the principal colonial powers fought very hard to maintain the far-flung empires which they had created for themselves during the past four centuries. They expended tremendous economic resources, both in absolute terms and relative to those of the insurgents who, in many cases, literally went barefoot. They employed the best available troops, from the Foreign Legion to the Special Air Service and from the Green Berets to the *Spetznatz* and the Israeli *Sayarot.* They fielded every kind of sophisticated military technology in their arsenals, nuclear weapons only excepted. They were also, to put it bluntly, utterly ruthless. Entire populations were driven from their homes, decimated, shut in concentration camps or else turned into refugees. As Ho Chi Minh foresaw when he raised the banner of revolt against France in 1945, in *every* colonial-type war ever fought the number of casualties on the side of the insurgents exceeded those of the "forces of order" by at least an order of magnitude. This is true even if civilian casualties among the colonists are included, which often is not the case.

Notwithstanding this ruthlessness and these military advantages, the "counterinsurgency" forces failed in *every* case. The British lost India, Palestine, Kenya, Cyprus, and Aden, to mention but the most important places where they tried to make a stand. The French spent six years fighting in Indochina and another seven trying to stave off defeat in Algeria; having failed in both cases, they gave up the rest of the empire without a struggle, a few minor possessions only excepted. The Belgians were forced to surrender the Congo, a country with a population so backward that the number of high school graduates did not perhaps exceed 100. The Dutch lost Indonesia, though not before an attempt was made to hold on by military means, and proved hopeless. The Spaniards had enough sense to yield the Sahara almost without a struggle, but the Portuguese in Angola and Mozambique fought for years before they, too, were forced to capitulate. Even the South Africans, who held out longer than anybody else, ended up by agreeing to withdraw from Namibia.

Against these defeats, numbering in the dozen, there is just *one* shining (and often-quoted) example of a former colonial power "winning" a struggle in the Third World. The British armed forces in Malaysia successfully put down a communist insurgency which, truth to say, was largely confined to the Chinese minority and unsupported by most of the population. By this feat they acquired a high reputation, also learning "lessons" from which others have since sought to benefit. What is often overlooked, however, is that this particular struggle was conducted in a vacuum. It was perhaps the only time in history when a country, far from using war for expansionist ends, from the beginning announced its intention of *not* doing so. The British Conservative Government headed by Winston Churchill entered the struggle with the promise that Malaysia would be evacuated once the insurgency was defeated. When it was defeated, the British kept their word.

Even worse were the defeats suffered, not by the old colonial powers themselves, but by those who sought to take their place. By 1964 the process of decolonization had already gone far, and the end was in sight. That was also the year when America under the Johnson Administration decided to show that, unlike the Europeans, it *did* have both the will and the muscle to impose itself on the Third World. For nine years the Americans fought in Vietnam. Over 2 million troops were sent out— the largest number present inside the country at any one time was approximately 550,000—and over 50,000 were killed. The United States, at that time the world's undisputed technological leader, also threw in every kind of device, from giant B-52 intercontinental bombers all the way down to "people sniffers" and remotely-controlled listening devices. The cost of the war has been put at $150–175 billion (and three or four times as much, in 1990 dollars). Yet long before the last helicopter took off from the roof of the American embassy in Saigon, catastrophic defeat had become evident. Once again a rich, powerful, industrialized, sophisticated country had tried to trample on a poor, weak Third-World society, and once again it had failed.

The failures of conventional forces during the period 1975–90 have been numerous and painful. Perhaps the outstanding case was that of the Soviet Union in Afghanistan. When the invasion took place in 1979 many in the West stood aghast at the unfolding power of the Red Army. There was talk of the irresistible momentum which would finally enable the Russians to realize a centuries-old dream and take them to the Persian Gulf. The United States under the Carter Administration was sufficiently disturbed to set up a Rapid Deployment Force to deal with such a contingency, even though the logistic realities were such that the RDF never stood the slightest chance of repulsing a serious Soviet onslaught by conventional means. Inside Afghanistan, opposition to the Red Army consisted of a motley collection of guerrilla organizations. Their members had little formal training, were unable to cooperate among themselves, and never learned to operate in forces larger than a battalion. Yet nine years later, and (the Soviets say) with over 30,000 men killed in action, that Army was staggering back across the border, jeered by *mujahideen* who did not even take the trouble of shooting at it.

Nor have armies belonging to less developed countries done much better against LIC. To mention but a few of the best known cases, the Syrians have been killing off Lebanese for a decade and a half without, however, bringing about a situation where Assad's writ will run unquestioned. Cuban units experienced little difficulty in overrunning Angola in 1976, but subsequently found themselves unable to deal with the UNITA Movement in its jungle hideouts. Time after time the tough South Africans slugged the guerrillas in Namibia, Angola, and Mozambique, always to good effect and always to no avail. Indian intervention in the Sri Lankan civil war not only failed to achieve its objectives but ended in a humiliating retreat, thereby opening the door to similar trouble in Kashmir. Much the same fate befell the North Vietnamese Army, a force so tough that it first defeated the American war machine and then inflicted a stinging reverse on the Chinese. However, they too had to concede defeat—or at least a stalemate—after almost a decade of trying to cope with the Khmer Rouge guerrilla movement in Cambodia.

Perhaps most interesting of all is the case of the Israeli Army which, since its 1967 victory over the Arab countries, had been considered perhaps the world's best. In 1982 six Israeli divisions with about 1000 tanks between them invaded Lebanon. They quickly (though not as quickly as they had hoped) overran the PLO, reaching Beirut after six days. They also pushed back the Syrians, inflicting a heavy defeat on the

Syrian air force in particular. These victories won, it gradually dawned on the Israelis that their tanks, aircraft, artillery, missiles, and remotely piloted vehicles—including the most modern models ever deployed by any army—were of no use against the kind of opposition which, to their cost, they now confronted. For three years they floundered about in "the Lebanese swamp," trying to maintain themselves amid a bewildering array of different militias who butchered each other even as they hounded the Israel Defense Forces. The Israelis may not have been as ruthless as the Soviets in Afghanistan, but they were ruthless enough. The parallel with Afghanistan is remarkable—when they finally retreated across the border, the Israelis too organized a victory parade. At the time of writing they are having the greatest difficulties in dealing with the *intifada,* a rebellion in the occupied territories mounted by Arab youths armed with little but sticks and stones.

The Record of Failure

The great majority of wars since 1945 have been Low Intensity Conflicts. In terms of both casualties suffered and political results achieved, these wars have been incomparably more important than any others. While developed countries on both sides of the Iron Curtain have participated in these wars, the colonial legacy has meant that, on the whole, Western states have been much more involved than those from the Eastern Bloc. Afghanistan apart, the largest Soviet presence in any country outside Eastern Europe since 1945 has consisted of some 20,000 advisers in Egypt. From 1969 to 1972, they manned much of Egypt's antiaircraft defense system, flew a number of combat sorties against the Israeli Air Force, and also trained the Egyptian Army. The Cuban presence in Angola has been equally large and more protracted, protraction being itself an indication of failure. For the rest, even the Soviet effort in Afghanistan was dwarfed by the American effort in Vietnam. In terms of numbers, though of course not of equipment, the forces committed by the Soviets to Afghanistan were comparable with the expeditionary forces which France supported in Indochina from 1948 to 1953.

Whatever their relative involvement, so far neither Western nor Eastern countries have been forced to fight foreigners waging on LIC on their own territory. The most important reason for this is technical. Ours is an age of telecommunications and of modern means of transport which, perhaps for the first time in history, give their owners a truly global reach. However, these means are largely controlled by a small group of states, perhaps 25 out of some 1500. As has been the case since Vasco da Gama first reached India in 1498, the most powerful among these states can "project force" against less developed ones without running the risk of reciprocity. For example, France has the wherewithal to send troops to fight in the Central African Republic. French troops could if necessary make a forced entry and probably even occupy the country's capital, not that this would bring the "war" to an end. Conversely, the idea of the Central African Republic invading France amounts to a bad joke. Whatever ragtag forces it could raise would never get anywhere near its enemy's shores. It follows that when the logistic superiority of these most important powers is added to their armaments, then those powers ought to be able to do what they like with— and to--the rest of the globe.

The military gap between developed and undeveloped countries is, however, nowhere as evident as on the pages of the many glossy international magazines devoted to praising modern weapons systems. An observer relying solely on this literature might be pardoned for thinking that the gap is greater today than ever before. After all, when the British conquered India in the eighteenth century they were only marginally superior in the quality of their weapons and, of course, vastly inferior in numbers. The few thousand troops in question were not even an army in our sense of the term; rather, they were soldiers of fortune serving what was still officially a private corporation, the East India Company.

But the notion that superior weaponry in itself can prevail is misleading. If war were a tournament, with two equally matched sides meeting on some neutral field, then today's British Army might still be "superior" to the Indian. That, however, is not how things are. Today, the only way Britain could prevent India from infringing on its interests would be by threatening to use—perhaps by actually using—nuclear weapons. That possibility apart, Britain cannot face even some third-world country that has hardly any military forces at all. The government of such a country might very well be involved in kidnapping and robbing, perhaps even killing, passport-carrying British subjects. Such acts may take place—*have* taken place—in that country's own territory, on the high seas, in the air, or even on British soil. Since 1970 things have been done to British property and lives which, not so long ago, would have caused the Royal Navy to use its battleships' 16-inch guns, or else the Royal Air Force would have been sent in to bomb entire villages to smithereens.

The British are not alone in their predicament. So unhappy was the 1983 American experience in Lebanon—a country so mired in chaos that its government cannot even control its own capital—that it is unlikely that American troops will be sent in again even in the face of the most severe provocation; future American hostages will have to be released by negotiation, not force. Nor, since Afghanistan, is there much reason to think that the USSR would do much better in such a conflict, a factor that helps explain the restraint shown by the Kremlin in handling attempts at secession. The cold, brutal fact is that much present-day military power is simply irrelevant as an instrument for extending or defending political interests over most of the globe; by this criterion, indeed, it scarcely amounts to "military power" at all. When it comes to preventing acts of terrorism closer to home, the military services and their arms—fighter bombers, tanks, armored personnel carriers, etc.— are even less useful. All this is true of developed countries in both West and East, and also on either side of the equator.

Were our observer to ask for the reasons behind this extraordinary situation, he would find experts aplenty to explain them to him. No doubt the list would be headed by "democratic traditions" and "Western humanitarianism." Both are laudable, to be sure, but there is a price to be paid. It would be stated that they prevented the United States from doing whatever was necessary to win in Vietnam: i.e., imprison its own dissidents, muzzle its press, mobilize its economy, put its population into uniform, and bomb the enemy back into the stone age. However, other factors besides democracy would also be cited as posing a problem. America's civilian leaders would be blamed for misusing the country's military might, never telling the armed forces just what it was that they were supposed to accomplish. The forces' own deployment, was made difficult by the vastness of the Pacific, thus turning a war that was merely very expensive into a financial black hole. Finally, the Vietnamese received tremendous support from the Soviets, or else the United States would have quickly prevailed.

On the whole, these are nothing but feeble excuses. To proceed in reverse order, rival imperialist powers have obstructed each other ever since their colonial expansion began—the Spanish fought the Portuguese, the Dutch battled the Spanish, the French beat the Dutch, and the English fought it out with the French, to name but a few conflicts. Often, the imperialists formed alliances with local rulers, supplying them with arms and know-how. These wars did not prevent Europe from dominating the world. Nor, perhaps, did they even slow down the process whereby that domination was achieved. As to conquering distance, Columbus discovered America with his three wooden cockle-shells. Steamships capable of transoceanic voyages only made their appearance during the second half of the nineteenth century, and the same is true of telecommunications. Thus, throughout the great period of colonial expansion, relative technological backwardness meant that the problems of space were greater than anything most people can even imagine today.

Proximity in itself does not guarantee victory in Low-Intensity Conflict. Fighting guerrillas on their own doorstep, in Cambodia, Lebanon, Afghanistan, and Sri Lanka respectively, the Vietnamese, Israeli, Soviet, and Indian armed forces did not exactly gather laurels. A military failure that affects a small force fighting far away can be tolerated. However, failure to defeat an insurgency taking place near the homeland may carry disastrous consequences insofar as discontented groups within the affected countries take heart, causing the fighting to spill over the border. Thus it was not distance that prevented the former colonial powers from maintaining their empires; distance is what saved them from having to fight LICs, possibly even civil war, on their own national territories. As the events surrounding the *Organisation Armée Secrète* and the Generals' Revolt between 1958 and 1962 demonstrated, had the Mediterranean not existed to separate Algeria from France it would have had to be invented.

Returning to the American forces in Vietnam, their mission actually was clear enough; i.e., they were to kill Communists/Viet Cong/North Vietnamese soldiers until there were none left. True, the United States never mobilized anything like its full resources—had such mobilization been considered necessary to win then public opinion would not have tolerated the war in the first place. Even so, the resources that Lyndon Johnson did commit to the struggle were, comparatively speaking, greater than anything in history. It is difficult to see what more the United States could have done. "The best and the brightest" were sent into the jungles, or else proffered their advice on how the war should be won. The most modern technologies were used, including some never before seen in any theater of war, such as satellite communications, and bombs capable of clearing landing-zones in the jungle. Every weapon system in the arsenal was tried out, often unnecessarily and always to no avail.

The Americans could have hurt North Vietnam's economy even more than they did by bombing the dams near Hanoi. However, this would probably have caused the Soviet Union to step up food supplies in addition to weapons, and in any case the destruction of North Korea's dams by bombing had not brought that country to its knees. They could have invaded the North (as they did invade Cambodia and Laos), but only at the cost of increasing still further the extent of the jungles to be combed and the number of guerrillas to be searched for and destroyed. They could have depopulated the entire South-Vietnamese countryside instead of only parts of it. Finally, they could have followed the counsel of a few hotheads and used nuclear weapons to wipe Hanoi—and much else—off the face of the earth. This might conceivably have "won" the war in some Strangelovian sense, but only at the price of breaking the taboo and, therefore, giving others license to use similar weapons against the United States.

The West prides itself on allowing humanitarian considerations to influence its conduct of war at home and abroad, though the merits of such a claim are often doubtful. Be this as it may, the most favorable interpretation can scarcely attribute humanitarian motives to such figures as Syria's President Assad. The Soviets in Afghanistan (like their predecessors, the Egyptians in Yemen) resorted to every conceivable weapon including, it is alleged, gas. The Vietnamese in Cambodia reportedly engaged in biological warfare, employing an agent supplied to them by the Soviet Union and known as "Yellow Rain." At the time these events took place the countries in question were nothing if not totalitarian dictatorships. The rulers of each would not have dreamt of allowing their citizens to criticize the conduct of the war, let alone to stage sit-ins or burn their draft cards. It goes without saying that torture and terrorism—the killing of civilians *pour encourager les autres*—have been systematically employed by all those trying to cope with Low-Intensity Conflict, without exception. From Algeria to Afghanistan there have been cases when the scale of the operations was so large as to make them look like genocide, yet even so the end of the conflict was by no means guaranteed.

In fact, there are solid military reasons why modern regular forces are all but useless for fighting what is fast becoming the dominant form of war in our age. Perhaps the most important reason is the need to look after the technology on which the forces depend; between maintenance and logistics and sheer administration this ensures that the number of troops in their "tails" will be far too large, and the number in the fighting "teeth" far too small. For example, even the most pessimistic intelligence estimates never doubted that, throughout the war, the Americans and the Army of the Republic of Vietnam outnumbered the Viet Cong/North Vietnamese forces confronting them and indeed that they did so by a considerable margin. The catch was that, among the

American troops in particular, more than three quarters served in an enormous variety of noncombat jobs from guarding bases to welfare. At the place where it mattered, in the jungle, the number of "maneuver battalions" actually available was about equal on both sides.

Designed as they are for conventional war, the command-structures of modern armed forces tend to be too tall, battle procedures too cumbersome; in Vietnam, according to one source, the USAF required fully twenty-four hours advance warning to tailor planned missions to available ammunition. This case may be extreme but it is not atypical. In the jungles of Vietnam, the mountains of Afghanistan, and the closed, heavily populated, Lebanese countryside, forces on foot were often as mobile tactically as their mechanized opponents. They were also capable of making much better use of the terrain, with the result that it was always the conventional forces who were pinned down or blown up. The nimble guerrillas got away, usually suffering heavy casualties only on those occasions when they chose to stand and fight. Attacked by swarms of gnats, all the conventional forces could do was flounder about in helpless fury, destroying their environment and themselves. They are about as relevant to war in our age as Don Quixote was in his.

A special chapter in the failure of conventional forces is formed by their weapons systems. During most of history the principal weapons were hand-held, operated by, and against, individual soldiers. There have been some ups and downs (Napoleon once wrote that it was with artillery that war was made), but on the whole the relative effect of those arms was probably greatest in the mid-nineteenth century—in the American Civil War and the Austro-Prussian War, also known as the Needle Gun War. Since then, their role has declined. They now provide a small and still diminishing proportion of the firepower at the disposal of armed forces. By far the greatest part of that firepower is generated by motorized, crew-operated weapons systems, which also account for the bulk of the cost. Some systems currently in use can fire as many as 6,000 rounds a minute. Others are accurate enough to hit a missile in flight, and others still are so powerful that they can blow to pieces virtually anything that moves, including even sixty-ton tanks covered by several layers of composite armor. Some weapons systems can fly at twice the speed of sound; others can reach an enemy dozens or even hundreds of miles away. At such speeds and such ranges, very often the pilots and crews that operate these systems cannot see their opponents. Instead, targets are detected by radar and appear as blips on fluorescent screens. They are acquired, tracked, and engaged with the aid of technical, read "electronic," instruments.

Thus, modern aircraft, helicopters, ships, tanks, antitank weapons, artillery, and missiles of every kind are all becoming dependent on electronics to the point where this dependence is itself the best possible index of their modernity. Now electronic sensing devices and the computers to which they are coupled are very sensitive to environmental interference. They work fairly well in simple media such as air, sea, even open plains and deserts. However, the more complicated the surroundings the greater the problems. Many sensors can distinguish friend from foe only if the target cooperates by sending out an agreed-on signal as was shown when the Syrians shot down numbers of their own aircraft in 1973, and again when an Iranian airliner was downed in the Persian Gulf in 1988. In addition to being easily misled by clutter of every kind, the computers that process the information sent by the sensors can only respond to such eventualities as were explicitly foreseen by their programmers. Often the net effect of complex environments is to cause the wrong signals to be picked up and sent out, either sounding false alarms or none at all.

What is more, once the principles on which these gadgets operate are understood they are easy to spoof, overload, or jam. Often all that is needed is a similar gadget, modified to do the opposite job. For example, once the Iranians started using surface to surface missiles against oil installations in the Gulf States, devices were quickly installed that caused them to home on rafts anchored off the coast. It is not too hard to build an apparatus that will give out the acoustic "signature" of a submarine where in fact there is none (active sonar may be harder to mislead, but gives away its own presence at much longer range). A flare worth perhaps a few dollars may mislead a heat-seeking antiaircraft missile costing tens of thousands of dollars, sending it on a wild-goose chase. The possibilities are endless and, in fact, within the capabilities even of countries possessing only a modest technological infrastructure.

These factors help explain why U.S. Forces—which pioneered the field—repeatedly succeeded in shooting down Libyan Migs above the Gulf of Sirte. They also help explain why the same forces failed to make much of an impression either in the jungles of Vietnam or, on a much smaller scale, against the mountains surrounding Beirut. Israeli electronic hardware, perhaps equally sophisticated, suffered a similar fate. In 1982 the combination of Advanced Warning and Control (AWAC) systems, Remotely Controlled Vehicles (RPVs), fighter bombers, missiles, and computer-networks behind them performed marvels against the simple, clearly defined targets offered by the Syrian air force and antiaircraft defenses. The Israeli Air Force was able to win complete command of the air. Nevertheless, in sharp contrast to 1967 (or even 1973) its contribution to the winning of the ground battle below was minimal. Similarly the fact that Israeli tanks in 1982 were the most advanced ever fielded availed them little when it came to controlling the heavily-populated, built-up, areas of Lebanon. What is more, the argument can be turned around. So expensive, fast, indiscriminate, big, unmaneuverable, and powerful have modern weapons become that they are steadily pushing contemporary war under the carpet, as it were; that is, into environments where those weapons do not work, and where men can therefore fight to their hearts' contents.

Weapons do not grow in a vacuum. Even as they help shape ideas concerning the nature of war and the ways in which it ought to be fought, they themselves are the product of those ideas. The same is even more true of the social organizations—armed forces, general staffs, and defense departments—which produce, field, and use the weapons. My basic postulate is that, already today, the most powerful modern armed forces are largely irrelevant to modern war—indeed that their relevance stands in inverse proportion to their modernity. If this is correct, then the reasons must be sought on the conceptual level as represented by modern strategic thought.

CHAPTER
II

By Whom War Is Fought

The Clausewitzian Universe

The Clausewitzian Universe is named after Carl Philipp Gotlieb von Clausewitz, a Prussian officer who was born in 1780 and died in 1831. At the age of 12 he entered the army as an officer-candidate and took part in the campaign of 1793. Later he studied at the Berlin War Academy where his intellectual capacities were first discovered. Appointed *aide de camp* to Prince August of Prussia, he fought in the disastrous Jena Campaign of 1806 where he was captured. On being released, he served on the General Staff which was being rebuilt by Gerhard von Scharnhorst. He took a hand in the reform of the Prussian Army while simultaneously acting as military tutor to the Prussian princes royal, who later became Frederick William IV and William I. Like many of his colleagues, Clausewitz was disgusted by King Frederick William III's decision to join Napoleon in the fight against Russia in 1812. He joined the so-called German Legion, a body of anti-French officers, and stayed with it throughout the Russian campaign. Following the Peace of Tauroggen in 1813, he reentered the Prussian Service, received an appointment as chief of staff to an army corps, and served through the Wars of Liberation from 1813 to 1815.

With the return of peace, Clausewitz—like many of the former military reformers—came to be distrusted as something of a revolutionary by the Prussian Government. Though promoted to the rank of general, he was never permitted to realize his ambition and command troops. Instead, he was appointed administrative director of the *Kriegsakademie,* a sinecure which left him with time on his hands. He devoted

33

his leisure to writing, working mornings in his wife's drawing room. His repeated attempts to have himself transferred to some other military or diplomatic post—at one time there was talk of an ambassadorship in London—met with failure. Finally, in 1831, Clausewitz was appointed chief of staff to the Prussian Army which was being deployed to observe the Polish rebellion against Russia. Accordingly he packed his papers and left Berlin for Silesia. Following the death of his revered commander in chief, General August von Gneisenau, Clausewitz took over. He had only occupied his new position for a few days, however, when there arrived from Berlin another general sent to replace him. Thereupon Clausewitz, too, fell ill and died, whether of cholera or heartbreak is not clear.

Clausewitz's writings span a period of almost thirty years and include works on art, education, philosophy, and current politics, as well as military history and theory. His magnum opus, *vom Kriege (On War)*, in which he invested some twelve years, was left incomplete and had to be published posthumously by his wife and brother-in-law. The book's fame spread slowly at first, but by the 1860s it had established itself as a classic. The preeminent position of *vom Kriege* was confirmed when Moltke, fresh from the Prussian victories of 1866 and 1870–71, called it "the military work which most influenced my mind." The work was praised by Engels ("a strange way to philosophize, but, on the matter itself, very good") and read by Marx. Lenin during his stay in Zurich provided it with perceptive footnotes. Hitler is said to have been able to quote it "by the yard," and Eisenhower grappled with it during his days at the US Army War College. To this day, it is regarded as the greatest work on war and strategy ever written within Western civilization.

Among military theorists, Clausewitz stands alone. With the possible exception of the ancient Chinese writer Sun Tzu, no other author has ever been remotely as influential, and indeed to this day his work forms the cornerstone of modern strategic thought. His continuing relevance is perhaps best illustrated by the fact that he is one of the few military thinkers to whom homage is paid on both sides of what, until recently, used to be the Iron Curtain. The man who at one point was regarded, not entirely without reason, as a typical Prussian militarist is now highly esteemed in both German democracies. His works have been translated into many languages, including Hebrew and Indonesian. Spurred by an excellent new translation of *vom Kriege* by Michael Howard and Peter Paret, Clausewitz-studies have enjoyed a renaissance in the United States during the last decade. The National War College in Washington D.C. has a Clausewitz-medallion which it awards to the best instructor of the year. A bust of him is on display at the US Army War College, Carslyle Barracks. As it happens, all we know about Clausewitz's appearance (apart from the fact that his face was permanently tinted red by the rigors of the Russian campaign) originates in a single portrait; hence, the bust probably owes even more to imagination than does the medallion.

Trinitarian War

To appreciate Clausewitz's contribution to the understanding of war, his work has to be seen in its proper context, a context provided by the late European enlightenment and the age of reason. *Vom Kriege* is mainly deductive in character: starting from first principles, the nature of war and the goal that it serves, the book seeks to progress step by step towards the most important question of all—namely, how armed conflict ought to be conducted. Given this axiomatic method, the role played by military history was limited. It was used as a source of examples (many of which have long become dated), and also as a kind of control designed to prevent theory from straying too far away from reality. However, no very great value was put on the past as such. Clausewitz always considered himself a practical soldier, albeit one with a philosophical bent of mind, writing for the benefit of other practical soldiers. As he says, the significance of this was that history was appreciated to the extent that it was recent, for only recent history was at all like the present and therefore capable of offering insights relevant to it.

Precisely which history should be considered "recent" was a question with which Clausewitz occupied himself, but to which he never gave an unambiguous answer. Among his voluminous writings on military history, a few go back as far as Gustavus Adolphus and Turenne in the seventeenth century however, the majority are concerned with the eighteenth century, the Seven Years' War, and Napoleon. *Vom Kriege* itself proposes several different possible starting-points. One is 1740, selected because it saw the outbreak of the first Silesian War and thus the first conflict commanded by Frederick the Great. Another is 1703, marking the outbreak of the War of the Spanish Succession, the first war to do without that ancient weapon, the pike. *Vom Kriege* was, however, much too profound a work to be governed by such technicalities. It was one of Clausewitz's most important contentions that war is a social activity. As such, war is molded by social relationships—by the type of society by which it is conducted, and the kind of government which that society admits. The dominant form of government in Clausewitz's own time, and as far into the future as he could see, was the state. Hence he saw little point in a detailed study of those periods in history which antedated the state; in other words, earlier than the Peace of Westphalia in 1648. And indeed those earlier periods are mentioned in *vom Kriege* mainly by way of illustrating their utter otherness.

Clausewitz's own military career is also relevant to the problem at hand. It began during the War of the First Coalition and ended, more or less, at the Battle of Waterloo. Fired by a passionate love of his own country and hatred of "Bonaparte," he was an active (although, to his own mind, not active enough) participant in these events. His entire thought can only be understood against the background of the very great historical changes which took place in front of his eyes; in one sense, indeed, it represented an attempt to understand and interpret those changes. This is not the place to discuss and analyze French Revolutionary and Napoleonic warfare, a subject that gave rise to an impassioned debate even as the events themselves unfolded. Suffice it to say that, between 1793 and 1815, a new form of war arose which smashed the *ancien régime* to smithereens. In the process, the organization of armed conflict, its strategy, and command—to mention but a few features—were all transformed beyond recognition. More important still, the scale on which war was waged also increased dramatically, and, above all, so did the sheer power with which it was waged.

The sound and fury of these years notwithstanding, when we ask not how war was conducted but by whom—what the social relationships behind it were, to use Clausewitz's own terminology—a plausible case can be made that little change took place at all. Except perhaps for a brief period of revolutionary fervor during the nineties, war remained something waged by one state against another. Both before and after 1789 it was not people who made war, nor armies on their own, but governments. Nor, when everything is said and done, had even the nature of government itself changed all that much. Napoleon, once he had become firmly established, behaved like any good contemporary monarch, marrying into the greatest ruling house of the times and creating dukes and princes galore. He spoke of the war against Prussia as *mes affaires,* and addressed his marshals as *mes cousins.* Whatever the exact differences between government and state, both are artificial creations not identical either with the persons of the rulers or with the people whom it claims to represent. That organized violence should only be called "war" if it were waged by the state, for the state, and against the state was a postulate that Clausewitz took almost for granted;

as did his contemporaries, including even the most pacific among them, such as Emmanuel Kant in his *Project for Perpetual Peace*.

The extent to which war was identified with the state is, paradoxically, attested to with particular force by those cases when non-governmental bodies did try to wage war on their own initiative, subject to no orders from above. Such cases had not been unknown even during the "civilized" eighteenth century. During Louis XIV's expansionist wars, the Savoyards—a backward people whose home was in the mountains between France and Italy—often resorted to violence to try and prevent their horses (to say nothing of their women) from being requisitioned by the army. The German Palatinate was another favorite target of French invasions. Its inhabitants were occasionally so impertinent as to take pot-shots at the occupation forces, earning the sobriquet of *Schnappeurs,* said to be derived from the sound made by a firing mechanism when the trigger is pulled. The French reaction to such outbreaks of "unofficial" warfare resembled that of other conquerors before and after them. They killed, burned, and looted with little or no restraint, turning entire districts into deserts and calling it peace.

From our modern point of view, what makes these reprisals remarkable is that they were supported by international law which condemned the uprisings. This was true even of Emmeric Vattel, the great and humane Swiss jurist whose works were standard on the subject and continued to be so to the time of the American Civil War. As Vattel, writing during the 1750s, saw the problem, war was an affair for sovereign princes and for them only; indeed it was defined as a way by which princes, *faute de mieux,* could settle their differences. Princes were supposed to wage war in such a way as to minimize the harm done both to their own soldiers, who deserved humane treatment if they happened to be captured or wounded, and to the civilian population. In return, that population had absolutely no right to interfere in quarrels between their sovereigns, not even when they resulted in their property being robbed and their lives put in jeopardy. Neither unworldly nor a fool, Vattel would have been the last to deny that war was the province of many an outrage. Still, the distinction between the military and civilians had to be observed at all costs. Should it break down, then Europe would revert to the Thirty Years' War with all its attendant barbarism.

Nevertheless, when the Spanish guerrillas rose after 1808 and began the struggle against Napoleonic tyranny, much of Europe was prepared to applaud. Russian partisans and German *Freikorps* followed their example, fighting for their countries' liberation with varying degrees of success. What makes these cases interesting to us is the fact that, in every single instance, the appearance of the guerrillas excited the suspicions of the powers-that-be and of the classes that supported them. No doubt there were many reasons for this, some political, others socio-economic in nature. The Tsar and his noblemen could scarcely be expected to show enthusiasm for a movement that put muskets on the serfs' shoulders and taught them how to fight. The Prussian monarchy thought it had everything to lose at the hands of a people in arms. In these two countries reaction triumphed with comparative ease, but in Spain it took some twenty years and a whole series of civil struggles (the Carlist Wars) to put the people back where they belonged. Though these states' attitudes to the guerrillas, leading to their ultimate suppression, may have had their origins in class interest, they were rooted at the same time in the existing juridico-military-theoretical outlook. The popular uprisings might be considered useful, patriotic, even heroic. However, they did not tally with conventional ideas as to who was entitled to wage war, and as to what it was all about.

If it was governments that made war, their instrument for doing so consisted of armies. Though the methods by which armies were raised underwent some changes, their fundamental nature was not trans-formed either by the French Revolution or by the wars that followed it. Armies were defined as organizations that served the government, whether monarchical, republican, or imperial. They were made up of soldiers; that is, personnel who were drafted into the organization at the beginning of their career and formally discharged when it ended. Contacts between soldiers and civilians were generally discouraged; for example, by recruiting foreigners, moving the troops from one province to the next, and obliging the population to assist in arresting deserters. The military had their own separate customs, such as drill, the salute, and—for officers—honor and the duel. They swore to obey their own separate laws and dressed in their own separate costumes. Following the end of the War of the Austrian Succession in 1748 there was also a growing tendency to house them in their own separate institutions, known as barracks. Often they were even supposed to carry themselves differently from ordinary mortals, an affectation that has lasted to the present day.

In Europe, the first standing armies originated in the midst of feudal disorder as paid private instruments at the disposal of monarchs such as Charles VII of France. This meant that they were also frequently used for purposes which we today would regard as nonmilitary, such as administration, enforcing law and order, and tax-collecting. However, such use decreased as the eighteenth century drew to a close. One reason for the change was the disarming of the population that accompanied the shift from countryside to city; burghers generally did not like to have weapons at home. Another was the steady growth of civil services, including both tax-collecting agencies (England was the first country to institute a permanent income-tax in 1799) and police forces. Finally there was the rise of military professionalism—the idea that war represented an art or science in its own right which had to be exercised by specialists and by them alone. After 1815 there appeared the idea of the nonpolitical army which, under ordinary circumstances, was prohibited from engaging in any activities except those related to waging war against foreign powers. Paradoxically, this even applied, where most soldiers were themselves conscripted civilians, as was the case in the French and later the Prussian armies.

As postulated by *vom Kriege,* the third vital element in any war consists of the people. Between 1648 and 1789 jurists and military practitioners were in agreement that, since war was a question of state, the people should be excluded from it as far as possible. This was carried to the point where they were prohibited from taking an active part in hostilities; as is also evident from the fact that, when speaking of "small" war, contemporaries had in mind not guerrilla operations but merely those of light troops, such as the Austrian Croats, who operated away from the army's main body. There arose, as a result, the idea of the civilian or "civilist" as he was sometimes called. All that absolute monarchs such as Louis XV, Frederick II, and Maria Theresa asked of civilians—their own and their enemies—was docility. They should pay taxes to whatever government happened to be occupying the province in which they lived; this demand satisfied, they were not expected to hate, cheer, or feel a lump in the throat, but merely stay out of the way. After Jena the Governor of Berlin simply announced that, the King having lost a battle, it was the citizens' first duty to remain quiet.

Faced with the disintegration of the Old Royal Army, the French National Assembly in 1793 "permanently requisitioned" all citizens for the national service, including not just men but women, children, and old people. Confronted with the huge new armies that the *mobilisation générale* made possible, other states were compelled to follow suit to a smaller or greater degree. Later, during the nineteenth century, even reactionary states such as Austria, Prussia, and Russia caught on to the nationalistic wave. They began to demand that the people display proper patriotic enthusiasm and, increasingly, contribute not just their possessions but their persons to the war effort. Education, public art, and ceremonial, as well as propaganda of all kinds, were mobilized. In each country the masses had to believe that their state was great and strong, always right and never wrong. Still, the magnitude of the change should not be exaggerated. Cynics might say that, whereas most educated persons before 1789 agreed that war was made at the people's expense, after that date it was supposed to be waged on their behalf. However this may be, the "trinity" by which war was and was not made, the Clausewitzian trinity consisting of the people, the army, and the government, remained unaffected by the Revolution.

The idea of war as something that could be waged only by the state was, if anything, reinforced by the decades of reaction that followed upon the Congress of Vienna (1814–15). This was a period when the incipient industrial revolution led to social unrest and upheavals. The ever-present specter of another French Revolution, as well as sheer war-weariness, meant that most European princes feared their own peoples more than they did each other. The last thing they wanted was to give those peoples arms; on the contrary, they attempted to deprive them of the arms they already had. The best-known of these struggles took place in Prussia. Assisted by the Regular Army, the Monarchy set about to dismantle the largely middle-class Civil Guard, or *Landwehr,* which was no longer needed now that Napoleon had been sent to Saint Helena. Regarded as the last resort against Revolution—*gegen Demokraten hilfen nur Soldaten,* as King Frederick Wilhelm IV of Prussia once put it—standing armies became even more professional than before. In some countries a system of recruitment that allowed the well-to-do to purchase substitutes ensured that the rank and file would be drawn from the lower classes. Soldiers continued to be strictly isolated from society at large. This was carried to the point that, in France under Louis Philippe, orders were issued for them to wear whiskers and for the whiskers to be black.

A whole series of international agreements, most of which date to the period between 1859 (the battle of Solferino) and 1907 (the Second Hague Conference) codified these ideas and converted them into positive law. To distinguish war from mere crime it was defined as something waged by sovereign states and by them alone. Soldiers were defined as personnel licensed to engage in armed violence on behalf of the state; as part of this, the ancient practices of issuing letters of marque and privateering were prohibited. To obtain and maintain their license, soldiers had to be carefully registered, marked, and controlled, to the exclusion of privateering. They were supposed to fight only while in uniform, carrying their arms "openly," and obeying a commander who could be held responsible for their actions. They were not supposed to resort to "dastardly" methods such as violating truces, taking up arms again after they had been wounded or taken prisoner, and the like. The civilian population was supposed to be left alone, "military necessity" permitting. In return, they were supposed to let the soldiers fight it out among themselves. Civilians who broke the rules, failing to procure a license before resorting to armed violence, did so at their own risk and could expect reprisals when captured. Their fate had been depicted by Goya who, in the midst of the Spanish uprising against Napoleon, did a series of pictures entitled "The Horrors of War."

Whether intended or not, one result of these agreements was that non-European populations that did not know the state and its sharply-drawn division between government, army, and people were automatically declared to be bandits. Whenever they tried to take up arms, they were automatically considered *hors de loi*. The way towards atrocities of every kind was thereby opened. In the colonies, European troops often acted as if what they were waging was not war but safari. They slaughtered the natives like beasts, scarcely stopping to distinguish between chiefs, warriors, women, and children. Even within the so-called civilized world violations of the rules were not unknown: Sherman's burning his way through Georgia in 1864 provides one example that has still not been forgotten in the American South. The Germans after defeating the French Army in 1870 complained bitterly about the *franc-tireurs* and took savage measures to suppress them. Still, as far as the "civilized" world was concerned, by and large the distinctions held up well. The period from 1854 to 1914 witnessed a whole series of "cabinet" wars. Each was declared by a government for some specific end, such as occupying a province, assisting an ally, or—in the case of Prussia against Austria—deciding who would be master in Germany. Paradoxically the best example of all was presented by the United States. The Civil War was officially considered a rebellion. Nevertheless, the Union text on international law (the Lieber Code, known after its author, Francis Lieber) decreed that it would be waged, and the rebels treated, *as if* it were an international conflict on both sides.

To sum up, Clausewitz's ideas on war were wholly rooted in the fact that, ever since 1648, war had been waged overwhelmingly by states. A brief period of revolutionary fervor and guerrilla uprisings apart, these ideas turned out to be even more applicable during the nineteenth century. It was a period when the legal separation between governments, armies, and peoples became, for various reasons, even stricter than before: 1848–9 marked the end of armed uprisings. Intrastate political violence was largely restricted to the anarchists, a term that speaks for itself. The occasional bomb apart, states all but achieved their aim of monopolizing armed force; nor did it take long before they had the monopoly codified into formal international law. Indeed, so firmly entrenched is trinitarian doctrine even today that we commonly add some adjective such as "total," "civil," "colonial," or "peoples," to those cases—actually, the majority—where it fits barely or not at all. As the existence of such cases makes clear, however, it is not self-evident that the trinity of government, army, and people is the best way to understand either "uncivilized" war or the great wars of the twentieth century. This is even more applicable to those periods, comprising most of history, that Clausewitz did not consider worth discussing in detail.

Total War

The man who first discerned that trinitarian war would not necessarily be the wave of the future, and who also tried to work out the implications of such a possibility, was Colmar von der Goltz. Von der Goltz was a German officer and writer who was destined to become a field marshal. During World War I he served as commander of German forces in the Middle East. In this capacity he was responsible for mounting an abortive invasion of Egypt before dying—officially of typhus, unofficially perhaps of poison—in Mesopotamia. Long before these events, the then Major von der Goltz published a book called *Das Volk in Waffen* (1883) which, thirty years later, was translated into English as *The Nation in Arms*. This work was not intended as an anti-Clausewitizian polemic. Like most of his fellow-officers, von der Goltz regarded himself as a disciple of the master, whom he praised fulsomely. *Das Volk in Waffen* took particular delight in the Clausewitzian emphasis on war as an exercise in unrestricted violence.

The point where von der Goltz clashed with *vom Kriege* was, instead, precisely the one which interests us here. However great the emphasis that Clausewitz had put on the changes brought about by the French Revolution, ultimately he presented war as something made by armies. Such a point of view might have been valid in his own day, but during the second half of the century it began to be undermined by modern economic, technological, and military developments. The greatest challenges were posed by those twin instruments, the railway and the telegraph, which Clausewitz did not live to see and which from the 1840s on started transforming every aspect of life. As to their use in war, nobody had done more to further that use than the Germans themselves. In 1864, 1866, and 1870–71 railways and telegraphs were put under the command of the Prussian General Staff. Meticulous planning and careful preparation enabled mobilization and deployment to be carried out with unprecedented effectiveness, so much so that a huge military advantage was acquired before the first shot was fired. The demonstrated ability of modern technology to integrate the resources of entire countries, wrote von der Goltz, pointed to the conclusion that future wars would no longer be fought by armies as traditionally understood. The rhetoric of 1793 could now be put into practice: called to the flag, the entire nation would put on its uniform, take up its arms, and hurl itself on the enemy.

The second point where *Das Volk in Waffen* differed with *vom Kriege* was over the vexed question concerning the relationship between politics and war at the top level. Clausewitz himself had discussed this problem at some length, finally concluding that civil and military functions were best concentrated in the hands of a single man. Again, this solution may have had its merits in Clausewitz's day, though Napoleon's ultimate fate makes one doubt even this. By the late nineteenth century it had become perfectly anachronistic. On the military side, war had become much too large and complicated to be managed by the ruler in person in addition to his other duties; that could only be done by a dedicated, full time, professional commander in chief with a suitable organization at his beck and call. Conversely, the time had long passed when modern states could be run on a part-time basis by a ruler-*cum*-supreme commander who spent weeks and months away from the capital campaigning in the field. In 1870–71 these problems were highlighted by the power-struggle which broke out between Moltke and Bismarck. It became clear that, if war was to be subordinated to politics, it would also have to be subordinated to politicians.

It was against this aspect that von der Goltz revolted, along perhaps with the majority of his colleagues. As the contemporary military—and not just the German military—saw the problem, war was the most serious, certainly the greatest, possibly the most wonderful, thing on earth. War was the way in which God effected His choice among nations; as such it was much too important a business to be left to the "idiotic civilians" (the Kaiser's phrase). Hence, war was the appropriate time in which to put the politicians back in their place, and the same applied to the commercial and industrial bourgeoisie, which during those very years was using its economic muscle to challenge the social position of the officer corps. War, it was hoped by many, would bring about a "reversion to traditional values." Accordingly the supreme commander ought to be the Emperor in his suit of shining armor, not some politician in black coat and top hat.

At the time when these doctrines were first put forward they were little more than a militarist's dream. They were, however, destined to be turned into reality by World War I, the first "total" conflict in modern history. The conflict began like any other, a limited "cabinet war" for limited ends. The Sarajevo Crisis was just one more crisis much like previous ones. There had been a crisis over Morocco in 1904, one over Bosnia-Herzegovina in 1909, and another over Morocco in 1911, all of which were resolved and dissolved. Nor was the drama taking place in June 1914 taken seriously at first, what with the Kaiser refusing to interrupt his sailing holiday in the Baltic. This particular time around it was Austria, incensed by the killing of the Archduke Karl, that wanted to crush Serbia. Serbia appealed to Russia for help. Germany decided to teach Russia a lesson, and France saw an opportunity to recover Alsace-Lorraine. When Italy entered the war in 1915 she even entered into a formal agreement with the Entente, specifying just how much she would be paid and which provinces she would get for her aid. In each country crowds cheered as the opposing teams, dressed in khaki, field-grey, horizon-blue, or earth-brown took the field. It was thought that the war would be short, and the victors were expected home by Christmas.

Things, however, soon changed. The initial battles failed to produce a decision, but instead produced mountains of casualties. The armies had to be backed up by the massive mobilization of military manpower of all ages. Next came the mobilization of civilians of both sexes to staff the factories that produced the wherewithal for the war effort—the tremendous supplies that modern armed forces require to operate and to exist. This was complemented by that of agriculture, raw materials, transportation, finance, technical-scientific talent, and every other kind of resource. The nineteenth-century doctrine of economic *laissez faire,* which had already taken some body blows before the war, died a sudden and unnatural death. It was not long before governments started taking a hand in everything considered even remotely relevant to the war effort. This included people's health, their living conditions, their calory-intake, their wages, their professional qualifications, their freedom of movement, and so on ad infinitum.

To supervise mobilization, vast bureaucratic structures were called into being as if by magic. Soon the organizations set up by Walter Rathenau, David Lloyd George, and (later) Bernard Baruch acquired a momentum of their own, spending money and devouring resources on a scale that would have been considered inconceivable before the war. The greater the scale and intensity of mobilization, the more the hostilities escalated; by the 1918 the daily consumption of shells by the leading armed forces had increased fiftyfold over that of 1914, with other indicators following suit. The more hostilities escalated, the stronger the pressure on entire social systems to join the conflict until they became locked in a murderous embrace. By 1916, the year of Verdun and the Somme, the war had grown into a self-sustaining monster from which even the most determined statesmen saw themselves unable to escape. So far from "using" war as its instrument, the state now threatened to be devoured by it, people, economy, politics, government, and all.

One man who did as much as any other to bring this situation about was Erich Ludendorff. Ludendorff was a German staff officer who won his spurs at Liege in 1914. Later he served on the Eastern Front, where he was the brain behind the great victories at Tannenberg and the Masurian Lakes. When his superior, Field Marshal Paul von Hindenburg, was appointed Army Chief of Staff in July 1916, Ludendorff went with him. Assuming the post of First Quartermaster General, he became Germany's military dictator in all but name. He used his position to mobilize the country's resources, waging war on a scale and with an intensiveness that overshadowed even the already considerable achievements of 1914 and 1915. In the early summer of 1918, having defeated Russia and launched a series of mighty offensives on the Western front, he came close to winning the war. When fortune deserted Germany later in the year he collapsed, leaving his country leaderless. After the war he became temporarily involved with Hitler. Later still, assisted by his second wife, he set up a publishing house which specialized in confused antisemitic tracts.

The last of Ludendorff's books was called *Der Totale Krieg (Total War)*, and was published in 1936. In it he tried to summarize his experiences and explain his mistakes away. The core of the work was formed by a direct attack on Clausewitz, whose definition of war as the continuation of politics Ludendorff wanted to "throw overboard." Modern conditions had rendered it imperative that politics be made the continuation of war, now understood as a national struggle for survival with no holds barred. *Der Totale Krieg* was rife with complaints about people and organizations which, so its author complained, had obstructed him and prevented all of Germany's resources from being committed to the war effort. Among those whom he denounced were the various states comprising the German Empire; parties and trade unions; industrialists, media-barons, even the chancellor himself. All of them were presented as having stood in his way, preferring their own selfish interests to those of the country.

Der Totale Krieg was, however, as much a blueprint for the next war as it was a summary of the last one. To prevent the same situation from recurring, and to enable maximum efficiency to be attained, Ludendorff demanded that the usual distinctions between government, army, and people be scrapped. Whether in of out of uniform, the entire country was to become the equivalent of a gigantic army with every man, woman, and child serving at his or her post. At the head of the machine there was to stand a military dictator. *Der Feldherr*—Ludendorff himself, needless to say—was to exercise absolute power, including that of overriding the judiciary and putting to death members of the national community who in his judgment were standing in the way of the war effort. Perhaps most radical of all, this kind of organization would not be limited solely to wartime. Modern armed conflict was waged on such a scale, and needed such lengthy preparations, that the only solution was to make the dictatorship permanent.

Ludendorff's views were indeed extreme, representing the acme of German militarism. Even so, they were rooted in a much wider Western school of thought; it was the school that, starting around the turn of the century, came to see "efficiency" as the ultimate human achievement, and sought various ways in which social structures might be transformed in order to achieve it. More important to our immediate purpose, it did not take long for Ludendorff's views to turn into horrible reality. The outbreak of World War II caused the old mobilization-plans to be taken out of the drawers and dusted; this even applied to countries such as the Netherlands which were at first uninvolved but which bitter experience had taught about the economic difficulties arising from war. For the second time in a quarter century the belligerents flexed their every muscle. This time they did so on a scale, and with a ruthlessness, that might have made even Ludendorff—who had died in 1937— blanch.

As mobilization proceeded and the war became total, the process of government was split into two halves. Its most important functions were amalgamated with the war. The process is well illustrated by the career of Albert Speer, an architect-turned-manager who headed the German *Rüstungsministerium* (Ministry of Armaments), a post that did not even exist before 1939. By 1943 Speer had reached the point where he was second only to Hitler in the *Grossdeutsche Reich*. Theoretically, and to a large extent in practice as well, he possessed absolute authority as to who was to produce what, by what means, on the basis of what raw materials, and at what prices. In terms of the funds that he commanded as well as the manpower that worked for him—some 20 million people—Speer totally eclipsed any other minister. As he himself proudly notes in his memoirs, compared with him the generals who commanded the armed forces were not even in the running as candidates for power. Hitler's long-time second in command, Hermann Göring, was thrust aside by Speer, who went on to engage the fearsome Himmler in a struggle over slave labor. Nor, truth to say, were things so very different on the Allied side. Stalin's mobilization was quite as ruthless as Hitler's and any striking Russian worker would have been shot out of hand. Thanks partly to democratic traditions, partly to geographical circumstances that rendered their situation easier, Britain and the United States did not go quite so far. However, in order to assist mobilization they put in effect many restrictions on personal freedom, whereas the scale on which their war effort operated was if anything greater still.

Even as some parts of government became identical with the running of the war, those that were not immediately vital to its conduct were reduced to impotence or irrelevance. Perhaps the worst affected were the various financial agencies. Before the war these agencies had held governments by the throat, obstructing or delaying rearmament. As expenditure mounted and dwarfed income, such considerations became irrelevant and the very meaning of money changed. The principal task left to state finance was to print money and supervise its distribution, with the result that there were times when in Britain, for example, the Secretary of the Exchequer was not even a member of the war cabinet. Much the same happened to those who, in peacetime, had been responsible for their countries' foreign policy. When Hitler in 1941 declared a war of extermination against the USSR, German foreign policy shrunk almost to zero; henceforward it consisted merely of attempts to enlist the aid of minor neutrals, and later of preventing them from joining the Allies. When Churchill and Roosevelt declared their aim to be unconditional surrender, policy in the ordinary sense of the word was also forced to take a back seat. Incidentally, the ground lost by treasuries and foreign offices during the war has not been recovered to this day. Treasuries have so far lost control over money that steady inflation was built into the economy of most advanced countries. Foreign offices have had to renounce many of their original functions, which have been taken over by defense departments, another indication of the changing relationship between policy and war.

Finally, many of the distinctions between army and people which had been established by eighteenth- and nineteenth-century international law also broke down. Armed violence, far from being limited to combatants, escaped its bounds. Terrible atrocities, including even the planned starvation of tens of millions, were carried out against the inhabitants of occupied countries both in Europe and in Asia. The populations themselves did not acquiesce with their lot. Occupation per se was now regarded as a monstrous injustice and resisted. In places such as Yugoslavia, Tito's partisans, though comprising neither government nor army, came close to waging full-scale conventional conflict; and indeed in retrospect this may have been the most important of all the changes which the War brought about. Meanwhile the sky was filled with mighty fleets of heavy bombers—later, flying bombs and ballistic missiles—headed in both directions. They deliberately set out to kill civilians, women and children not excluded. Entire cities were destroyed by firestorms in a manner not seen in Europe for three centuries. A climax of violence was reached in 1945 when two nuclear bombs were dropped on Japan, killing 150,000 people in flat disregard of the fact that peace negotiations were already going on in Moscow at the time. Officially the destruction of enemy civilians was justified by their wickedness. In practice, often they had to be declared wicked so that they could be destroyed by the indiscriminate weapons available.

In 1815 the delegates at the Congress of Vienna made a brave attempt to restore the *ancien régime,* putting the blame for the years of disorder on "the Ogre"—Napoleon—personally. Similarly, the overriding purpose of the War Criminals' Trials held in Nuremberg and Tokyo was to help patch up the damage done to international society by defining the things which were and were not permissible. To do this, the political, economic, social, military and technical factors that had been responsible for the breakdown of the traditional trinitarian distinctions had be largely ignored. Instead, that breakdown was put at the door of a particular group of people, namely, the losers. Their principal leaders were to be put on trial, convicted, and for the most part executed. The armed forces of the defeated side were disbanded, their main economic organizations (such as the Japanese *Zaibatsu*) scattered, and their resources expropriated as reparations by those of the victors who chose to do so. The trials themselves helped crystallize a whole new series of juridical concepts, such as "conspiracy to break the peace," "waging aggressive war," and something known as "war crimes." All these were duly defined by lawyers and, in one form or another, became a recognized part of international law.

Metternich, looking back from the eve of his resignation in 1848, might have felt satisfied with the results of the Congress of Vienna despite several limited revolutionary outbreaks that had taken place in the meantime. Similarly, a backward glance from the perspective of 1990 makes the attempt to put the genie back into the bottle appear successful up to a point; those who set out to establish a new world order after World War II did their work reasonably well. The principal reasons for this outcome were the ever-present fear of nuclear Armageddon and, of course, sheer war-weariness. At any rate, to date there has been no repetition of "total" conflict on the model established by both World Wars. When the principal military powers went to war—always excepting the "low-intensity conflicts" which, though they formed a large majority, hardly counted as a war—they usually abided by the rules. Whatever may be said about the Falkland War, it did not witness either the breakdown of distinctions between the military and civilians or, consequently, large-scale atrocities. The same is true about the Arab-Israeli Wars, except perhaps for the first; though in this case things might have looked different had victory gone to the other side.

The point, however, had been made and would not be forgotten. Whatever else total war may have done, it put an end to any idea that armed conflict, including specifically the largest ever fought, is necessarily governed by the Clausewitzian Universe. Historically speaking, in fact, trinitarian war—in other words, a war of state against state and army against army—is a comparatively recent phenomenon; hence, the things that the future has in store for humanity may also be very different indeed.

Nontrinitarian War

The Clausewitzian Universe rests on the assumption that war is made predominantly by states or, to be exact, by governments. Now states are artificial creations; corporate bodies that possess an independent legal existence separate from the people to whom they belong and whose organized life they claim to represent. As Clausewitz himself was well aware, the state, thus understood, is a modern invention. Though there are always precedents, by and large it was only since the Peace of Westphalia in 1648 that the state became the dominant form of political organization even in Europe; and indeed it is for this reason among others that we speak of "the modern age" as opposed to whatever came before. Moreover, most non-European parts of the world had never known the state until it emerged during the nineteenth- and twentieth-century processes of colonization and decolonization. It follows that, where there are no states, the threefold division into government, army, and people does not exist in the same form. Nor would it be correct to say that, in such societies, war is made by governments using armies for making war at the expense of, or on the behalf of, their people.

If it was not the state and armies who made war, who did? The answer depends on the period one selects. Proceeding in reverse chronological order, the early modern age witnessed a whole series of struggles, that among other things were waged precisely in order to determine who was, and who was not, entitled to use armed violence. Nor was the outcome predetermined by any means. England during the second half of the fifteenth century sank into civil war between the great baronial factions and all but disintegrated. Much the same fate overtook France a century later. The German *Landesfrieden* of 1595 was intended to end the war of all against all, but instead merely acted as a prelude for worse things to come. Even as late as 1634, the Habsburg Emperor saw himself constrained to have his own commander in chief, Wallenstein, murdered for fear that he would use his independent army to establish an equally independent state. The ultimate victors were, nevertheless, the great monarchs. Allied with the urban bourgeoisie, and thanks in part to the superior financial resources at their disposal, they could purchase more cannon than anybody else and blast the opposition to pieces. By the 1620s Cardinal Richelieu in France was proceeding systematically against the aristocracy's castles, blowing them up one by one; a clear sign of things to come.

Before the triumph of the monarchies could be completed, however, it was necessary that many contenders be fought off. Among them were great independent noblemen such as the *frondeurs* who made the France of Louis XIII such an uncomfortable place to live. War was also waged by religious associations, be they the French Catholic League, their Huguenot opponents, or—before them—the Bohemian Hussites; all of these set up military organizations that were sovereign in all but name. In the Netherlands from the 1560s on, war was made by the so-called *geuzen* or beggars, all kinds of riff-raff led by disaffected noblemen who had rebelled against Philip II of Spain. In Germany during the 1520s there was a Peasants' War of serfs against barons which was savagely suppressed, claiming tens of thousands of victims. In all these struggles political, social, economic, and religious motives were hopelessly entangled. Since this was an age when armies consisted of mercenaries, all were also attended by swarms of military entrepreneurs out to make a personal profit. Many of them paid little but lip service to the organizations for whom they had contracted to fight. Instead, they robbed the countryside on their own behalf, even building fortified strongholds where they collected loot and held prisoners for ransom.

Given such conditions, any fine distinctions that may have existed between armies on the one hand and peoples on the other were bound to break down. Engulfed by war, civilians suffered terrible atrocities— during the Thirty Years' War one third of Germany's population is said to have perished by the sword or else by hunger and disease. Provinces, districts, and towns found themselves faced with the threat of imminent ruin; making use of the old organizations for territorial defense that still existed in many places they sometimes rose in self-defense, whether in the name of some recognized authority or not. Having once risen, they were no different from the gangs of ruffians serving with military entrepreneurs, nor from the bands of peasants rising against their lords, nor from the retainers attending the warring noblemen. All of them engaged in war, which itself was scarcely any more distinguishable from simple rapine and murder. When "public" authority caught up with people waging war in any of the above capacities they were sometimes hanged for their pains. Often, however, they obtained a pardon by agreeing to switch sides, which in practice meant pursuing the same activities under a different name.

Meanwhile the most powerful monarchies were valiantly trying to create order out of chaos by setting up their own *militum perpetuum* or standing armies. Sometimes they were successful, sometimes not. The principal reason for failure was financial. Armies were extremely expensive to raise and maintain, with the result that their pay was almost always in arrears. When things got bad the troops mutinied. They would raise the standard of revolt, elect leaders, formally disown their allegiance to the crown, and set out to plunder the countryside like anybody else. This even applied to the best-organized armed forces of the time, namely, those of Spain. For example, a year after Philip II went bankrupt in 1575 the Army of Flanders mutinied. For three days the troops ran amok, plundering and burning the great commercial city of Antwerp. The shock waves spreading from "the Spanish fury"—an ironic name, since the men were an international lot—decisively influenced the seven northern Dutch provinces' decision to sign a treaty for mutual self-defense. A somewhat disorganized rebellion was thereby turned into a full-fledged struggle destined to last for another seventy-two years, finally ending when the Netherlands became an independent country.

When we retreat from the early modern age into the Middle Ages the distinction between government, army, and people becomes more tenuous still. As the term "feudal" implies, this was a period in which politics did not exist (the very concept had yet to be invented, and dates back only as far as the sixteenth century.) So closely intertwined were a man's political power and his personal status that his ability to conclude alliances could well depend on the number of marriageable daughters he had sired. Politics were entangled with military, social, religious, and, above everything else, legal considerations; feudalism before it was anything else comprised a network of mutual rights and obligations. The resulting witches'-brew was utterly different from the one we are familiar with today, so that to use the word politics probably does more harm than good. The medieval context hardly even makes it possible to speak of governments, let alone of states. Both concepts did exist, but only in embryonic form, as it were. Often their use carried nostalgic overtones, as if people were harking back to the days of the Roman Empire, from which government at any rate had been derived.

Under such circumstances, to speak of war in modern Clausewitzian terms as something made by the state for political ends is to misrepresent reality. For a thousand years after the fall of Rome armed conflict was waged by different kinds of social entities. Among them were barbarian tribes, the Church, feudal barons of every rank, free cities, even private individuals. Nor were the "armies" of the period anything like those we know today; indeed, it is difficult to find a word that will do them justice. War was waged by shoals of retainers who donned military garb and followed their lord. The identity of those retainers who owned military service changed over time. When the foundations of the feudal system were being laid during the ninth century the *fyrd* or levy counted the entire free population, including even the lowliest villagers who responded to the call armed with whatever weapons they possessed. Later the situation changed. As free villagers were reduced to serfdom, there rose above them a class of people, known first as *bellatores* or *pugnatores* and later as knights, who made war their vocation and who fought on horseback. Thanks partly to their equipment, partly to their training, the military superiority of the knights over the popular levy was such that the latter languished and gradually disappeared.

Depending on the time and place, some of those who habitually fought on horseback might be "free" and noble, others not. A few, like the German *ministeriales*, were simply retainers, maintained by the lord in his own household and at his own expense. However, the majority probably received a fief and fought to fulfill their feudal duty, usually consisting of forty days' obligatory service a year. From the fourteenth century on there was a tendency to commute feudal service for money-payment—the so-called *scutagium*—which, in turn, could be used to employ mercenaries. Whatever the arrangements under which their members were engaged, during the high Middle Ages armies were small, impermanent bodies, which in many ways scarcely even answered to the term "organization." Far from being separate from society, their members themselves *were* society or at any rate the only part of it that mattered (except for priests). Far from obeying a separate code, the chivalrous one that they professed to obey was *the* social code (excepting, again, the code imposed by religion). The identity between army and society even extended to dress. Armor was the knights' dress *par excellence,* and at the churches where they are buried it is in their armor that we can see their brass effigies today.

The third element in Clausewitzian trinitarian war, namely the people, did not come into the equation at all; precisely because they were excluded from war, the great mass of serfs did not form part of society either. Low-born personnel who were not knights participated in war by attending their masters as baggage-carriers, servants, grooms, and the like. For them to take up arms was considered distinctly unsportsmanlike; usually when they did so they would be slaughtered, more in jest than in anger. The population at large entered war mainly in the role of victims. The simplest way to hurt an enemy while enriching oneself was to attack and despoil the serfs from whom he derived his income. Conversely, so little did feudal war concern itself with the protection of the population at large that the garrisons of besieged castles often expelled noncombatants, regarding them as so many useless mouths. Hoping to apply psychological pressure, the besieging commander would then refuse to let them pass through his lines, with the result that the unfortunates ended up starving or freezing to death.

Given that war was no concern of ordinary people, little is known about what they thought of it, the more so since their views were considered as hardly worth recording by the two upper classes, the aristocratic and the ecclesiastic. Though the great French fourteenth-century peasant uprising claimed more lives than did most contemporary wars it was not even dignified with the name of war, but was called the *Jacquerie* instead. The *bonhommes* were regarded as scarcely human, nor was chivalrous custom followed in the process whereby they were suppressed. Judging by literary sources such as the fourteenth century *Piers Plowman,* members of the lower classes seem to have looked at war as the product of baronial vice and greed. Far from being a deliberate instrument in the king's hands, it was considered akin to a plague inflicted on the people by wanton noblemen. Always in theory, and often in practice as well, they did this without the king's knowledge or else against his will.

When we come to the classical world, the Clausewitzian Universe appears to be much more relevant than it was during the middle ages. Such an impression is, however, incorrect. Even the term "Roman Empire" is misleading, since the proper translation of *Imperium* is "authority" or "domination." Beginning in the first century A.D. there was an attempt to turn Rome itself into a divinity. However, the idea of the state as an abstract legal entity standing apart from the ruler did not exist, nor were contemporaries able to conceive of a conflict of interest between the two. Augustus' attempt to disguise his true position by bedecking himself with republican titles such as consul could not deceive anyone: he was *Imperator*—victorious commander—before he was anything else. As time went on, his successors did not even bother to keep up the pretense until the term *princeps* was replaced by *dominus,* first unofficially and then officially as well. All this was reflected in contemporary "political" theory which, properly speaking, did not concern itself with politics at all. The object of doctrines such as epicurianism, cynicism, and stoicism was to reconcile the individual to his fate in a world apparently destined to be ruled by despotism; somewhat later, the same applied to early Christianity.

Despotism, too, was the normal form of government during the Hellenistic age. So closely identified with each other were the god-king and his realm that the principal officials of the kingdom were known simply as the king's "friends" and "companions"; originally, indeed they *had* been precisely that, living in or around his tent and sharing with him the dangers of battle. Nobody put the idea more clearly than Seleucus I, the successor who, after the death of Alexander the Great, established himself in Asia Minor, Syria, and parts of Iraq on the basis of no right except that provided by the force of arms. In front of his assembled army he gave his own wife, Stratonike, to his son by a previous marriage, Antiochus, adding that since both were young they would surely have children. This act of incest was justified "not because it is the law of gods or men, but because it is my wish." He was emphasizing the obvious: namely, that the Seleucid Kingdom was a military dictatorship, a haphazard collection of peoples and provinces subject to a single man who had the spears to back him up.

If late antiquity did not know the state, at least it recognized the division into "government," army, and people. The culturally homogeneous Hellenistic world in particular regarded war as the business of the former two, and not of the people, and some rules were established as to who might do what, to whom, under what circumstances, and for what ends. However, these distinctions did not apply in the same form either to Republican Rome or to the classical Greek *polis.* The translation "city state" is, in this respect, misleading. Admittedly the *polis* was sovereign in the sense that it recognized no superior above itself while possessing and exercising the right to go to war. Nevertheless it was not a state, nor do such words as *arche* or *koinon* correspond to our modern idea of "government" as an institution. Those responsible for the day-to-day running of Republican Rome and the Greek *polis* were not rulers but officials elected on an annual basis. They were in charge, not of the state but, to use the Latin expression, of the *res publica:* which may be translated either as "the association of people" or "the public domain."

The *res publica* embraced religious, cultural, and social affairs in addition to political ones. The citizen's gods were the gods of the city. The same applied to the festivals he celebrated and to the calendar by which he regulated his life. Therefore the role played by these entities in the individual's life exceeded that of the modern liberal state in many ways, approaching that of the totalitarian one. Nevertheless, neither the Greek *polis* nor the Roman *respublica* had an independent legal identity; that idea does not antedate the seventeenth century. Whereas territoriality lies at the root of the modern state, the Greek and Roman counterparts could exist even without a territorial base, and indeed many a Greek colony dated its existence from the moment the men set foot aboard ship. As if to emphasize the essentially associative character of the "political" organization, the vital decisions concerning war and peace were made not by the magistrates but by the Roman (or Athenian, or Spartan) people in their various assemblies. This system reflected earlier, more primitive, forms of organization.

Having voted for war, the citizens proceeded to the place where a levy was held. The magistrate in charge at the time raised his own force, either taking volunteers or selecting those who had not yet completed their obligatory number of campaigns. An army as a permanent, specialized organization separate from the people did not exist; originally the term *populus* could mean either concept. Accordingly the best translation of the Latin *exercitus* and the Greek *stratos* is not army but host, and the same applies to the Biblical *tsava,* meaning "mass" or "throng." So closely identified were "host" and "people" that the Athenians, isolated in enemy territory during the Sicilian expedition, could dream of setting themselves up as an independent *polis*. Nor did it ever occur to the citizens of a city-state that they were fighting on behalf of anybody except themselves. The absence of an abstract entity is reflected in the language that our sources use. From Herodotus through Xenophon and all the way to Polybios, it is always "the Athenians" or "the Lacedaemonians" who declare war, fight, and conclude treaties, never "Athens" or "Sparta" as such.

We end our historical survey by pointing to the numerous tribal societies which, until recently, existed all over the world and which even in Europe continued to play an important role until well into the Middle Ages. From the North American Sioux through the Amazonian Jibaro and the East African Masai to the Fijians of Fiji, many of them were extremely warlike. Some, such as the ferocious headhunters of New Guinea, even centered their entire lives around martial exploits; which was one reason why, when colonization made the continuation of such exploits impossible, their culture tended to wither and die. The fact that these people were warlike did not mean that they were familiar with the state or that they fought on its behalf. On the contrary, tribal warriors often found it hard to understand why anybody should fight for anybody but himself, his family, his friends, or allies. Nor were these distinctions simply academic. When tribal societies clashed with the white man it was often the result of misunderstandings, with each side accusing the other of treachery. For example, a North American Indian chief might promise the representatives of some American state to refrain from hostilities and smoke the pipe of peace with them. However, he did not necessarily consider his undertaking binding on the members of his nation. Even if he did, very likely he did not have the authority to make sure it was observed.

It is worth pointing out that tribal societies, which do not have the state, also do not recognize the distinction between army and people. Such societies do not have armies; it would be more accurate to say that they themselves *are* armies, in which respect they are not so different either from the Greek city-state or, to select a contemporary example, the various terrorist organizations at present fighting each other in places such as Lebanon, Sri Lanka, or Aberdjan. Nor, in their case, would it be correct to speak of soldiers. What they have is warriors, with the result that there are many languages—Masai, for example, or North American Indian languages—where the term for "warrior" simply means "young man." As the comparison with terrorist bands already shows, the rudimentary nature of tribal organizations does not mean that they are irrelevant to the present. Instead they may point to the future, perhaps more so than the world of states from which we seem to be emerging.

Low-Intensity Conflict Resurgens

If the argument advanced here is correct, then trinitarian war is not War with a capital W but merely one of the many forms that war has assumed. Nor is trinitarian war even the most important, given that, some previous parallels notwithstanding, it only emerged after the Peace of Westphalia. Based on the idea of the state and on the distinction between government, army, and people, trinitarian war was unknown to most societies during most of history. Had somebody tried to explain it to the members of those societies, probably they would not have understood any more than they would have grasped the idea of a modern corporation (the two, incidentally, arose at the same time). Given that one's understanding of the nature of war necessarily under-lies the way it is conducted, the problem is anything but academic. For example, during the great period of colonization, primitive tribes all over Africa and Oceania were never able to grasp why soldiers in red coats should risk their lives for some great woman-chief living beyond the ocean, who knows how far away. Unable to understand, they as-sumed that the invaders' real purpose was simply robbery. Treating their opponents as if they were robbers, they themselves received similar treatment.

One could, of course, follow some modern political scientists—not, it should be emphasized, Clausewitz himself—and identify all war with the state. This line of reasoning leads to the conclusion that, where there is no state, whatever armed violence takes place does not amount to war. The effect of such an arbitrary classification would, however, be to leave out the great majority of societies that have ever existed, including not just the "primitive" but some of the most civilized from Pericles' Athens down. Worse still, in the recent past such a view has often prevented low-intensity conflict from being taken seriously until it was too late. In both Algeria and Vietnam, to say nothing of the West Bank, the first limited uprisings were at first dismissed as simple bandi-try that "the forces of order" would suppress easily enough. For practi-cal as well as theoretical reasons, it seems much more reasonable to take the opposite tack. If any part of our intellectual baggage deserves to be thrown overboard, surely it is not the historical record but the Clausewitzian definition of war that prevents us from coming to grips with it.

So far, the past. Considering the present and trying to look into the future, I suggest that the Clausewitzian Universe is rapidly becoming out of date and can no longer provide us with a proper framework for understanding war. Modern, nontrinitarian, low-intensity conflict owes its rise in part to World War II. The peculiarly monstrous nature of the German and Japanese occupations were widely considered to violate established ethical norms. Hence, people had the right to revolt even though their armies had capitulated and their governments had surrendered. Having been upheld by the Allies, the principle took root. Before long it was turned against its original proponents, causing wars waged by entities other than states to multiply, so much so that *none* of those currently being fought anywhere around the world—perhaps a score or so in all—fits the traditional trinitarian pattern.

The news that present-day armed violence does not distinguish between governments, armies, and peoples will scarcely surprise the inhabitants of Ethiopia, the Spanish Sahara, or—to select an example from the developed world—those of Northern Ireland. Nor will it astonish the inhabitants, say, of Peru, El Salvador, and other Latin American countries who over the last few years have fought civil wars costing perhaps 70,000 in dead alone. It is hardly necessary to remind the reader that developing countries, the *locus classicus* of nontrinitarian war, have as their populations approximately four fifths of all people living on this planet. If anybody should be startled at all, it is the citizens of the developed world and, even more, the members of their defense establishments who for decades on end have prepared for the wrong kind of war.

It is easy to find the reasons why, until recently, large numbers of intelligent people in both East and West have missed the truth or else preferred to put their heads in the sand. In 1945, having just gone through the horrors of total war, most developed countries heaved a sigh of relief. They were only too happy to return to the good old days when wars were directed by governments and fought by armies, preferably in the territory of some far-away third country. During the fifties there arose a whole "limited warfare" school of thought that sought to codify those ideas. Meanwhile most people were content to watch war on TV or else to play it on their personal computers. They had not the slightest intention of risking their lives, however, and when President Johnson hinted that mobilization might be necessary to win the war in

Vietnam he found himself out of a job. A curious vicious circle was created. Regarding each other as their most important enemies, the superpowers in particular thought in terms of trinitarian war. Estimating armed force in terms of what it takes to wage trinitarian war, they looked at each other as their most dangerous enemies. Thus the military establishments of developed countries clung to trinitarian war because it was a game with which they had long been familiar and that they liked to play. It was also one in which they themselves held virtually all the cards, be they military, technological, or economic.

As far as many developed countries were concerned, the exercise in make-believe probably could have gone on for ever. After all, preparing for trinitarian war (so long as it remained safely below the nuclear threshold) did not endanger anybody in particular. It was expensive, to be sure, but its very cost kept a vast military-industrial complex happy and prosperous. Unfortunately, there were those who regarded conventional ideas about war as part of a vast plot designed to perpetuate the rule of developed countries over the undeveloped. All over the so-called Third World numerous movements of national liberation sprang into being. The majority did not have any army, let alone a government, though without exception they did claim to represent the people. Usually they called themselves by some local variant of "freedom fighters" and claimed a link with either God or (until about 1975) Karl Marx. Others called them guerrillas and terrorists, or else resorted to a large repertoire of other epithets which were less complimentary still. If their aims did not resemble those of criminals, their methods often did. So, as a result, did the treatment that they received. Semantics apart, very often they were both able and willing to employ warlike violence to achieve their ends.

Judged by the ordinary standards of trinitarian war, none of these movements stood the slightest chance of success. Often the economic resources at their disposal were nil. Some had to resort to bank-robbing or drug-dealing, causing the distinction between war and crime to become blurred. Militarily they were very weak, especially at the outset. They had neither a regular organization, nor experience, nor heavy weapons. They were too weak to carry arms openly, nor could they afford to wear uniforms and thus turn themselves into easy targets. If only for these reasons, they could not and did not abide by the established rules of war. They did not agree to fight as if it were a tournament, one army against another. Far from observing the distinction between combatants and noncombatants, from Kenya to Algeria and from Rhodesia to Vietnam that was just the distinction they tried to abolish.

They regarded both soldiers and civilians as legitimate targets, meanwhile striking out at governments as best they could. Using a combination of violence and persuasion, they drew the population to their side and intimidated the enemy. Their methods were, admittedly, not nice. However, there was nothing particularly nice about the methods of conventional war which, to select but two recent examples, included gassing opponents to death and destroying entire cities by fire.

Nice or not, nontrinitarian methods were very effective—so much so that the insurgents seldom had to close to the kill before the regular forces broke and evacuated the field. Often withdrawal was occasioned by the feeling that counterinsurgency was not "their" kind of war, and that it would end up destroying them even if, as happened once or twice, something like military victory seemed within reach. Either way, over much of the world nontrinitarian war has already taken over. Though decolonization is now all but complete, low-intensity conflict has not been interrupted in its march of conquest. Even today it is tearing to pieces many developing countries from Colombia to the Philippines. Much of this is the work of ragtag bands of ruffians out for their own advantage, hardly distinguishable from the *ecorcheurs* ("skinners") who devastated the French countryside during the Hundred Years' War. Now as then, they have turned entire societies into bloody chaos.

Nor is there any reason to think that the comparatively small number of developed countries can continue to enjoy immunity forever. On numerous occasions in the past their embassies have been attacked, their ships hijacked, their aircraft bombed out of the sky with heavy loss of life. Some of their citizens have been taken hostage and held for ransom. Others were murdered, others still threatened with execution unless they bowed to the dictates of some fanatical leader in a faraway capital. To make matters worse, many developed countries now contain sizeable minorities—whether Muslims, as in Western Europe, or Hispanics, as in the United States—who sympathize with the struggles going on in their countries of origin and who may themselves resort to violence to protest social and economic discrimination. Today, to believe one is safe from nontrinitarian war one has to be either very foolish or blind.

Long-established, stable countries like Britain, France, West Germany, Italy, and Spain, to mention but a few, all have their own indigenous *ecorcheurs,* usually known as terrorists. Some terrorists claim to be on the left of the political spectrum; others, on the right. Many are inspired by nationalist considerations pertaining to the ethnic communities in which they are rooted. All have this in common, that they are dissatisfied with the existing order and determined to use violence to alter it. Excluding those active in the developing world, the organizations with which they are affiliated number in the dozens and may soon exceed 100. Many of their members are strongly motivated, highly educated, and fully capable of taking advantage of modern technology from computers to plastic explosives. In the past such organizations have proved themselves willing and able to cooperate with each other, forming a kind of terrorist international. Nor have they refrained from establishing contacts with other organizations whose motive for resorting to violence is not primarily political, such as drug traffickers, Mafiosi, and the like.

Usually these movements have been able to obtain finances, weapons, training, and asylum from one source or another. Like self-transplanting weeds, they cannot be eradicated simply by being uprooted at one particular place. The prevalence of terrorism has often been blamed on the unwillingness of liberal-democratic countries to take the tough measures necessary to suppress it. Advocates of this view pointed to the fact that, through much of the post-war period, East Bloc totalitarian states with the Soviet Union at their head had been able to contain terrorism within very narrow bounds. However, Russia itself has a history of terrorism as long as anybody else's. As the eighties gave way to the nineties there were abundant indications that people living within the borders of the USSR, Muslims in particular, were about to follow the example of their brethren outside. As Soviet dominance weakens East European national rivalries are expected to make a comeback; in Yugoslavia and Romania, this has already led to violence. Finally, the United States as the most violent "First World" society by far has always had something resembling nontrinitarian warfare within its borders; except that, in this case, even organized violence is seldom politically motivated and is usually known as crime.

However spectacular the effects of nontrinitarian war, and however tragic the fate of its victims, at present it is incapable of seriously threatening the security of Western states—unless one includes Lebanon, which for most intents and purposes has ceased to be a state at all. Still, any number of spectacular bombings will testify that the dangers does exist. Terrorism will not be eliminated so long as it can find support, either in certain states or else among important dissatisfied social groups inside the target-countries themselves. Already today, scarcely a government exists that has not been forced to negotiate with terrorists and thus accord them at least a limited degree of recognition. Aware of the danger, here and there states are beginning to think of joining forces to combat low-intensity conflict, even at the price of surrendering parts of their treasured sovereignty. Considered from the point of view of the identity of those by whom it is waged, such conflict is much closer to the most primitive forms of nontrinitarian war than to war as conducted, say, in the days of Moltke or even those of Eisenhower. The same applies to the weapons that it employs, the methods that it uses, and even the reasons why it is waged. Much of what follows will consist of an attempt to make good this claim: starting with the role that right and might, respectively, play in war.

CHAPTER
III

What War Is All About

A Prussian Marseillaise

If modern trinitarian ideas as to who wages war can be shown to have their roots in *vom Kriege,* the same is even more true in regard to another question, namely, what war is all about. The first chapter of the first book of *vom Kriege* addresses this problem; as a bold-lettered headline informs us, war is "an act of violence carried to its utmost bounds." Accustomed to the violence of two World Wars, the modern reader is likely to consider the point obvious, even trivial. And so, in a certain sense, it is.

Clausewitz's theories should be seen against the historical background in which they originated. Like many others of his generation, he was trying to understand the secret of Napoleon's success. Well-known contemporary military commentators, such as Dietrich von Bülow and Antoine Jomini, believed they had found it in the realm of strategy, a subject around which they wove elaborate intellectual systems. Clausewitz disagreed. Though he called Napoleon "The God of War," the Grande Armée did not owe its victories to some arcane wisdom that was possessed by the Emperor alone. Rather, the elemental violence that had been unleashed by the French Revolution was incorporated in the Grande Armée and harnessed to military ends. Such force could only be answered by force. "Since the use of utmost force by no means excludes the use of the intellect," when hard clashed with hard the side least subject to restraint would triumph. Nor was the problem of a theoretical nature only. Prussia, still harking back to the Frederickian world, had been defeated as badly as any state in history. Unless the monarchy was prepared to let go of eighteenth-century "limited" methods in war, its future appeared bleak.

Never one to mince his words, Clausewitz serves explicit and emphatic warning against introducing "moderation" into the "principle" of war. Armed force is presented as subject to no rules except those of its own nature and those of the political purpose for which it is waged. He has no patience for the "philanthropist" belief that war could (or should) be restrained and waged with a minimum of violence: "In dangerous things such as war, errors made out of kindness are the worst." Again, he said: "Let us hear no more about generals who conquer without bloodshed." Whether Clausewitz himself, the "philosopher in uniform," was capable of practicing what he preached is open to doubt. This character remains something of a riddle to us; it does not seem to have included that ruthless streak that perhaps is essential to the great commander.

It is not easy to answer why this "hard-headed" line of reasoning has had such a tremendous impact on many of Clausewitz's successors—and thus on modern strategic thought at large. The popularity of *vom Kriege* owes little to its style which, while it does contain an occasional brilliant metaphor, is often turgid and certainly does not make for bedside reading. Two explanations suggest themselves. First, the favourable reception accorded to Clausewitz is probably linked to the rise of nationalism as a popular creed. Not only was he himself an ardent Prussian patriot, but, even as he wrote, the agitator "Father" Jahn was telling his fellow Germans that whoever taught his daughter French was selling her into prostitution. Later in the nineteenth century swelling national feeling, deliberately spurred and abetted by the state, was turned into chauvinism. Earlier restraints, whether imposed by religion or natural law, were discarded as irrelevant. Every major European nation now proclaimed itself to be the crown of creation, the guardian of a uniquely precious civilization deserving to be defended at all cost. The time was to come when, as each employed every available means and went to the utmost lengths to defeat its rivals, it brazenly proclaimed its right, and even its duty, to do so.

Second and possibly more important still, Clausewitz's ideas seem to have chimed in with the rationalistic, scientific, and technological outlook associated with the industrial revolution. Modern European man, his belief in God destroyed by the Enlightenment, took the world as his oyster. Its living beings—and its raw materials—were regarded as his to exploit and plunder, and indeed plundering and exploiting them constituted "progress." The final step in this direction was taken when

Charles Darwin showed that humanity, too, was an integral part of nature. Now Darwin himself was a gentle character who hesitated to draw the logical conclusion from his beliefs. However, his scruples were not shared by his "socio-darwinistic" disciples. Herbert Spenser, Friedrich Häckel, and a legion of lesser luminaries on both sides of the Atlantic lost no time in proclaiming that man was simply a biological organism like any other, subject to no rule but the law of the jungle. With war considered God's (or nature's) favorite means for selecting among species and races, it became hard to see why one's fellow humans should not be treated as animals allegedly treat each other in "the struggle for existence"; that is, with the utmost ruthlessness and regardless of any considerations except expediency.

Be this as it may, *vom Kriege* became—in the words of the British military critic Basil Liddell Hart, who was one of the few to resist its lure—"a Prussian Marseillaise which inflamed the body and intoxicated the mind." Clausewitz himself seems to have looked at war's barbarities with quiet resignation. Later writers took his words as a clarion call for action, applauded them, and turned them into a positive good. The list of those who, claiming to be his disciples, have gleefully piled brutality upon brutality is long and replete with famous names, beginning with Colmar von der Goltz and ending with some of the nuttier characters among today's nuclear strategists. Nor was the impact confined to theory. The nineteenth century for all its nationalist bombast and socio-darwinistic rhetoric still managed to restrict war between European countries and limit its horrors. However, the next century saw two "total" World Wars that were waged with precious little regard to constraints of any kind. They employed every weapon, sought to destroy whomever and whatever could be reached, and ended with an escalation to nuclear violence the horror or which is only now beginning to subside.

According to Clausewitz, the law of war consists of "self-imposed restraints, hardly worth mentioning." If, in the days before Auschwitz, civilized nations no longer exterminated each other in the manner of savages, this was not because of any change in the nature of war but because they had found more effective means of fighting. *Vom Kriege* dismisses the entire tremendous body of international law and custom in a single irreverent sentence. In this it has set an example that has been followed by subsequent "strategic" literature down to the present day, even to the point where works on the law of war are usually stored in some separate, slightly out-of-the-way, library. However, war without law is not merely a monstrosity but an impossibility. To show this we shall work our way through history, consider the present, and try to get a glimpse of the future.

The Law of War: Prisoners

To understand how wrong Clausewitz's dismissal of international law and custom really is, consider his own fate when captured. The event took place two weeks after the disastrous Battle of Jena when his unit, fighting a rearguard action near Prenzlau, halfway between Berlin and the Baltic Coast, was cut off by French cavalry. Together with Prince August of Prussia he was taken to Berlin. While the young Clausewitz was made to cool his heels in an anteroom, the Prince was interviewed by Napoleon. The meeting over, the two young noblemen gave their word of honor to refrain from further participation in the war and were sent home. A month later they were ordered to proceed to internment in France. Their journey was made at a leisurely pace, and Clausewitz even took the opportunity to visit Goethe in Weimar. Having reached France, they spent time first at Nancy, then at Soissons, and finally at Paris. Though the authorities kept an eye on them, they moved everywhere freely and were able to frequent the best social circles. The sojourn ended after ten months when, following the Treaty of Tilsit, they were allowed to go home. They traveled by way of Switzerland, stopping to stay with Napoleon's great literary opponent, Madame de Stael, in whose house Prince August seems to have had a love affair.

Clausewitz was a captain at the time. Had he been captured in some modern conflict—say, in Italy or France during World War II—his fate would have been entirely different. In all likelihood he would have been taken to some interrogation-center, possibly after being deliberately starved and roughly handled for a day or two. International law would have required him to disclose his name, rank, serial number, and blood type, and no more. Nevertheless, had he impressed the interrogators as being one who possessed important information, they would have tried to squeeze it out of him, though probably without resorting to actual torture. This phase over, he would be sent away and locked behind barbed wire in some prisoner-of-war camp. He would not be asked to give his word not the escape: on the contrary, as an officer and gentleman it would be his *duty* to try. So long as he did not take up weapons or kill a guard in the process, even repeated attempts to escape did not constitute an offense and were not supposed to be punished.

In practice, German prisoners in Allied camps were reasonably, though by no means luxuriously, looked after. Allied prisoners in German hands generally received similar treatment, even if they were Jews. However, the Soviet Government had not ratified the 1907 Hague Convention. This served the Germans as an excuse, if one was needed, to shoot Red Army Commissars out of hand. Others who survived the subsequent death-marches were herded into camps, where hundreds of thousands were deliberately starved and frozen to death before it occurred to the Germans that their labor had value and could be exploited. The Soviets ill-treated German prisoners, often by making them work under the harshest conditions, but not as much as the Germans had mistreated them; normally it was only captured SS who were shot out of hand. Allied personnel in Japanese hands suffered atrociously. Their treatment does not seem to have been the result of systematic brutality ordered from the top, however, but merely reflected the normal way in which Japanese commanders at all levels slapped and kicked their own subordinates. Since numerous camps were located in remote jungle sites, prisoners in Japanese hands also tended to be neglected and perish of hunger or disease. Finally, Japanese servicemen were told that the Allies took no prisoners, which often enough was actually the case. Hence they not infrequently preferred suicide to surrender; Japanese troops who were taken prisoner, however, generally received decent treatment.

Had Clausewitz been captured as few as four decades earlier, i.e., during the Seven Years' War, his fate would also have been different. Very likely he would still have been well treated, even pampered by being invited to wine and dine with his peers among the captors. A captive officer who had given his word not to escape and not to take up arms again was free to move about, even to contact his friends and relatives on the other side. However, his final release had to wait until after the payment of a ransom. The amount of money involved varied from one war to the next and also depended on rank. In Clausewitz's case it might have amounted to a few thousand French *livres,* say up to three years' income for one of his station in life. It was a sign of the growing professionalization of armies that, during the last decades of the *ancien régime,* the question of ransom ceased to concern individuals but was taken over by governments. Acting either directly or else by way of their field commanders, either during or after the war, they negotiated with the enemy, fixed prices, and settled accounts. However, had Clausewitz been so unfortunate to be captured even as late as the War of the Spanish

Succession (1701–14), the ransom would have had to come out of his own pocket. Since officers at that time were independent businessmen as much as they were anything else, this was considered a normal risk of war. Nor would he have received reimbursement except, perhaps, by throwing himself on the King's mercy and citing "difficult circumstances."

Looking further back to the early modern period and the late Middle Ages, armies as armies did not take prisoners at all; this was done only by individual soldiers who might or might not grant quarter when asked. Once their surrender had been accepted, the prisoners' persons and whatever property they carried on themselves were regarded as belonging to their captors to do with as they pleased. A prisoner considered sufficiently important (and rich) might find himself well housed and well looked after; he might be invited to wine and dine at his captor's table, giving and receiving elaborate compliments. At the other end of the scale, captives might be subject to imprisonment deliberately made harsh, both by way of punishment for transgressions committed and as a means to make them pay up quickly. Since the prisoner was regarded as private property, it was not rare for him to become the subject of disputes among different would-be captors, even to the point where violence was used. The natural authority to settle such disputes was the commanding king or prince, who in this way was able to demand, and receive, one-third of all ransoms.

Medieval *Livres de chevalerie* and early modern treatises on international law were in accord that noble prisoners—the only kind considered worth bothering with—should not be mistreated without cause. Some thought that captors were within their rights to pressure captives in order to force them to pay; others disagreed. Scholars debated whether a prisoner whose word could not be trusted might be, to quote the fourteenth-century French writer Honoré Bonet, "held in a high tower," put in chains, or otherwise constrained. Prisoners who tried to escape were supposed to have broken their word. They could be punished if caught, though there was no unanimity on the kind of penalty involved. Until about 1450, prisoners who made good their escape might have their arms displayed in reverse, a grievous insult. The act of asking for quarter and its acceptance by the victor was supposed to establish a treaty akin to an IOU. Though slavery was never very important in medieval Europe and tended to fall into disuse as time went on, prisoners were regarded as an investment. Hence they could be sold, bartered, or otherwise transferred by one captor to another without their respective rights and duties being affected thereby. Just as we today have the white flag, so the medieval chivalric code had certain widely-recognized verbal formulae and signals by which intent to surrender could be conveyed.

In respect to prisoners who were not officers the ideas of previous ages also differed from our own. Modern international law makes few distinctions between the two categories, the most important one being perhaps that enlisted men, but not officers, can be made to work. Previous ages did not share our democratic ideas and treated them as if they belonged to two different races, one of baboons and one of men. The eighteenth century took the view that, since personnel who did not hold the King's commission could have no honor, their word was worthless and they could not be put on parole. Instead they would be held in the cellars of some fortress and, by way of making them earn their keep, rented out as hired labor whenever the opportunity presented itself. Thus they were in no position to make arrangements for paying their own ransom; nor was it possible to extract very much from men who were, in the Duke of Wellington's famous phrase "the scum of the earth, enlisted for the drink." During the War of the Austrian Succession a common soldier's ransom was fixed at a very low sum—4 *livres*—as opposed to 250,000 for a *maréchal de France*. Apparently even that sum was paid not by the soldier but, following the general settling of accounts, by the state. Having been paid, it could either be waived or, in case of some particularly stingy government, deducted from the soldier's future pay.

In a period when sieges were as important as battles, and more numerous, the fate of prisoners might depend on the circumstances under which the surrender had taken place. Particularly during the early eighteenth century, sieges rarely had to be pushed to a bloody conclusion—even the Ottomans, whose religion forbade them to give up any place that contained a mosque, finally learned that it was better to live like a dog than to die like a lion. In the age of Vauban, Coehorn, and their colleagues, siege-warfare had developed to the point where it became a question of scientifically applying cannon to walls. Sound logistics always presupposed, this left little doubt about the outcome, attackers and defenders alike being able to forecast with considerable precision the time an operation would last. It became the normal practice for the two sides to agree that, in case no "succor" arrived within such and such a time, the garrison would surrender. The surrender-instrument itself was drawn up in the form of an elaborate legal document. While terms varied from one case to the next, very often the defending commander undertook to deliver fortress, equipment, and stores intact. In return, he and his army were allowed to evacuate the fortress and proceed where they would. Sometimes they had to give their word not to fight again, sometimes not.

The agreement having been signed, both sides collaborated to arrange the so-called *belle capitulation,* following one of the numerous handbooks in circulation. A mixed party of officers would be sent to inspect the fortresses' storerooms, drawing up lists which were duly verified and signed. The two sides might then join forces to enlarge the breach in the wall so as to enable the ceremony to take place in splendid form; an artist would be commissioned to paint the occasion and produce a picture such as Rubens' *Las Lanzas,* which shows the Dutch town of Breda being surrendered to the Spanish general, Ambrosio Spinola. As the garrison came marching out, drums beating and banners flying, the victors formed a guard of honor and the opposing commanders exchanged compliments. To sweeten the pill, officers who surrendered in this way were usually allowed to retain their personal effects, including arms, horses, carriages, servants, and mistresses. The net effect of such arrangements was that the besieged force was saved to fight another day, or at any rate they obviated the need to pay ransom; hence they normally received the blessing of governments. There is even a case on record when Louis XIV threatened to cashier an officer because, alone in his garrison, he "presumptuously" refused to surrender.

Another factor that helps account for attitudes to prisoners was the cosmopolitan character of warfare. Early modern governments down to the eighteenth century gladly employed foreigners in their armed services, since this had the effect of sparing their own subjects and leaving them free to pay taxes. Many armies contained entire units consisting of nonnationals. Some were volunteers, often coming from poor regions such as Switzerland and, later, Scotland or Ireland; nationals of those countries often found themselves confronting each other in battle while enlisted in the French or English services. There were also cases when troops were sold or rented out *en bloc* by their princes, as happened to the unfortunate Hessians who did much of Britain's fighting during the War of the American Revolution. When such soldiers and such formations were taken prisoner they were sometimes made to change sides. Frederick II in 1756 impressed an entire Saxon Army, lock, stock and barrel, promising a bounty to those who joined more or less out of their free will and making liberal use of the knout to persuade those who did not. This particular case owes its fame to the fact that it was among the last. However, between about 1500 and 1650, a period when war was a form of capitalist enterprise and armies consisted of mercenaries, it had been standard practice and excited scant comment.

Still, there were exceptions even during this period. If the war was considered a rebellion against legitimate authority, or else when religious ideas were at stake, then the treatment that prisoners could expect was very different. The Thirty Years' War in Germany became notorious for the number of massacres that it witnessed. Often, as in the case of Magdeburg in 1631, they were the handiwork of a blood-crazed soldiery acting in defiance of the commander's wishes. No such explanation can be found for that famous Spanish commander, Fernando Alvarez de Toledo, Duke of Alva, during his campaigns in the Netherlands between 1567 and 1574. Supported by his Auditor General—the celebrated jurist Balthasar Ayala—the Duke developed the nasty habit of tying the members of defeated garrisons back to back and throwing them into the fortress moat. At the battle of Agincourt (1415) Henry V of England ordered his followers to massacre their prisoners, an order that was obeyed with some reluctance because it meant that ransom would be forfeit. The English knights present left the killing to the low-class archers, or so they later claimed. The incident gave rise to much bad publicity, and had to be justified by the claim that the French were putting their captors in danger by trying to escape *en masse*.

Whatever the outcome in each individual case, the outstanding fact was that, contrary to the situation today, there was no universal rule obliging the victors to grant quarter if that was asked. Certainly the medieval chivalric code, as represented by Froissart, for example, frowned on knights who did not permit their opponents to surrender. However, even in this case the defeated party did not have an absolute *right* to be spared. Then, as later, he who killed an opponent under such circumstances acquired a sinister reputation. Such a reputation might have its uses—witness the terror inspired by the Swiss, well-known for their refusal to give quarter. However, it also exposed the slayer to similar treatment if fortune deserted him. Unless the dead opponent happened to be some particularly great baron who thus might have paid a large ransom, the killer had no fear of being formally reprimanded, let alone brought to justice. As late as the early seventeenth century, wrote Hugo Grotius, all that the members of a defeated force who were not commanders could do was to appeal to tender Christian mercy. We shall soon see that the same applied to people who did not form part of an armed force, but were nevertheless so unfortunate as to be captured. Sometimes the appeal worked, sometimes not. Very often whether it did work depended on whether the person asking for quarter looked as if he would be able to pay.

The fate of prisoners of war at times and places before the fourteenth century will not be discussed here. This is not because war in those periods was not subject to rules, nor does it mean that those rules were less important than those existing in our own time. The point to make is that the rules exist. To understand their real importance, one only needs to watch them change. Today, most people would be outraged by a system that distinguished between individual prisoners of war on the basis of their financial means or, in plain words, their ability to respond to blackmail. Conversely, our ancestors from about 1650 to 1800 would resent and ridicule the modern system which, unwilling to recognize the concept of honor, causes captives to be housed, clothed, fed, and generally looked after at their captors' expense. None of this is to deny that the rules of war, those pertaining to prisoners as well as others, are frequently violated. But they do exist, and once we give up a narrow contemporary point of view their role in defining what war is all about turns out to be very great.

What is more, the further back into history we go, the greater the problems of terminology and classification. Where armed force is directed by social entities that are not states, against social organizations that are not armies, and people who are not soldiers in our sense of the term, trinitarian concepts break down. The same applies to present-day legal distinctions between officers and noncommissioned personnel, soldiers and civilians, combatants and noncombatants, all of which are modern inventions. Not even the category of "wounded" holds up; though people were always injured in battle, "the wounded" as a distinct group having special rights and deserving special treatment represent a trinitarian concept that only made its appearance in the eighteenth century. So different are historical circumstances before about 1350 that the modern term "prisoner" itself does more harm than good. It is therefore proposed to break off the discussion at this point, and devote the next section to the treatment of noncombatants.

The Law of War: Noncombatants

Except when war is waged in a desert, noncombatants, also known as civilians or "the people," constitute the great majority of those affected. Recognizing this fact, Clausewitz considers them as one leg in his trinity; he explicitly says that a theory that does not take them into account is not worth the paper it is written on. However, all over the world today, the traditional distinction between peoples and armies is being broken down by new, nontrinitarian, forms of war collectively known as Low-Intensity Conflict. Often this is because the line between the two may have been shaky to begin with. Many developing countries in Africa and Asia have never had the time to engage in "nation building," let alone to establish proper armed forces on the model of the more developed nations. In other cases the distinction is being subjected to deliberate attack. This has become quite a common phenomenon in developing and developed countries alike, and those who engage in it are usually known as terrorists.

There is an obverse side to this coin. But for the fact that traditional distinctions between combatants and noncombatants are still being observed to some extent, many contemporary low-intensity conflicts would have been altogether unintelligible. For example, the Palestinian uprising in the West Bank and the Gaza Strip would have ended within days if the Israelis had come to the conclusion that enough was enough. They could, had they been willing to ignore international public opinion and their own self-restraint, have treated people who hold demonstrations and throw rocks as if they were real enemies. In that case the tanks and self-propelled artillery would have been trundled out of the emergency depots where they are stored. Many Palestinians would have been killed, the great majority probably driven across the border into Jordan. Potential international complications apart, all this could have been done at the cost of negligible Israeli casualties or none at all. The benefits to Israel, in the short term at any rate, would have been immense. Thus understood, the Israeli attitude has been a model of self-restraint—though it is by no means certain that, should the uprising continue, things will not end otherwise. As this and a hundred other examples prove, present-day ideas concerning the nature of "civilians" and "noncombatants" are of vital importance to modern war. To a large extent, these ideas determine the way wars are planned, prepared for, and conducted.

Given the importance of such distinctions in shaping present-day conflict, it is all the more remarkable that they were not recognized during much if not most of history. Take the case of tribal societies of the hunting-gathering and farming types. Such societies, both ancient and modern, are usually organized according to sex and age. The most fundamental distinction is between males and females. With the exception of a few cases to be discussed later in this book, members of the female sex do not play an active part in war; their role is to encourage the warriors, participate in the celebration of victory, or be victimized in the case of defeat. Typically the males are divided by age into children, adolescents, warriors, and old men. The name "warriors" speaks for itself. While most tribes include a handful of males, such as the shaman, who do not actually fight, by and large just being a warrior—in other words, an adult male—is synonymous with membership; witness, for example, the Book of Exodus where it is only *yotsei tsava* (members of the host) who are counted among the 600,000 "Sons [not daughters] of Israel," to the exclusion of women and children.

Tribal societies tend to hold old people in high regard. Often they are allowed privileges that are not granted to younger groups. Since in their case it no longer matters, women in the postmenopausal state are often free to have sex with whomever they choose. Old men are exempt from war, and in their case too the privilege is an ambiguous one. The remaining groups that are excluded from war by reason of age or sex are, legally speaking, wholly "owned"; this remained true even in a comparatively advanced society such as Republican Rome where the *paterfamilias* had unlimited power over his dependents, including the right to kill his wife and sell his children into slavery. Insofar as in any society women and children provide for the future, and are in fact the future, the warriors depend on them, a fact that they usually realize and sometimes resent. Women and children may be treated kindly or otherwise. However, this does not affect their legal position as people who do not form part of "society" and are therefore without any "rights."

When tribal societies waged war on each other they did so in one of two ways. One arrangement, known from places as far apart as North America, East Africa, and Melanesia, was for one side to challenge the other to a collective duel. The duel was held at an appointed time and place, normally a spot especially designated for the purpose and located midway between their respective villages or camps. Attired in all their finery, and often carrying special blunt arrows or spears, the warriors presented themselves. What took place next is best described as a cross between a festival, a picnic, and some particularly dangerous form of sport. The role of noncombatants, that is females and males who are either too young or too old (or who may just not want to participate on that particular day) was to act as spectators. The women encouraged their menfolk and insulted the enemy, sometimes by raising their skirts and making all sorts of obscene gestures. They also offered refreshments to warriors taking a break and dressed the wounds of those, normally not many, who were hurt.

From South America to New Guinea, most tribal societies also had another form of war which was less innocuous and, from the noncombatants' point of view, less pleasant. A group of warriors might go out and ambush the members of a neighboring tribe. Alternatively they might raid their village, an operation which usually took place before dawn and could result in the destruction of entire settlements. Whatever the exact tactics used, the role of enemy males was to be killed, usually on the spot but sometimes—as in Melanesia and Brazil—later on as part of some cannibalistic rite. Women and young children might also be killed, but it was more normal for them to be captured. Using the captured women's own hair for the purpose, the New Zealand Maoris bound their prisoners and took them back to their village. In the absence of either a state or even a *res publica,* human captives as well as captured property belong to those who made the catch, that is, to individual warriors. The fate normally reserved for them was to be forcibly adopted into the victorious tribe which treated children as children and women as women. Since institutionalized slavery was unknown, usually after a generation or two captors and captives could no longer be told apart.

An interesting transitional phase between tribal and "civilized" society may be found in the Biblical Book of Deuteronomy. It was ordained that the sons of Israel, having gained a victory in war, might come unto the women of their fancy and take them for their wives. They were, however, required to allow the fair captives one month of mourning for their dead relatives. Women who failed to please were to be set free; it was expressly forbidden to sell them or to treat them harshly. The fate of the Trojan women was similar, except that this time there was no Pentateuch to prescribe either the time that sex had to wait or the treatment they should receive after it had taken place. The men of Troy were killed out of hand. Their children were either killed, as Hector's son Astianax was, or else enslaved. The women captives were put on board the "black ships" and "dragged back in chains" to Achaea. There such of them as were found suitable were made to perform menial tasks in their master's household and to share his bed when required. However, the society described by Homer differed from the Biblical one in that it was already monogamous. Hence, though captives might be sexually exploited, there was usually no question of marrying them. Those heroes who did so—Agamemnon and Achilles' son, Neoptolemus—paid the penalty and were murdered by their original wives.

Modern scholarship tends to regard the time when the Biblical injunctions were composed as roughly contemporary with the Trojan War, placing both in the last third of the second millennium B.C. From then on, and for some 3,000 years, armed conflict continued to fall naturally into field warfare on the one hand and siege-operations on the other. One of the most persistent divisions in all military history, it even survived the gunpowder revolution by several centuries: it held true regardless of whether the heaviest weapons in use were spears, cata-pults, or cannon. Seen from our special point of view, the outstanding fact about field warfare was that it consisted of tournaments between armies, whatever their organization or the tactics that they used. The rule was that, when a battle took place in the open field, noncombatants were nowhere to be found. Plato in the *Republic* suggested that young children of the ideal *polis* should be taken to the battlefield where, properly chaperoned, they would observe the proceedings and strive to learn from them. Aside from the primitive wargames described earlier, I do not see that his suggestion has ever been taken up.

An army around 1200 B.C., like its successor in 1648 A.D., would encounter noncombatants principally in the course of marches or else during foraging operations. The way they were treated varied from case to case and also depended on the prevailing social institutions. In friendly or neutral territory, the troops might be ordered to pay for what they took. Sometimes this also applied in enemy territory, but such cases were very rare until the second half of the seventeenth century. It was customary for armies on campaign to act like swarms of locusts, eating all that could be eaten and setting fire to the rest. Members of the population who looked as if they were able to pay would be put to ransom or else tortured to reveal their treasure's whereabouts. Where slavery existed they would be rounded up and sold, either directly by the soldiers or, more likely, through the specialized dealers who fol-lowed in the wake of Roman armies in particular. Thus, throughout the period the least that the inhabitants could expect was to see themselves relieved of their possessions. If they tried to resist, and frequently even if they did not, they would be enslaved or killed.

To escape the enemy, people whose country was threatened by invasion took refuge in fortified cities or castles, carrying along as many of their possessions as possible. Hence it came about that, when a fortress was captured, large numbers of noncombatants of both sexes and all ages were usually found within its walls. From the days of Greece right down to the Thirty Years' War, Xenophon's dictum that "the losers' life and their property belong to the victors" held good. True, the attackers often entered into negotiations with the defenders, agreeing to spare their lives and (sometimes) their property in return for a speedy capitulation. Even the Mongol Tamerlane, whose march of conquest in Central Asia was marked by pyramids built out of thousands upon thousands of human skulls, preferred to offer a city terms before engaging in the tedious business of a formal siege. The longer and the more difficult the siege, however, the more likely it was that the troops would wreak vengeance in an orgy of murder, plunder, and rape.

Faced with the prospect of an imminent sack, the position of victorious commanders was ambiguous. A sack might damage their reputation in the face of history, particularly if the place in question was sacred or otherwise famous. Too, it meant that control over the army would be temporarily lost and that much valuable property would be destroyed. Hence many commanders tried to prevent it from taking place, sometimes successfully and sometimes not. Titus in 69 A.D. did his best to prevent Jerusalem from being sacked, or so Josephus claims. In Europe during the early modern age commanders sometimes paid their troops "storm money" *en lieu* of permitting them to run amok, the idea being both to prevent disorder and to make organized spoilage possible. On the other hand, there were also many cases when commanders made deliberate use of the sack, either to terrorize other cities that might refuse to surrender or else as a reward to their own troops. For example, the Romans in 146 B.C. sacked and utterly destroyed the city of Corinth. The resulting shock-waves of horror were such that, for centuries thereafter, Greece never once dared rise in revolt.

In Europe, the last time when a besieged city was put to an old-fashioned sack was probably during Wellington's capture of Badajoz in Spain in 1811. Already during the eighteenth century trinitarian ideas concerning the nature of war began to affect its conduct. Against the background provided by the rise of professional armies, there was a growing tendency to leave the inhabitants of captured towns un-molested, at any rate officially and as far as their lives were concerned. Though methods changed, the same did not apply to their property. Even as late as the 1870–71 War the invading Prussians demanded "contributions," meaning that the inhabitants of occupied French towns were summarily ordered to come up with horses, provisions, and cash. The Grande Armée turned "feeding war by war" into a fine art; even during the supposedly civilized eighteenth-century, levying of contributions and "eating all there is to eat" was the method recommended by quartermasters such as Puysegur, who served Louis XIV and XV. Seventeenth-century armies were even more notorious for the way in which they extracted "contributions." When a town was entered a special officer known as *Brandschaezter* went around accompanied by a guard, assessing the value of the citizens' residences with his expert's eye. He would then summon the mayor, take his wife hostage, and tell him to come up with an equivalent sum in cash. Though bargaining was usually possible, a town that refused to comply would be burnt down, sometimes with the citizens themselves being thrown into the flames.

Though over two centuries have passed since the death of Emeric Vattel in 1767, present-day notions concerning the treatment of noncombatants are still based on his work, *Droit des gens,* and date to the time of the absolute states. From his time to ours, the central idea upon which everything else rests is that the military constitute a separate legal entity that, alone among all the organs of the state, is entitled to wage war. Under modern international law, people who are not members of armed forces or accountable to established authority are not supposed to take up arms, fight, or resist in any way. In return, their persons are not supposed to be violated by an invading army. Now this is not to say that today's international law does not permit civilian property to be destroyed or taken away. However, such things are supposed to take place only so long as active operations last, and then only to the extent that "military necessity" demands.

It is also in keeping with the lasting influence of eighteenth-century ideas that the end of hostilities does not signify the onset of unlimited license as was the case during much of history. On the contrary, the law treats the inhabitants of occupied territories almost as if they were children who have been temporarily deprived of their political rights and, for that reason, are all the more in need of care. Public property may be occupied by the invaders, but not that of private individuals. Existing law is supposed to remain in force, subject only to such modifications as are necessary to ensure public security, that is to say, that of the invaders. The latter are supposed to do everything in their power to allow the population to lead normal lives. They must institute a government, either military or civilian, whose task is to look after the people's welfare until peace comes. They are permitted to levy taxes to cover the expenses of the occupation; but they may not forcibly appropriate economic resources, deport manpower (this offense brought Hitler's Labor Czar, Fritz Sauckel, to his Nuremberg scaffold), strip away artistic treasures, and the like.

Most of the international conventions that embody these ideas date to the age of "civilized" warfare from 1859 to 1937. Though both the Franco-Prussian War and World War I saw them violated to some extent, at least the principles behind them were widely recognized. However, World War II caused the distinction between combatants and noncombatants to break down in two principal ways. First, "strategic bombing" destroyed men, women, and children indiscriminately—to say nothing of religious and artistic treasures of every sort. Second, and historically perhaps more important, there was the tendency of occupied peoples in many countries to take up arms again after their governments had surrendered. The Germans, to their credit, adopted something like the American Union's Lieber Code when they treated de Gaulle's Free French as if they were bona fide soldiers serving a legitimate government. The same line was not followed when it came to the resistance movements in various countries. Their members, whoever they were and however they operated, were tracked down, imprisoned, tortured, and executed.

The Nazis regarded as murderers those civilians who attacked their soldiers while not wearing a distinguishing mark and not carrying arms openly. What is more, from the standpoint of international law as it then stood the Nazis had right on their side. Partly because the absurdity of such a position came to be widely recognized after the War, partly because of the sheer number of national liberation struggles since 1945, international law is slowly being amended. In 1977, a meeting assembled in Geneva decided that "freedom fighters" would also be granted combatants' rights. This may not have been as positive a development as appears on first sight. For one thing, each government insists that, whatever the situation elsewhere, their homegrown variety of rebels are not freedom fighters but bandits, assassins, and terrorists who don't come under the protection of the law. And possibly more important, if terrorists are entitled to be treated as combatants, then combatants might also be treated as terrorists. It is difficult to see who has benefitted from the change, aside from the terrorists themselves.

The rules of war as they exist today are far from perfect, nor is it possible to deny that they are being violated every day. Still, at least they no longer grant the victors automatic access to the losers' persons and property, let alone their womenfolk. The records of the US Army Judge Advocate during World War II show that more servicemen were executed for rape than for any other crime, particularly if they were black and particularly if the victim ended up dead as well as violated. By contrast, the Israelis in the occupied territories may have killed numbers of Palestinians, but to this day not even Jordan TV has been able to report a single case of rape. Had these facts been reported to our ancestors, surely they would have wondered why Americans, Germans, and Israelis were fighting at all, given that they were not even permitted to indulge the natural needs of heroes. By comparing the present situation to that prevailing in the past, it becomes clear that the distinction between combatants and noncombatants, far from being negligible and irrelevant to the practical business of conducting modern war, defines what that war is all about.

The Law of War: Weapons

In the field of weapons, too, war has always been limited by rules. Had armed conflict been simply a question of employing whatever force is necessary to achieve one's ends, as postulated by the Clausewitzian Universe, then there should have been no such limitations; in fact, however, they exist in every civilization that has known war, including our own.

The list of weapons that, for one reason or another, have been declared "unfair" is long, starting already in the ancient world. An early example is associated with Paris, the man who abducted and later married Queen Helen. A better lover than he was a warrior, Paris' preferred weapon was the bow. As a result the *Illiad* calls him by various nasty names, "coward," "weakling," and "woman" being but three out of a considerable collection. Similarly among the two sons of Telamon, Ajax and Teukros, the former fights with the spear and is counted among the great heroes. The latter is a champion bowshot who, though quite effective on the battlefield, shelters behind his larger comrade's shield "like a child in his mother's dress." Nor was contempt for the bow limited solely to the epics. According to Plutarch, Lycurgus when he wanted to make his Spartans brave forbade them to use the bow.

Given that Greek religion was anthropomorphic, it will not come as a surprise that similar distinctions prevailed on Olympus. Eurypides in one of his plays accuses none other than Heracles himself of cowardice, saying that he prefers shooting from afar to fighting, man to man, in the front row and exposing himself to the gash of the spear. The sea-god Poseidon, whose characteristic weapon was the trident, was much stronger and more manly a figure than Apollo of the silver bow. Goddesses, too, were classified by the weapons they used. The strongest was Athene, the virgin goddess of war, who wore armor and whose weapon was the *dorus* or spear. She was her father's favorite among the younger generation, and much stronger than her sisters, the hunting-goddess Artemis and the love-goddess Aphrodite, both of whom used the bow.

The reasons why weapons that could kill from afar were disliked are not hard to discern. As Homer makes quite clear, they did not constitute a proper test of manhood, given that they enabled a weakling such as Paris first to wound the mighty Diomedes and then to kill Achilles, the greatest hero who ever lived. The Persians on the other hand expressed their ideal of virility by saying that a man should do three things: namely, ride a horse, shoot the bow, and speak the truth. By contrast, Western military tradition regarded the bow as somehow sneaky. While well suited for sport and hunting, in war its use could be justified only by the force of circumstances. How persistent such traditions could be is evident from the fact that, throughout the millennium and a half known as antiquity, long-range devices such as the bow and the sling were regarded as the poor man's weapons. No self-respecting hoplite or legionary would condescend to use them. Units of bowmen and slingers, often even of javelin men, typically consisted of men drawn either from the lowest social classes or from foreign, semi-civilized peoples such as the Scyths who were used to police Athens. In the Roman army such units and such men never even attained proper military status. Though their contribution to the conduct of war was considerable, they were called *auxilia* and made to serve for a longer period, and for less pay, than legionaries.

As antiquity turned into the Middle Ages, the bow's fortunes became dependent on geography. The Byzantines, many of whose forces consisted of mercenaries originating in the Russian steppe, adopted the latter's method of fighting on horseback and using long-distance weapons. In the West, the Franks who established the Merovingian Kingdoms preferred to fight hand to hand using spears, swords, and axes. Later, when the Franks took to horse and became knights, they still fought hand to hand. The bow remained what it had been in antiquity, a second-class weapon. The opening verses of the great epic of Carolingian chivalry, the *Chanson de Roland,* deride the Muslims for refusing to fight at close quarters and relying on missiles instead. The Second Lateran Council in 1139 sought to impose a ban on the crossbow, the reason being that it was considered too cruel—in plain words, too effective—a weapon to use against Christians. The best way to understand the ban is, however, to examine the social position of the bow. Edward I, Edward III, and Henry V—as well as William the Conqueror—owed their victories largely to the bow, using it first as it was carried by the Normans and then adopting the long version from the Welsh tribesmen whose national weapon it was. Nevertheless, these monarchs themselves did not use it, nor would they have dreamed of making their sons or great barons train with it for any but sporting purposes. The equation can also be turned around. One reason why the bow was disliked was precisely because it was cheap, hence accessible to anyone and hardly worth bothering with as a status-symbol.

Another indication of the bow's inferior position is its role in fights that did not amount to war—that is, in games and amusements of every sort. Already in the *Illiad* shooting with the bow is the last, and least, among the contests organized by Achilles in honor of his dead friend, Patroclus. Similarly, in the medieval tournament, that showpiece par excellence of chivalry, the bow's position was ambiguous. Its use in combat of knight against knight was prohibited, although this rule was sometimes violated in the early days. True, the days set aside for a tournament often also witnessed competitions in archery. Just as the pause in modern soccer games is sometimes filled by dancing girls or light athletics, so the function of the bow in the tournament was to fill gaps in the program or else bring it to an end. Those who competed with the bow were not knights, nor does the record tell us that noble ladies awarded the prizes. Ladies did, however, sometimes use the crossbow for target-practice or hunting—another indication of its problematic nature as a first-class weapon of war.

The early firearms, by enabling a commoner to kill a knight from afar, threatened the existence of the medieval world and finally helped bring it to an end. Firearms originated in the fourteenth century, but took more than two centuries before they became truly respectable. In Mamluk Egypt and Samurai Japan they were regarded as incompatible with the social status of the ruling groups, and banned. In Europe, too, they were resisted: Ariosto, Cervantes, Shakespeare, and Milton are but four out of a long list of famous names who derided them and described them as Satan's own special creation. Though firearms were originally considered low-status weapons, those who specialized in their use were perhaps more akin to technicians or magicians than to mere peasants. These factors in combination explain why those who did employ firearms in war were sometimes subjected to punishment. The fifteenth-century Italian *condottiere* Gian Paolo Vitelli used to blind captured arquebusiers and cut off their hands, whereas his near-contemporary Bayard—he who went down in history as the *chevalier sans peur et sans reproche*—had them executed.

The ease with which firearms killed from a distance was not, however, the only reason why they were disliked. Early firearms were difficult if not impossible to use on horseback. Hence, in Europe as well as among the Egyptian Mamluks, they threatened to bring to an end an

entire social order that for hundreds of years had divided humanity into
those who rode and those who did not. Firearms were also messy, dirty,
and dangerous. The charge consisted of black powder that, before the
introduction of the metal cartridge at the end of the nineteenth century,
had to be loaded separately from the ball. Hence, firing a weapon was a
complicated operation that always fouled the firer, and sometimes
ended up with an explosion in front of his face. Whatever the reason, the
prejudice against firearms persisted, in some respects, into the nineteenth century and beyond. Even during the years immediately preced-
ing World War I, members of the European nobility typically preferred
the cavalry to any other arm, one reason being that its principal weapon
continued to be cold steel.

One very important reason for disliking a weapon was, of course,
that it was new. A new weapon might or might not be effective, but
whenever one was introduced it always threatened to upset traditional
ideas as to how war should be waged and, indeed, what it was all about.
This explains why weapons classified as "unfair" often make their
appearance during periods of rapid technological progress; good examples are provided by the Greek catapult (invented in Sicily around 400
B.C.) and, of course, early firearms. Coming closer to the present day,
one such period opened around 1850 and ended in 1914. Except
perhaps in the United States, whose professional military forces were
small and whose commitment to traditional forms of war was correspondingly less, the development of military technology came as a
shock and a surprise. Writing in the 1820s, Clausewitz neither listed
military technology among the principal factors governing war, nor
expected it to undergo any very great development. How wrong he was
became clear a year after his death, when the first breechloading
needle-guns emerged from the factory of Johann Dreyse, a Saxon
locksmith.

As the industrial revolution spread and began to affect war, one
new device after another made its appearance. The breechloaders were
followed by rifles, rifles by repeating guns, repeating guns by ma-
chineguns firing smokeless powder and spitting out death at 600 rounds
a minute. Artillery, too, was revolutionized. Where barrels had been
made of bronze they were now cast in steel. Muzzle-loaders with a range
of perhaps a mile, scarcely changed for three centuries, were turned
into breechloading rifled steel monsters weighing up to 100 tons. The
rate of fire was also increased by the invention of the modern recoil
mechanism, first introduced by the French in 1897. By the time of World
War I the largest guns, mounted aboard ship or else on rails, could put

one shell a minute, each close to a ton in weight, on a target more than fifteen miles away. Their introduction was accompanied by that of ancillary devices, such as the railway and the telegraph, that had not been invented for the purpose of war but soon made their impact felt. The telegraph, the steamship, the submarine, the balloon, dynamite, and barbed wire were among other important devices.

The fascinating story of how the new technologies were received provides many insights into the social dynamics of invention. Railways provide a good example. Railways, wrote the famous German economist Friedrich List in a prize-winning essay, would help the defender (whose network would be intact) and obstruct the attacker (faced by scorched earth), to the point that war itself might become impossible. When Alfred Nobel invented dynamite in 1887 he expressed similar hopes, based on the belief that his was an explosive too powerful to be used in war. Very often both the military and their political masters displayed a "not invented here" syndrome. Consequently they were anything but eager to adopt devices pressed upon them by dubious characters out to make a fast profit. Their ambivalence, however, also rested on deeper causes. Both soldiers and others—for example, the Jewish banker Ivan Bloch in his six-volume work on future conflict— feared lest advancing technology would transform war into something new, monstrous, and unprecedented.

Attempts to regulate the new weapons started at St. Petersburg in 1868 and ended at the Hague in 1907, with numerous less important meetings taking place in between. The key problem with which they had to grapple was defining what did, and did not, constitute war; for which purpose "fair" means had to be separated from those that were "dastardly," and measures constituting "military necessity" from those that would merely cause "unnecessary suffering." Since each delegation had its own ideas on these subjects the results were meager enough. It was agreed to ban explosive projectiles weighing less than 400 grams. It was further agreed that explosives should not be dropped from balloons, not that the latter were exactly ideal for the purpose. Finally, it was agreed that submarines would not use their torpedoes to sink unarmed merchantmen without first warning the crew and allowing them to take to their boats. All three prohibitions were later violated, the first when the British used dum-dum bullets to stop "savages" in Afghanistan, and the other two during World War I. Nevertheless the debates that brought them into existence, as well as the rules themselves, provide very good insight into contemporary understanding of war.

One weapon that was also banned at St. Petersburg, and was destined to become more controversial than any other, was gas. Now asphyxiating agents in the form of smoke had been used in war since time immemorial without being considered in any way special. Since effectiveness depended on concentration, its use was usually associated with the constricted spaces characteristic of siege warfare and, even more, the mining and countermining operations it involved. As the nineteenth century witnessed the rise of the modern chemical industry, the nature of the problem changed. Poison gas, which previously could be synthesized only in the laboratory and only on a minuscule scale, could now be manufactured in whatever quantity was needed to turn it into an effective weapon. Just as today there is sometimes talk of unleashing "weather warfare" and artificial earthquakes, so a century ago the looming possibilities of chemical warfare frightened the military almost out of their wits. It was therefore agreed that they should be banned, and for close to fifty years the ban was observed.

Those who formulated the conventions and added their signatures to them were thinking in terms of open warfare of the Napoleonic kind. They did not consider trench-warfare of the kind that took place in front of Richmond in 1864. The idea of using so-called "stinkbombs" was, in fact, raised during the American Civil War, and the only reason they were not used was because the struggle ended too early. In 1915, faced with what was to them (and to most combatants) the entirely unprecedented situation of stationary trench warfare, German reasoning resembled that of the Union Army in its time. A Nobel-prize winning German chemist of Jewish ancestry, Fritz Haber, was put in charge and used his expertise to produce chlorine gas. The gas was pumped into steel containers and released, when the wind appeared favourable, at Ypres in April 1915. Its use caused a panic in the British lines and thus represented a great success, except that the Germans themselves did not realize its magnitude and failed to follow up.

This breach of international law was vehemently denounced on all sides. Volumes were written to show that the use of gas reflected some particular Teutonic form of wickedness, the same type that allegedly had caused them to cut off the limbs of Belgian children and violate fair Belgian maidens. These denunciations did not prevent the Allies themselves from resorting to gas. The war was not yet a year old when both sides engaged each other in a race to produce more poisonous chemicals and better protective masks. Even the suspected presence of gas forced men to put on their protective gear, thus immobilizing them and turning them into half-soldiers (conversely, the fact that it did not allow them free play as soldiers was one reason why men disliked gas). It was a very effective weapon, particularly when used in combination with high explosive. The idea was to force the defenders into their dugouts, and then smoke them out like rats. Paradoxically, though a man going blind or else drowning in his own fluids even as he coughed his lungs out was not a sight for pretty eyes, gas as a weapon was relatively humane. This was because, compared to other devices, a much lower proportion of those who became casualties died.

The interwar period saw gas employed by the Italians in Abyssinia, and possibly also by the British in putting down the rebellions of remote Indian villages. In 1937, with World War II already looming over the horizon, the ban against gas was formally reaffirmed. During the War itself both sides produced and stored gas on a massive scale. Their arsenals included not just the comparatively primitive asphyxiating and blistering agents available twenty-five years earlier but novel, far more lethal compounds aimed at paralyzing the central nervous system. The pros and cons of gas were debated in every country; in Germany, for example, the military had to fend off pressures brought to bear by the manufacturers (I.G. Farben), who hoped to see their product put to use. Perhaps the decisive reason why chemical weapons were not employed was that they are ill-adapted to motorized, mobile warfare. To use gas against a well-defined line of fortified positions is one thing; to drench entire provinces and even countries with it is quite another.

Today many countries, the superpowers included, produce and store chemical weapons. Partly because their employment is difficult to verify, however, reliable reports of their use have been comparatively few. The Egyptians during the sixties used gas against Yemenite tribes. Two decades later their example was followed by the Iraqis, who used the weapon first against the Iranians and then against their own Kurdish fellow-citizens. The Americans in Vietnam resorted to defoliating agents in order to deprive the Viet Cong of cover, and also employed chemicals in order to destroy rice-crops in areas considered to be "infested" by the enemy. Though some of these agents were later discovered to cause cancer, whether this amounted to chemical warfare as defined by international law is debatable. The CIA at various times came up with allegations accusing the Chinese of using gas in Cambodia and the Soviets of using it in Afghanistan—not that it did either power much good. A few cases may have gone unreported, yet considering the number of conflicts that have taken place since 1945, the total number in which gas was used is small.

A logical reason for this reluctance is difficult to find. Already in World War I, fear of retaliation did not deter the belligerents from resorting to gas—the Germans in particular ought to have been worried, given that the winds blew mostly from west to east. Nor did developed countries waging low-intensity conflicts in some faraway colony have to fear retaliation, given that most guerrillas were incapable of producing chemical weapons even if they had wanted to. Perhaps the best explanation is cultural. We today seem to regard as acceptable blowing people to pieces by artillery bombardments or burning them with napalm. However, we generally do not like to watch them choking to death. As often happens when imagination has to substitute for reality, dislike may become self-reinforcing. A weapon that is considered horrible is not used. If the weapon is left unused for any length of time, the horror with which it is regarded tends to grow. Unfortunately time can make people forget as well as remember, with the result that the cycle may not last. As the twentieth century is drawing to its end, there are indications that the horror with which chemical weapons are regarded in much of the modern world is not unmixed with curiosity.

Thus, the distinction between chemical and other weapons exists solely in man's mind. It is a convention like any other, neither more logical nor less—a historical phenomenon with a clear beginning and, most probably, a clear end. It remains to ask, however, what all this teaches us about the nature of war, and the things that war is all about.

The War Convention

While the field of international law and custom associated with prisoners, noncombatants, and weapons is vast, it represents only a fraction of a much larger body of conventions and usages. From the dawn of history to the present day, men—far from discarding all restraint when they went to war—have sought to regulate it and subject it to limitations. Even some of the earliest historical societies known to us, such as the Biblical Hebrews and Homer's Greeks, already surrounded armed conflict by rules that defined the way it should be declared and terminated. The same societies also sought to establish procedures by which the two sides could communicate even as they fought (parleys), ways in which the fighting could be temporarily halted (truces), places that would be exempt from it (sanctuaries), and so on ad infinitum.

Modern international law originates in the late Middle Ages, which in turn built upon foundations laid by Roman and Canon Law. Like some long-lived reef of coral, it is still growing every day, adding layer upon layer even as older ones degenerate and are forgotten. Present-day international law, besides covering every one of the problems just mentioned, also rules over a very large number of other issues. The status of enemy diplomats, of enemy citizens, of enemy property, have all been subjected to an enormous body of scholarship as well as numerous international agreements, most of them dating back to the eighteenth and nineteenth centuries. Another large body of law is concerned with the rights and duties of neutrals, particularly as regards assistance to belligerents; asylum, internment, and right of passage; and questions involving neutral property being carried in enemy ships or vice versa. Some rules attempt to prevent the destruction of churches, libraries, cultural monuments, and even entire cities. There are rules that protect the wounded, the medical personnel attending them, and the facilities in which they are treated or transported. Others forbid shooting at members of the armed forces who are temporarily defenseless; for example, pilots parachuting to safety and ship's crews taking to their boats. I have yet to mention problems such as the right to carry arms and *ruse de guerre*. Merely to catalogue the rules would require several volumes.

Like any law, that which pertains to war is occasionally (some would say frequently) broken. The mere fact that the law in question pertains to war, however, does not prove that this happens more often than in other fields, let alone that the law does not exist or does not matter. To select but a single extreme example, World War II was as "total" a conflict as has been fought at any time and place. Still, social mores change. Not even Hitler when he went to war against Stalin followed the example of the Ottoman Sultan who, as he declared war against the Habsburg Empire in 1682, threatened to "bare the breasts" of any German woman who came his way. Though both Hitler and Stalin treated their own subordinates with the utmost ruthlessness, neither, as afar as we know, tried to assassinate the other as a method for waging war (Hitler is said to have rejected the idea when it was suggested to him). Neither used chemical weapons, though both had plenty in store. Neither was exactly considerate in his treatment of enemy noncombatants, yet not a single Soviet or German city was sacked in the manner that Wellington sacked Badajoz or the Japanese sacked Nanking. Both sides, it is true, treated prisoners harshly, often starving, freezing, or working them to death. Still, the great majority were not executed, as would have been their fate if they had been Dacian tribesmen, for example, falling into the hands of that paragon of civilization, the Roman Emperor Trajan.

Furthermore, and whatever atrocities may have been committed on the Eastern Front, in the West the struggle insofar as it pertained to the regular forces was tolerably clean, sometimes—as in Northern Africa—almost chivalrous. Between shipwrecked sailors, shot-down pilots, prisoners, the wounded, hospital ships, medical personnel, and so on, the number of those who owed their lives to the fact that the law of war was observed probably ran into several millions. Nor is this the end of the story. If we today are able to enjoy the splendors of Paris this is partly because the French in 1940 declared it an open city, a declaration the invading Germans understood, accepted, and respected. Again, when Hitler in 1944 ordered the bridges of Paris demolished and the city burnt down, the Wehrmacht commander in chief, General Dietrich von Choltitz, hesitated. In the end, prodded by the local Red Cross representative, he refused to cooperate. He declared Paris an open city, thus saving one of mankind's great cultural monuments and winning history's approval for himself.

The "strategic" view of the law of war is that it applies largely to marginal groups of people who are weak or *hors de combat* and therefore deserve protection; or else that it only pertains to "exceptional" weapons such as gas. However, nothing could be further from the truth. The purpose of the law of war is not, as Clausewitz and many of his followers seem to think, simply to appease the conscience of a few tender-hearted people. Its first and foremost function is to protect the armed forces themselves. This is because war is the domain of uncertainty and agony. Nothing is more likely than the terror of war to cause rationality to go by the board, nor is anything more conducive to make even the most even-minded start behaving somewhat strangely. The paradox is that war, the most confused and confusing of all human activities, at the same time is also one of the most organized. If armed conflict is to be carried on with any prospect of success, then it must involve the trained cooperation of many men working as a team. Men cannot cooperate, nor can organizations even exist, unless they subject themselves to a common code of behavior. The code in question should be in accord with the prevailing cultural climate, clear to all, and capable of being enforced.

As Plato puts it in the *Laws*, obedience always has held and always will hold pride of place among the military virtues. From the time of ancient Rome down to the present day, the best armies have ever been the most disciplined. Nor is it by accident that military law has always sought to be more strict, and military parlance more terse and precise, than its civilian equivalents. Whenever and wherever war takes place, it cannot occur unless those who participate in it are given to understand just whom they are and are not allowed to kill, for what ends, under what circumstances, and by what means. A body of men that is not clear in its own mind about these things is not an army but a mob. Though there have always been mobs, their usual reaction when confronted by an effective fighting organization is to scatter like chaff before the wind.

The need for the law of war does, however, go further even than this. War by definition consists of killing, of deliberately going out and shedding the blood of one's fellow-creatures. Now shedding blood and killing are activities which no society—not even a society of animals—can tolerate unless they are carefully circumscribed by rules that define what is, and is not, allowed. Always and everywhere, only that kind of killing that is carried out by certain authorized persons, under certain specified circumstances, and in accordance with certain prescribed rules, is saved from blame and regarded as a praiseworthy act. Conversely, the kind of bloodshed that ignores the rules or transgresses them usually attracts punishment or, in some societies both past and present, atonement. It is true that different societies at different times and places have differed very greatly as to the precise way in which they draw the line between war and murder; however, the line itself is absolutely essential. Some deserve to be decorated, others hung. Where this distinction is not preserved society will fall to pieces, and war—as distinct from mere indiscriminate violence—becomes impossible.

The last function of the war convention is to help determine the outcome by telling the vanquished when to surrender. If the vast majority of conflicts are not fought to the bitter end—if not every enemy person has to be slaughtered and not every enemy possession destroyed—this is because the rules also define what does, and does not, constitute victory. For example, there were two ways in which ancient Greek armies could "lose" a battle. Either one side ran, or else it asked the other for a truce to gather up its dead. Since there were occasions when one side escaped whereas the other asked for a truce, disputes sometimes arose as to who had "won" an engagement. Insofar as medieval encounters were simple tournaments taking place in the open field, the armies of the day saw themselves confronted with similar problems. To remove any doubt, and to enable the heralds to record the outcome in due form, chivalrous custom demanded that the victor remain on the battlefield for three consecutive days as the Swiss (who were not knights) did after the battles of Sempach in 1315 and Granson in 1476. Finally, the normal practice of early modern commanders was to celebrate victory by holding a religious ceremony and having the troops sing *Te Deum*. As Voltaire says, each did so in his own camp.

Today the war convention remains alive and well, continuing to rule over the life and death of possibly hundreds of thousands. True, physical possession of the battlefield is no longer as important as it used to be. Since Napoleon invented "strategy" as Clausewitz understood the term, strategy in the sense of using battles to win a campaign, war is no longer simply a question of one wrestler throwing the other out of the ring. From Moltke through Schlieffen to Liddell Hart, the shining goal of strategy has been just the opposite: namely, to outflank the enemy, encircle him, cut him off, deprive him of supplies, and bring about his surrender *without* actually having to fight for the ground on which he stood. From the Austrians at Ulm in 1805, all the way down to the Egyptian Third Army at Suez in 1973, the story of modern strategy is always the same. Large armed formations are regarded as having been defeated—and, equally important, regard themselves as having been defeated—as soon as they are surrounded and their lines of communication are severed.

Under modern rules, fights to the death usually ensue only when one or both sides find it impossible to cut each other off and score "victory points." For example, World War I on the Western Front was, as contemporary wisdom put it, "not war." Conditions were such that one side was unable to outflank—let alone encircle—the other, with the result that for four years they engaged in a battle of attrition and wore down each other half to death. In attacking the USSR in 1941 the Germans operated according to standard blitzkrieg doctrine, penetrating to the enemy's rear and creating vast pockets of troops; however,they soon found that the Soviets unlike the French in the previous year, refused to surrender when surrounded and had to be defeated one by one, thus slowing down the campaign and eventually causing it to fail. Finally, one reason why today's armies often fail when confronted by guerrillas and terrorists is precisely that such opponents have no bases or lines of communication. Hence they cannot be cut off in the ordinary sense of the word. If they run, nothing is achieved. Alternatively, as happened at Hamburger Hill, they make a stand—with the result that the ensuing fight is apt to be unusually tough and bloody.

All this leads to the conclusion that, in any particular kind of war, the meaning of "victory" is decided as much by convention—tacit or explicit—as it is by actual physical results. Like any other kind of law, the war convention consists partly of explicit rules and regulations and partly of norms that are rooted in the culture. Like any other kind of law, it represents a more or less porous, flimsy barrier built upon the shifting sands of reality. As circumstances cause one type of conflict to be replaced by another, the existing convention becomes inadequate and new definitions have to be found.

Nor is it difficult to see what fate will befall a force that, for one reason or another, does not abide by the rules. One possible outcome is that the army will turn into a mob, running amok in all directions, inflicting tremendous destruction on the environment and, even more, on themselves. So far removed is such uncontrolled violence from war proper that Greek mythology, always a good source of insight, had two different deities to represent the two. The patroness of orderly, regular war was the virgin goddess Pallas Athene. Springing directly from Zeus' brain, she was a powerful warrior who is often represented leaning on her spear, her helmet pulled back, lost in thought. The patron of unrestrained violence was Ares, "mad, fulminating Ares," to quote Homer, an outcast among gods and men, Athene was one of the great gods and had the Parthenon erected in her honor. Ares, born to the same father in the ordinary way, was a minor deity who had only a few worshippers and fewer temples. The *Illiad* tells how Ares on one occasion met Athene in battle and was soundly defeated. Bleeding and trumpeting his pain he ran from the field, ascended to Olympus and complained to Zeus from whom, however, he received scant sympathy.

While armies that were turned into raging, uncontrollable mobs are not unknown, over the long run the more likely outcome is somewhat different. In a situation like Vietnam, where regular forces are employed against guerrillas and terrorists, the distinction between combatants and noncombatants will probably break down. Unable to go by the ordinary war convention as expressed in the "rules of engagement," all but the most disciplined troops will find themselves violating those rules. Having, by the force of circumstances, killed noncombatants and tortured prisoners, they will go in fear of the consequences if caught. If caught, they are certain to blame their commanders for putting them into a situation where they are damned if they do and damned if they don't. The commanders, in turn, will hasten to wash their hands of the whole affair, claiming that they never told their subordinates to break the rules. There will be atrocities, as happened at My Lai, and attempts to cover them up. Where the cover-up fails a few low-ranking members of the military establishment may be turned into scapegoats, as Lieutenant Calley was, whereas their superiors will deny responsibility. With the men unable to trust each other, or their commanders, disintegration occurs. When this happened in Vietnam, tens of thousands went AWOL, and an estimated 30 percent of the forces were on hard drugs. Soon such an army will cease to fight, each man seeking only to save his conscience and his skin.

Without a law to define what is and is not permitted, there can be no war. Though written international law is comparatively recent, previous ages were no less dependent on the war convention for their ability to fight. Nor does the absence of a formal written code necessarily mean that our ancestors were more ruthless in their conduct of war than we ourselves; a century that has produced Dresden and Hiroshima—and Auschwitz—cannot in all fairness accuse its predecessors of barbarism. Before there was international law there were bilateral treaties between kings. These in turn were preceded by the law of nature, the code of chivalry, the *ius gentium,* Greek religion and custom, and, earlier still, the customs and usage of tribal societies. While not all these codes were laid down in writing, they derived their binding force from the fact that they were supposed to represent reason, God, tradition, and even—in the case of primitive tribes—"reality" itself. All in all they were probably as effective as today's international agreements which, having been made by man, are also capable of being abrogated by him.

Though the rules of previous ages differed from our own, then as today those who broke them were sometimes apprehended and brought to justice. Nor was fate necessarily more kind to those, probably the majority, who never stood trial. Western literature as presented by the *Illiad* begins at the point where Agamemnon, the mighty King, was punished by Apollo for violating the law and rejecting the ransom of a young woman whom he had captured. In later Greek mythology, warriors who desecrated temples or committed other excesses were overtaken by nemesis and persecuted by the erinyes, the monstrous goddesses of revenge who made one's very food inedible. During the Christian Middle Ages, knights who did not respect the rights of monks, nuns, and innocent people in general were destined to be hounded by the devil while they lived and carried off to hell after they had died.

The fate that the modern world reserves for those of us who cross the border between war and crime is, in some respects, worse still. Long gone are the days when, as in ancient Persia, armies were ceremonially purged of bloodshed by being marched between the two halves of a sacrificial dog. God may still exist, but to judge from the infrequency of His appearances in strategic literature He has turned His face away. The breakdown of belief and the absence of religiously-sanctioned rites for expiation has made it very difficult for people to come to terms with their transgressions. Visit the Vietnam memorial in Washington, D.C. on any given day and watch the crowd for the effects of repentance and guilt on both combatants and noncombatants who, even after fifteen years, have yet to come to terms with that war.

CHAPTER
IV

How War Is Fought

A Prussian Marsellaise Continued

The conduct of war is usually known as strategy, and the history of strategy is long and interesting. The word comes from the Greek *stratos,* meaning army or, to be exact, host. From *stratos* comes *strategos,* general, as well as *strategeia,* which depending on the context can mean a campaign, generalship, or the general's office. From *stratos,* too, comes *strategama.* In modern parlance, this is best translated as a trick or ruse, which may be directed either at the enemy or at one's own troops. The Roman commander and engineer Sextus Iunius Frontinus around 100 A.D. wrote a book called *Strategematon,* a collection of stratagems that had been tried by ancient generals and found successful. Some of those he lists were meant to mislead the enemy; for example, by reversing signals in such a way as to pretend to attack at one time while actually attacking at another. Others, however, were designed for internal use; for example, Frontinus recommended that the commander should fabricate favorable omens in order to raise his men's morale and inspire them with courage.

It is indicative of the state of military affairs, and also of Greek studies, that words derived from *stratos* were all but unknown in the West from late Roman times on. The Middle Ages did not use the term strategy. The normal term describing the conduct of war was, to quote from Christine de Pisan's fourteenth-century handbook, "*L'Art de chevalerie.*" The period of 1500 to 1750 dropped the *chevalerie* and spoke, as did Machiavelli, Frederick the Great, and many lesser luminaries, of "the art of war." The later eighteenth century, with its emphasis on rationality in every field of human endeavor, gradually came to distrust art as too vague and intuitive. It preferred to think of war's conduct as a "science" whose principles could be discovered, laid down in a "system", and taught in the military academies that were just beginning to open their doors. The term "strategy" itself is a neologism. Apparently the first to use it was a Frenchman, Jolly de Maizeroy, who was a writer active in the military field during the years immediately before the Revolution.

As defined by the late-eighteenth and early-nineteenth century dictionaries, the important distinction was between strategy and tactics. Tactics, derived from a Greek word whose original meaning was order, stood for the conduct of battle; in plain words, the actual act of fighting. By contrast, strategy signified everything that took place in war before and after the physical clash. The task of tactics was to see to it that the slaughter should take place in good order and with the best possible outcome. That of strategy was to enable it to take place under the most favourable circumstances, and to make use of it once it had been accomplished; the strategist prepared violence and exploited it, but he did not himself engage in it. Hence, strategy not long after its birth began to acquire an aura of mystery that has lasted to the present day. Directed from the office with the aid of impressive-looking desks, maps, colored pencils and (later) telephones and computers, it supposedly required mental faculties different from, and higher than, those needed in the hurly-burly of battle. The talents in question were not considered within the province of every ordinary soldier. As time went on they came to be concentrated in a body of specially-trained men, known as the staff.

The discovery of a new intellectual tool is often followed by baroque attempts to work out its implications, and strategy was no exception. Early nineteenth-century works on military theory bristle with attempts to discover the "best" strategy or, at any rate, to formulate principles for its operation. The basic terminology was laid out in 1800–1806 by Dietrich von Bülow, the confused genius whose ultimate fate was to fall foul of the Tsar, be extradited to the Russians by Prussia, and die on his way to Siberian exile. As he saw it, the essence of strategy consisted first of choosing the correct "lines of operations" for the army to follow, then of coordinating those lines with each other in conformity with certain well defined geometrical principles. Other authors developed von Bülow's thought. Jomini, Venturinus, and others argued that the theater of war could be represented by a huge, exceedingly complicated, chessboard, and attempts were made to construct actual chessboards that would do justice to this complexity. Whether on the board or in the field, the art of the commander consisted of maneuvering his forces in such a way as to concentrate the largest number of men (or counters) at the decisive point.

Here we are concerned with the greatest writer of them all, Carl von Clausewitz. One of the more enlightening chapters of *vom Kriege* presents a brief history of strategy until about 1820. Starting from siege warfare—the first to be subjected to methodical analysis—he lists the various systems then in vogue and discusses the strengths and weaknesses of each. Clausewitz was too self opinionated to mention by name even his most famous predecessors, but their identity is easily guessed from the text. He does not disguise his feeling that they had allowed themselves to become lost in technicalities. One and all, they had skirted around the issue but left out the single most decisive element, namely, sheer overwhelming force. To Clausewitz, who admired Napoleon whom he called "the God of War," "the best strategy is always to be very strong, first in general and then at the decisive point."

On the question as to how strength was to be achieved and used, and where the decisive point was to be found, Clausewitz is open to different interpretations. He himself discussed the matter at some length, putting due emphasis both on the geometrical element and on the correct use of space and time in order to achieve a preponderance of force when and where it was most needed. However, when everything was said and done Clausewitz had little confidence in clever combinations, even in human reason itself. As the organization of *vom Kriege* shows rather clearly, strategy was much more than an intellectual exercise to be planned on a map and tested by means of some exercise or war game. Before it was anything else, it was a question of mobilizing *all* mental and physical forces and forging them into a mailed fist. The fist might maneuver this way or that, but ultimately its purpose was to crash down on the enemy, shattering his body and breaking his will. Once that had been achieved, the rest, in his own words, was "nothing."

Psychologically speaking, it is perhaps surprising that such a delicate and sensitive character as Clausewitz should have represented the essence of war in this way. His successors took up his thought and turned it into a brutal marching song. As time went on, there was a tendency to extend the meaning of strategy further and further. Particularly after World War I, it grew to include the creation of military force as well as its use, even to the point that the two are no longer distinguishable. This chapter seeks to explain all the various aspects of strategy, starting with the way in which armed force is created, passing through the obstacles that stand in its way, and ending with its employment against a living, reacting enemy.

On Strategy: The Creation of Force

Even where armed conflict appears in its most primitive form, preparations for it usually fall into two separates parts, one pertaining to the men and the other to the equipment. The men must be mustered, put on a war footing, disciplined, trained, infused with the warrior spirit, and intellectually prepared for the fighting ahead. The equipment must be produced, stored, distributed, maintained, and in general prepared for use. Depending on the society by which war is waged, these functions may be known under different names. At some places they are separate, whereas in others they merge into each other. Our contemporary way of doing these things is certainly not the only one: historically many societies did not even recognize the division between men and equipment, given that certain weapons were credited with magic personalities and had to be catered to much in the way humans were. Nevertheless, and regardless of when and where war takes place, it is difficult to see how it would be waged unless these functions are carried out and armed force is created first.

Among the adult males comprising primitive tribes, the concept of organization itself—in the sense of an ordered division of labor subject to discipline—hardly existed. Like most other activities, warfare was considered the function of every individual warrior, which is almost the same as saying that it was the function of nobody in particular. Following some incident—such as the destruction of a garden, the theft of livestock, or the abduction of a woman by a member of a neighboring tribe—the decision to go to war would emerge spontaneously. Hostilities might involve either the entire tribe or only some of its members. The men would take up their weapons—largely the same as those used in hunting—and assemble at some customary place. They would elect a leader, whose authority, however, lasted only as long as did the war itself. The onset of war properly speaking would be celebrated by a grand ceremony. Even as the witch-doctor invoked the spirits and distributed charms, the warriors would chant and dance and prance. The expedition over, the "army" would disband itself, often by going through the same process but proceeding in reverse order.

In view of the small, intimate population, the identity between males and warriors, and the widespread availability of weapons, creating a military force presented few problems. No administrative machinery existed, and none was needed, to put the tribe on a war footing within a matter of hours. The same factors, however, also ensured that whatever strength was created would be small, unstable, and impermanent. There was little discipline, less organized tactical training, and hardly any attempt to set up disparate tactical units capable of coordinated action. Even the critical matter of supreme command was uncertain, given that the leader's authority rested on no institutional basis, and was temporary to boot. The upshot was that tribal war, though occasionally numerous, seldom lasted very long. Even if it did the results were seldom permanent, given that there was no standing organization in charge of enforcing them; quite often the idea of conquest, and indeed that of territoriality itself, did not exist.

More advanced societies used various means to overcome these problems. In classical Greece, as in Republican Rome, the elected warleaders—known as *strategoi* or, in Latin, *consules*—officiated in peace as well as in war; Rome also had the *dictator,* a war-leader elected for six months whose authority was absolute. These arrangements meant that the magistrates held power far in excess of that enjoyed by any tribal chief, enabling them to carry out a measure of warlike preparation and training even while peace lasted; still, neither the Greek city states nor Republican Rome before the end of the second century B.C. had permanent forces at their disposal. The Hellenistic monarchies to a certain extent, and the Roman Empire to a greater one, solved this problem. They made war under a single permanent head, the King or Emperor, who either commanded in person or else transmitted his orders by bureaucratic means. Their war-waging instruments consisted of standing armies, numbering in the tens of thousands, regularly paid, strictly disciplined, and well trained. Permanent tactical formations in the form of the century, the maniple, cohort, legion, and ala (cavalry squadron) made their appearance. Apparently, in some cases there even existed royal workshops where arms were manufactured, though the evidence on this is fragmentary.

Proportionally speaking, not even Rome at its zenith was able to mobilize anything like the military resources available to the modern state. The Roman army always included as many auxiliaries as it did legionaries. These were drawn from various barbarian tribes, served under their own chiefs, and were so little subject to control that they ended up taking over the Empire. A "ministry of defense" in our sense of the term either did not exist or has left no trace in the records. Nor, apparently, was there a question of a regular general staff responsible for planning and conducting operations. Apparently not all of the army's equipment was centrally issued, nor was complete standardization ever achieved. Though an efficient mail service operated over the famous Roman roads, the technological infrastructure of war was primitive. The absence of good maps, timekeepers, telecommunications, and statistical information prevented the emperors from mobilizing all available resources even if, they knew what those resources were—which seems unlikely. Consequently even the late Roman Empire under Septimus Severus, for example, never had more than perhaps 600,000 men under arms, representing perhaps 1 percent of the entire population. This proved too much; by the time of Diocletian the Empire began to crumble under the burden of maintaining the army, leading to far-reaching socio-economic changes and ultimately contributing to its collapse.

During the Middle Ages, the ability to create military force declined to far below the Roman level. The feudal system, being decentralized, only permitted the establishment of armies that were ill-disciplined and impermanent. They were also small, the largest numbering perhaps no more than 20,000 men, of whom a majority were not knights but an ill-assorted lot of squires and servants. After 1350 things tended to improve, but slowly. The late Middle Ages saw the reintroduction of an economy based on money, made greater use of written records, and finally invented printing. By 1550 the most powerful monarchies had the core of a standing army at their disposal, though the majority of troops still consisted of mercenaries enlisted on a temporary basis. A late sixteenth-century political theorist, Justus Lipsius, wrote that a "large" country should have at its disposal no more than two regular legions consisting of 6,600 men each. Louis XIV, in some ways the mightiest of all eighteenth-century absolute rulers, at one point was able to have up to 5 percent of the population on active service. The creation of an army numbering 400,000 men represented a considerable achievement, even though the number of those who could be concentrated at a single spot was much smaller.

Present-day military establishments all over the developed world typically concern themselves with all aspects of the force-creating process. Since 1945, this has been carried to the point where it affects every aspect of national life. However, even as late as the eighteenth century many aspects of the creation of force were not considered part of war as such. For example, armies did not carry out their own staff work; that was the function of the commander's secretary, a civilian, who by international convention was exempt from the fighting and had to be released when captured. Nor did armies procure their own enlisted manpower; that was considered to be the function of contractors and, in the case of the British Navy, the notorious press-gangs which roamed harbors and dragged off sailors for service aboard men-of-war. Much the same applied to logistics and transportation. to such questions as medical and spiritual care, market-tender wares, laundry services, and the like. Either the army contracted civilians to provide such services, or else they were provided on an individual basis and had to be paid for out of the soldiers' own pockets.

Thus, during much of history, either the war-making societies were too small to require a centralized war-making organization, or else—as in Imperial Rome—they were too large to make such an organization possible. Either way, the force-creating process remained defective. No more than a fraction of the available resources could be mobilized. The absence of an institutionalized central brain, of detailed information, and of efficient communications meant that even such resources as actually were mobilized could not be properly coordinated and looked after. All this resulted in severe limitations on the maximum size of the forces, both in general and at the decisive point. From the time of the battle of Rapha in 217 B.C. to that of Malplaquet in 1709, field armies much stronger than 100,000 men seem to have existed mainly in legend. Napoleon was perhaps the ablest general who ever lived; yet when he concentrated 180,000 men at Leipzig in 1813 even he lost control.

The turning point in this, as in so much else, was formed by the railway and the telegraph, both of which began to affect the conduct of war from the 1830s on. The railways increased the speed and volume of transport many times while simultaneously reducing its cost. They first permitted entire countries—and, later, continents—to be knit together and mobilized for war-fighting purposes. The telegraph represented a vital aid, both because it enabled the railways to be utilized to their full capacity and because it allowed the mobilization-orders to be quickly and efficiently distributed. Once mobilization had been completed, again it was the railways and the telegraphs that allowed the conscripts to be fed and controlled. Though experiments with the new devices were made by the war ministries of many countries, the first to grasp the potential of the new instruments and to utilize them to the full were the Prussians. Dress-rehearsals were carried out in 1859, when the Franco-Austrian War led to a Prussian mobilization on the Rhine, and during the 1864 war against Denmark. In 1866, and again in 1870, the speed with which they mobilized against Austria and France respectively left the rest of the world gasping, and went far to determine the outcome before the first shot was fired.

Railways and telegraphs were, moreover, but two out of a whole galaxy of new devices that included the radio, the telephone, the rotary press, the motor car and, in the last years before 1939, automated business machines that were the ancestors of today's computers. Enmeshing society in a fine network, these devices both accelerated the force-creating process and led to a vast increase in its scope. It became possible to put millions into the field and, what is more, to maintain them there almost indefinitely. These armies resembled nothing so much as ambulant, albeit somewhat dilapidated, cities. They had to be fed, clothed, equipped, trained, policed, and looked after in every way. As almost every function of civil society came to be duplicated in the army, the old haphazard administrative machinery for mobilizing the forces and supervising their operations no longer sufficed. A new supervisory institution was needed, and this new institution duly appeared in the shape of the general staff.

General staffs consisted of bodies of specially selected, specially trained, experts. Their preferred place of work was not the field but the office. Instead of fighting, they planned and administered, with the result that—given the exceptional prestige that they enjoyed—the impression sometimes arose that administration and planning was what war is all about. Like all other young and successful institutions, general staffs soon acquired a dynamic of their own, seeking to add to their power. Over time they assumed responsibility for every aspect of war, beginning with the operations of large units and ending—in the case of the Wehrmacht in World War II—by providing disease-free brothels for the troops' use. Functions that had never been previously considered part of war were now entering the military arena. Nor were soldiers the only ones expected to serve their country. Modern communications enabled everything and everybody to be included in the force-creating process; even eccentric university professors were put behind barbed wire and set to work breaking codes or inventing strange devices.

Taking their cue from the Prussian mobilizations in 1866 and 1870, the general staffs' aims were order, coordination, and—above all—efficiency. Creating the greatest war-making potential involved more than mobilizing all available resources: above all else, it was an exercise in meshing those resources with each other until they formed a single coherent whole. While general staffs were often credited with the invention of efficiency, the concept spread to other areas. No sooner had the Prussians demonstrated what could be done than popular writers, such as Edward Bellamy in *Looking Backward,* started demanding that society at large be made as efficient as Moltke's Army. Managers such as Frederick Taylor and Henry Ford spread the gospel. They adopted the conveyor belt, using stopwatches and recording the movements of workers in an attempt to make them as efficient as the machines they served. Humans, too, were to be bred and raised for their efficiency, an idea first proposed by the Eugenic Movement around the turn of the century and later caricatured in another best-seller, Aldous Huxley's *Brave New World.* By the 1930s British Foreign Office experts were using "efficiency" as a criterion by which to judge entire nations. Since Hitler's Germany came out on top, it was only logical that it should be appeased.

Though circumstances differed, the methods by which efficiency was to be achieved were the same everywhere. The first prerequisite was a strong directing brain, confident of itself and of where it was going. The brain was to consist of the best available personnel, carefully groomed for the task and supposedly without any self-serving interest whatsoever. The brain's authority was to be both all-encompassing and absolute. The first part of its activity would consist of taking a complete inventory of the nation's human and (later) material resources, including even the last coupling on the last railway-car. The inventory ready, plans would be made to mobilize available resources for the purpose of war. The plans would encompass hundreds of thousands, possibly even millions of components. These had to be carefully dovetailed, coordinated, and geared with each other so as to ensure maximum speed and smoothness in operation. The plans would be "debugged"—to use modern computer terminology—by being rehearsed time after time. Periodic reviews would adapt them to changing circumstances and also ensure that the latest technology was incorporated. Nothing was allowed to hold them up, not even the need to have the commander in chief permanently at the end of a telephone wire.

For the plans to be put into effect, all that was necessary was that the responsible minister sign a piece of paper that itself lay ready and waiting, requiring only the date to be inserted. Once the paper had been signed and the mobilization orders sent out, things would proceed automatically. Men would go to depots where they would be formally turned into soldiers, put into uniform, and issued with weapons. Companies would be formed into battalions, battalions into regiments, regiments into divisions and corps. The corps would be merged with their supporting services such as supply trains, heavy artillery, and reconnaissance aircraft. They would proceed toward the frontier using either rail-transport or, in a later age, motor vehicles. Arrangements were made to receive them upon arrival, and the final march itself took place in such good order that even the number of axles passing a given bridge in a given period of time was calculated in advance. Once the deployment areas had been reached and the force-creating process completed, the war properly speaking could get under way. Before it did, however, it was necessary to find ways to deal with the great obstacles to efficiency—namely, inflexibility, friction, and uncertainty.

On Strategy: Obstacles to Force

The great twin obstacles to warlike force, according to Clausewitz, are uncertainty and friction. He might have added inflexibility, thus completing a trio that has bedeviled military forces since the beginning of time. Nor are these problems limited only to the level commonly known as "strategy"; that is, to the grand operations of war. On the contrary, the whole point of discussing them is precisely that they exist wherever and whenever war is waged. Starting with an infantry squad trying to make its way in the mud, and ending in the posh offices where military, social, economic, and political problems meet and merge, inflexibility, friction, and uncertainty make their influence felt; so much so that the quality of the performance at each of these levels is judged very largely by their ability to neutralize those influences. Still, it is generally true that the higher the level the greater are the problems, and the greater also the difficulties of dealing with them. Which is one reason why those at the top usually carry heavier responsibilities, work longer hours, and are better paid.

As we saw, a cardinal component of force is sheer size. "Everything else being equal, the side with the larger battalions wins"—so runs the common wisdom that could base itself on Clausewitz and Napoleon. One reason for this is psychological. A preference for size, so long as it is not excessive, seems to have been programmed into the psyche of men and animals alike. Even today when their most important function is to attract tourists, royal guards all over the world consist of big, powerful men. Now war, before it is anything else, is a question of psychology; to quote vom Kriege again, it is "a mental and physical struggle conducted by means of the latter." Other things being equal, an army going to war should therefore take care to appear as large and as powerful as possible, thus intimidating the enemy, impressing neutrals, and encouraging its own men.

The remaining elements that make up force are excellent equipment, good organization, tough training, strict discipline, and high morale. These can overcome sheer size, within certain limits and as long as circumstances are not too unfavorable. Whatever the exact relationship between quality and quantity, a problem that has formed the subject of a vast literature, the preponderance of numerical force unquestionably plays a vital role in war. Among the manifold factors that make for victory, its importance is second to none.

The existence of a large force, however, also gives rise ro problems. Again applying the eternal caveat—other things being equal—the larger any given body of troops, the less flexible it is. A squad may be able to operate in any kind of terrain, but not a division with all its transport. A squad, but not a division with its tremendous logistic requirements, may cut loose from its administrative tail, live off the country, and operate independently for a time. A single warrior can turn around at a moment's notice to face an attacker coming from either flank. A line consisting of ten men will find the same maneuver more difficult to carry out, and the greater the numbers the worse the problem. Nor is this simply a question of geometry; the larger the unit, the more cumbersome the command-procedures involved, and the longer its reaction time. Sophisticated technology can help alleviate these problems to some extent, but it most definitely cannot solve them. For example, modern Standard Operating Procedure (SOP) rests on the assumption that an army corps will be able to respond to two to three orders per twenty-four–hour period, a figure that has remained unchanged for two centuries and, indeed, ever since the *corps d'armée* itself was invented.

What is more, the flexibility of tactical formations of troops tends to stand in inverse proportion to their power. Describing the battle of Pydna in 168 B.C., Polybios tells us how the Roman commander Lucius Aemilius Paulus trembled at the sight of the Macedonian phalanx, numbering 40,000 and apparently irresistible in its forward sweep. Irresistible it may have been, but it was also vulnerable since the very factor that made it so powerful—the long *sarisae,* or pikes, supported by the shoulders of as many as sixteen men—prevented it from turning around or dealing with breaches in the ranks. To adduce another example, eighteenth-century tactical formations consisted of long, thin lines designed to bring every available musket into play and deliver the

maximum possible firepower. Marching forward slowly, frequently halt-
ing in order to dress ranks, they presented moving walls of flesh. The
two or three volleys which they delivered each minute, though scarcely
accurate, were absolutely devastating: a few hours fighting might leave
as many as 40 percent of the troops present either dead or wounded. As
theoreticians knew, and as Frederick II proved at Leuthen in 1757, the
great weakness of these formations was their inability to turn around
quickly enough. Attacked in the flank, they were like lambs at the
slaughter.

These problems became even worse when, during the second half
of the nineteenth century, rails replaced feet as the preferred method of
strategic locomotion. Rail by definition is an inflexible instrument, since
trains can go only where the rails are. Timetables must be carefully
prepared in advance and strictly adhered to, since any attempt to tinker
with them will lead to delays, congestion, or even collisions. In addition,
loading and unloading the trains represent long and slow processes, so
much so that large units—divisions and up—moving over distances of
less than 70 miles or so are better off marching on foot. None other than
Moltke said that the rail-deployment of an army, once it had been
started, could never be altered, The increasing number of railway lines
that became available in Europe after his time may have modified this
situation to some extent, but left its fundamentals unchanged. During
World War I, to take the most famous example, the details of the German
Schlieffen Plan had been laid down years in advance. When the Kaiser at
the last moment proposed that the plan be altered to accommodate
what appeared—mistakenly—as a diplomatic opening, his chief of the
General Staff, a nephew of the great Moltke, threw up his arms to heaven
and swore it could not be done.

Modern armies are admittedly less dependent on rails than their
predecessors. However, in their case there is the enormous logistic
apparatus to be considered. A division during the Franco-Prussian War
consumed about 50 tons a day on average, consisting mainly of food and
fodder. By 1916 the figure had risen to approximately 150 tons, most of
the increase being accounted for by ammunition, fuel, spare parts, and
engineering supplies. In 1940–42, the German General Staff worked on
the assumption that an armored division in the Western Desert needed
300 tons daily to remain operational. Allied planners in 1944–45
postulated 650 tons a day per American division in Western Europe, a
figure that has probably doubled or tripled during the decades since
then. Given such tonnages, large armies need tens of thousands of
motor vehicles and millions upon millions of gallons of gas to haul their

supplies. Also needed is a vast technological infrastructure that will keep the trucks supplied with everything from maintenance to tires. The paucity of available data since 1945 makes it hard to say just what these facts mean, though cynics might claim that the small number of conflicts from which data might be drawn already speaks for itself. However that may be, there is little doubt that modern armies are, by virtue of their very power, like mighty dinosaurs; and, if my argument is correct, they are equally doomed to extinction.

Insofar as inflexibility is the product of size, it is a problem armed forces share with other large organizations such as industrial firms. The same is also true of another and related problem, namely friction. Friction is a term that seems to have originated with Clausewitz and that he borrowed from the field of mechanics. *Vom Kriege* defines *Reibung* as "that which distinguishes war on paper from the real thing;" it is, to use Clausewitz's own incomparable metaphor, the factor that causes the easy and graceful act of walking to appear difficult and clumsy when it is carried out in water. The more numerous the components in any machine—human or mechanical—the greater the likelihood of any one of them breaking down, affecting the rest and creating friction. This proposition can be turned around. The friction in an armed force consisting of many disparate parts is enormous to begin with, since each part has its own problems and interacts with all others, Unless due care is taken, and given some bad luck, it may even prevent the force from operating at all.

What makes the problem of friction so intractable is the fact that, the greater the efficiency demanded, the worse its effects. A wagon that lost a wheel presented no great problem to the Grande Armée, given that it could always be circumvented or else pushed off the road so that the rest of the column might continue on its march. A train that has gone off the rails cannot be treated in the same way, however, nor can a demolished section of a railway line be bypassed as easily as a crater in the road. In fact, the tighter the kind of coordination on which efficiency depends, the more flawlessly each part meshes with another, the greater the danger that the failure of any one will lead to the failure of all the rest, As anybody who has ever been caught in a traffic jam knows, the delays created by a single broken-down car are not limited to its immediate vicinity but reverberate throughout the system. They also tend to be self-reinforcing, since the need to maintain safety-margins means that each successive delay has to be a little greater than the one that preceded it. The adage that nothing succeeds like success also has a reverse face: once failure starts, it is difficult to stop.

The role played by friction in war is very great, so much so that armies going on campaign have been known to starve before they could ever begin to fight. Nor, is it easy to see how friction can be overcome, given that it is rooted in the nature of things. A strong-willed commander can—and under certain circumstances, he must—drive his force forward regardless of friction. The cost of doing so is very great, however, since the wear and tear are tremendous and the point may come where the engine simply stalls. Should it stall after the objective is gained, well and good. Should it stall before the decision falls, the result can be disaster. For example, the German General Rommel repeatedly drove his forces to the breaking point and beyond. In 1941 his dash to Sollum almost ended in the destruction of his forces. In 1942 he reached Alamein with no fuel left, his ammunition a thousand miles in the rear at Tripoli, and with only nineteen tanks left in working order. To make things worse, his impossibly long lines of communication were subjected to constant sea and air attack. The Afrika Korps had clearly shot its bolt; from then on it only attempted one more half-hearted offensive at Alam Halfa. That attack having failed, all it could do was cower and wait for the enemy, who was becoming stronger every day, to launch his counteroffensive. When the offensive came it spelled the end of the Korps.

According to Clausewitz, the one factor that can help an army deal with friction is experience. By acting like the oil among the cogwheels of a machine, experience can alleviate the worst problems of friction without, however, eliminating it. This proposition can also be turned upside down. Experienced troops who have known each other for a long time recognize that each man, each piece of equipment, and each unit are liable to an occasional failure, turning themselves into sources of friction. They help one another, often without words. A good army is one that, whether by foresight or experience or in any other way, has learned to avoid friction where it can and live with it where it cannot.

Another source of friction, apart from that which originates from inside the machine, is the environment. The rains come early, turning the roads into quagmires and causing the advance to slow or halt. The bridge marked on the map is found to be in a bad state and cannot carry the division's tanks. The one antidote to this kind of thing is, of course, careful preparation based on good intelligence. Resources, however, are always limited, with the result that preparation can never be perfect. If only because no one really knows what will have to be known, the same also applies to intelligence. What is more, it takes time to gather intelligence—even to the point that the need for additional information is very often used as an excuse for delay and inaction. An army that postpones the opening of a campaign until it has *all* the requisite information at its disposal will wait forever. Finally, when it makes its move, it will likely discover that too much intelligence can be just as harmful as too little. As communications become clogged and cause orderly procedures to be circumvented or discarded, the quality of decision-making will suffer. Intelligence is never perfect; nor will a good army expect it to be.

The point where information enters the picture is also where we encounter the third great obstacle to force, namely, uncertainty. Like inflexibility and friction, uncertainty is a natural product of size and tends to increase in direct proportion with it. A one-man army faces no uncertainty, at least not of the conscious kind. The larger the force, the more difficult the problem of transmitting orders and directing it towards some positive goal. What is more, a force that is large enough may escape control simply because the commander no longer has the ability to know where his own units are, what their situation is, and what they are doing. Faced with this problem, Moses took the advice of Jethro, his father-in-law, and instituted a regular chain of command, From his time to ours, delegating responsibility, establishing clear channels of communication, and instituting what, in another book I have called a "directed telescope" are methods that can alleviate the problem without, however, completely solving it. The paradox is that, though nothing is more important in war than unity of command, it is impossible for one man to know everything. The larger and the more complex the forces that he commands, the more true this becomes.

Another very important source of uncertainty in war derives not from the army's size but from the nature of its human components. War more than any other activity is the domain of anger, fear, pain, and death. People who are immersed in these most intense of experiences are likely to be less objective than a man sitting in an office and writing papers, and far less objective than a computer that does not even "understand" the information it is processing. Under such circumstances, the speed with which information is transmitted, its internal organization and coherence, and its reliability are all certain to suffer, a fact that a wise commander will take into account. Again, it is possible to alleviate the problem by instituting and enforcing strict procedures, checklists, forms, call-signs, regular hours at which information must be transmitted, and so on. Ultimately, however, the quality of the various channels will depend on the human factor. Not even the most advanced information-transmitting and processing system will be better than the people who feed it with data, pass the data on, filter it, present it, and finally make use of it; this is a problem that no number of computers can solve.

The uncertainty inherent in any organization can be understood as a special kind of friction, namely, that which originates in the difficulties of information-processing. However, in the case of war, uncertainty is not merely the result of the army's own structure or the environment in which it operates. Rather, the very fact that it is facing a living enemy, made up of flesh and blood and possessed of a will that is to some extent free and unpredictable, already introduces an additional large measure of uncertainty into our calculations. Nor is it advisable to forget that, behind the human will, there are often at work psychological forces that are uncontrollable, even unknowable, and that may cause even the most rational opponent to react in unexpected ways. As Moltke once put it, of the three courses that the enemy can take normally he selects the fourth.

In addition, a wise enemy, seeking to put obstacles in front of our force, will do everything in his power to increase our uncertainty. He will make use of camouflage, secrecy, speed, deception, and surprise in order to disguise his movements. He will try to mask his "signature" by jamming, overloading, or spoofing our sensors. He will institute tight security, hounding our spies and hanging them if he can. Perhaps more dangerous still, after arresting our spies he may use force or persuasion to turn them around. They may then be employed to feed us with disinformation, as British Counterintelligence did to the German *Abwehr* in World War II. The ways in which the information game may be played are as varied and complex as the human mind itself. There is no limit to inventiveness, nothing that has not been tried at one time or another, successfully or otherwise.

Thus, on both sides of the conflict, simply to create the greatest possible force is not enough. A force, once it exists, represents a source of problems, namely those of uncertainty, friction, and inflexibility; and the larger it is the more true this becomes. Whatever else may be involved in the conduct of war, it is very much a question of managing this inter-related trio, even to the point where victory depends on the army's ability to cope with them. Each of the three factors is rooted in the forces' own structure as well as the environment in which they operate. However, uncertainty differs from the rest in that it is also deliberately introduced by the enemy. Hence it must not just be overcome, it must be used; and it is by using uncertainty as much as anything else that war is, and should be, fought.

On Strategy: The Use of Force

Assuming force has been created and mobilized, and the obstacles affecting its use dealt with to the extent that it is functional, how should it be used? The first decision that has to be made always concerns the question of defense versus attack. Of the two, defense is, *in itself and everything else being equal,* the stronger form of war. As Clausewitz writes, there are three reasons why this is so. First, holding on to something is easier and requires less effort than taking it away. Second, since the goal of the defense is to protect things as they are, it has time on its side; whatever does *not* happen helps the defense. Third, to the extent that the offense involves a geographical advance, operating away from one's bases, and progressively occupying hostile territory, it causes the attacker's lines of communications to become longer even as those of the defender contract. This problem was less critical in ages when the nature of logistics was such that armies could live off the country. Alexander operated in Asia for years on end without receiving any sustenance from Macedonia except for an occasional reinforcement, and so did Gustavus Adolphus in Germany. However, its role has grown and grown since the eighteenth century, and in modern conventional warfare its importance is paramount.

A belligerent who limits himself to defense alone can only expect to win by attrition: that is, he can hope to hold out, husbanding his forces and using such opportunities as present themselves to inflict losses until the other side gives up. Given the correct combination of circumstances such a strategy may have much to recommend it, and indeed from the days of Pericles on it has often been put into practice. The normal outcome of a purely defensive approach is, however, not victory but a standoff. To force a decision it is usually necessary to attack, destroying the enemy's forces and occupying the centers of his power. The attacker enjoys the advantage of the initiative. He is in a position where he can impose his will on the enemy and, by that very fact, prevent many of the enemy's plans from bearing fruit and even from being initiated. On this rests the wisdom behind the popular adage, "when in doubt—attack." Nevertheless, it should never be forgotten that an attack *qua* attack is the weaker form of war. Therefore the side that intends to attack ordinarily requires a superiority of force, whether quantitative, qualitative, or both.

Assuming the conditions for launching an offensive exist, the question still remains how this is to be done. The simplest possibility is for the available force to be concentrated at a single spot and, once concentrated, hurled at the enemy like some huge bullet. Alternatively the force may be divided into two or three or more parts, each of which will advance separately. If this alternative is selected, the next question is whether they should advance simultaneously or in echelon. If in echelon, then again the question is which wing should be made to advance and which one refused. Echelons apart, where a force is divided into two or more parts the axes along which they advance may run in parallel; however, they may also diverge or converge. These problems are not trivial, and the literature that has been written to answer them is vast. Much of this literature dates to the period 1800–1914, and all of it is closely associated with the name of that master-strategist and contemporary of Clausewitz, Antoine Jomini. Depending on the circumstances actually prevailing—force ratios, geography, lines of communication, natural obstacles, and the like--each has its particular strengths and weaknesses.

The stuff of which strategy is made consists of such problems as defilade against enfilade, breakthrough against encirclement, the direct approach against the indirect one. These questions are not new, nor are they limited to any particular level on which war is waged. A Roman legion going to war, even a band of cavemen going on a raid, had to solve them just as much as did an army of Moltke's or Eisenhower's. A company of fifty ordered to attack a fortified trench faces much the same choices as does an army numbering a million men and advancing toward some important river. The strategic terminology of attack, defense, advance, retreat, decision, attrition, and all the rest is universal; it applies regardless of the engagement's size, the nature of the technology in use, and even the amount of violence employed. More remarkable still, it applies not just to war but to many types of games, beginning with football and ending with chess. So extraordinary is the ability of strategy to serve as an analytical framework for many different activities that the existence of some very basic common denominator is indicated. The nature and significance of this denominator will be explained in the next section.

The reader will recall that, for an attack to succeed, a preponderance of force is usually necessary. Therefore, launching an attack when one is stronger than the enemy presents no problem; the real question is what to do when this is not the case. Under ordinary circumstances, matching force against force will lead to attrition and an indecisive outcome. Such an outcome may be acceptable, provided the two sides are of equal strength to begin with, though even in that case it will scarcely be regarded as desirable. A belligerent who is weaker than the enemy cannot, however, afford to be worn down. Assuming that the losses both sides inflict on each other are equal, the result will be that one side will be exhausted while the other still has forces in reserve. Some authorities have used this line of reasoning to argue that the weaker opponent must either attack or perish; nor is it by accident that three of the most prominent proponents of this theory—Frederick the Great, the German Alfred von Schlieffen, and the Israeli armored general Israel Tal—originated in countries that were surrounded by enemies stronger than themselves. And in fact, unless a weak defender can inflict losses far in excess of those that are inflicted on him (which assumes a peculiarly stupid attacker), it is difficult to see what other choice he has.

If an army is to launch a successful attack against an opponent who is as strong as itself or stronger, it will have to *concentrate*. It will have to weaken its forces at one point and reinforce at another, deliberately creating and accepting a risk. The greater the disparity in force between the two sides, the greater also the risk that the weaker one will have to take in order to succeed. The greater the risk that a force takes, the more likely it is to succeed but the worse also the consequences if it does not. For example, the Germans in World War I concentrated seven-eighths of their forces in the West, leaving East Prussia almost uncovered. By way of another example, the Israeli Air Force in the 1967 War (the Six Day War) numbered some 200 modern combat aircraft and was faced by combined Arab forces perhaps two and a half times as strong. On the morning of June 5, wave after wave of gleaming jets was launched in a devastating strike against Egypt's airfields, destroying more than 200 planes in just three hours. Even as the operation was under way, just four aircraft—2 percent of the total—were kept at home to guard against the possibility of Syrian, Jordanian, and Iraqi air attacks against the Israeli rear. This example may be extreme, but it is certainly not atypical. Throughout history, the side best able to concentrate it's force even while taking a calculated risk was the one that emerged on top.

Concentration can take place in two forms, in space and in time. Concentration in space means that some sectors of the front are left denuded whereas others are reinforced. An object lesson in the way it is done was served by the Theban commander Epaminondas at the battle of Leuctra in 371 B.C. The Theban phalanx, instead of being deployed in eight ranks all along its width as was the normal Greek practice, was turned into an unbalanced formation. Its left wing was heavily reinforced, so much so that it consisted of no fewer than forty-eight ranks drawn up behind each other. To make this possible, the right wing was denuded of troops. The attack was then launched in echelon, with the left wing going in first and crashing down on the Spartan right opposing it. In a battle lasting perhaps two or three hours, concentration paid its dividends. According to Plutarch, the Spartans saw the danger but were inable to side-step in time. Consequently they suffered the heaviest defeat in their history from which, indeed, they never quite recovered.

Concentration in time, no less risky to carry out, is probably even more difficult to achieve. A numerically inferior force will seek to compensate by secrecy and rapidity of movement. It will try to keep its opponents separate and guessing about its own intentions. It will concentrate against each one in turn, beating them in detail. Often geography will help, as happened with Israel which, surrounded by enemies on three sides, was able to concentrate its forces first against Egypt, then against Jordan, and finally against Syria. Sometimes, however, it is necessary that the force in question deliberately place itself between two different enemies and operate on what is known as internal lines, It must hold off one enemy even as it seeks to destroy the other. An operation of this kind, as exemplified by Napoleon's first campaign in Italy and later by his defensive operations in France in 1814, involves extreme risks. It takes a bold commander to put such a plan into effect, one who has plenty of confidence in the instrument at his disposal and, equally important, in himself.

Another cardinal problem of strategy, whether in war or in football or in chess, is the question as to which objectives one's strength should be directed against, and in what order. There are, of course, many different kinds of objectives; some are geographical; others consist of the enemy's equipment and personnel. They range from the most concrete, such as territory and economic resources, all the way to the most abstract, such as an army's information-transmission system and its fighting spirit. In theory, the most desirable goal comprises the simultaneous destruction and/or occupation of all objectives. In practice, since resources are limited, in almost every case such a goal is impractical. If force is to be used effectively, if it is to be used at all, some objectives will have to be selected and others be neglected. Therefore, the key question facing the strategist is which ones to neglect and which ones to select.

Though objectives may be classified in many ways, probably the most fundamental classification concerns the question of strength *versus* weakness. The problem is best explained by an example. For twenty-five years before World War I the German General Staff faced the question as to which opponent, France or Russia, should be attacked first. Of the two, France was considered the strongest and the most dangerous. Its elimination would therefore bring the greatest gains—so much so that, once this had been achieved, Germany would be able to fight Russia in a long conflict and even forever if the need arose. Precisely because it was so critical to victory, however, the France-first strategy also carried heavy risks. Should the march to Paris fail, then Germany would be faced with the prospect of a two-front war against opponents whose combined resources were greater than her own and who would therefore probably prevail in the end. The famous "Schlieffen Plan" was debated for years. All kinds of plans were drawn up, and many war games held, but the conclusion was always that Germany did not have a real choice. In 1914 a modified version of the plan was put to the test and failed. The outcome was just what a few wise heads had feared all along, namely, defeat.

As against this strategy of dealing with the strongest opponent first, a case has been made by Liddell Hart and others that the correct way of proceeding is just the opposite. To attack the enemy where he is strongest is folly; it is unlikely to succeed, and failure may well lead to disaster. Much better therefore to concentrate on his weakest parts, systematically chopping off limb after limb until the remainder of the body is left defenseless. This was just the strategy that Pericles recommended to the Athenians during the Peloponnesian War. For almost two decades it worked fairly well, until one morning the Athenians decided to take on a limb that proved too large for them to swallow. The expedition against the Sicilian city of Syracuse was a disaster, leading to the loss of the flower of the Athenian navy and army. Even then, she need not have lost the war if Sparta had not used Persian money to build a fleet and attack Athens where she was strongest, namely, at sea. Going for the jugular, the Lacedaemonians and their allies fought and won the great naval battle of Aegospotamoi. Athens' lifeline was thereby cut, leaving her with no option but surrender,

In theory, the best objective of all is one that is both essential and undefended. In any war there is the temptation to try and discover some vital target whose elimination will carry consequences far greater than itself and bring the entire system to a halt. While the logic is attractive, in practice it tends to work only on a small scale. Often this is because intelligence is lacking; to select an actual case from World War II, while stocks of nonferrous metals may have been absolutely indispensable to the German economy (and therefore seemed to present an attractive target for bombing), the quantities needed were relatively minuscule and difficult to target. At other times the logic does not work because the means of delivery are insufficiently accurate. A decentralized modus operandi relying on numerous autonomous units can frustrate pinpoint attacks on vital objectives; but so can the existence of redundant communications that is such a characteristic feature of any well-coordinated modern social system. Probably the best example of the logic being put into action—and failing—is found in the US Air Force attacks on the German ballbearing manufacturing plant at Schweinfurt in the summer of 1943. The first raid was successfully carried out but failed to halt German production of war-matériel because alternative sources could be found. The second raid found the Luftwaffe ready, with the result that a quarter of the attacking force was shot down. The experiment was not repeated.

The above list far from exhausts the dilemmas of strategy. Between military and nonmilitary objectives, strong and weak opponents, defended and undefended targets, those that can be reached and those that must be reached, and so on, the number of possible combinations is endless. An intellectual system sufficiently powerful to encompass all of them, and thus provide a complete guide for the employment of force, does not exist. Had it existed, it would be too complicated for any single man or organization to encompass—even an organization using the most powerful computers. Any attempt to construct such a system is itself an act of *hybris,* strongly reminiscent of the one which caused people to build the tower of Babel, and deserving similar punishment. Theory can aspire to save the strategist from the need to think out everything from the beginning, and provides him with a starting point for thought. Insofar as the theory is sound, such a starting point is certainly not without value. However, there always comes the time where it is necessary to cast loose and use one's brain instead; for when all is said and done, it is as much by brains as by force that war is fought.

The Paradoxical Logic

Strategy as presented so far consists of two basic elements; namely, creating force on the one hand, and using it against the opponent on the other. Of these the first in some ways is the most straightforward. Though creating force has always represented a necessary condition for waging war, in Clausewitz's day and even during most of the nineteenth century it did not count as part of strategy properly speaking. The idea that strategy also comprises preparation for war, even if it takes place in time of peace, does not antedate the period between the world wars, when it was advocated by Ludendorff. Even today, the use of the term in this particular sense is misleading. To quote Clausewitz, the art of preparing for war stands to war like that of the blacksmith who forges the sword to that of the fencer who uses it. Cynics might go further, arguing that much of strategy as understood in today's developed countries is, in fact, a vast exercise in make-believe. Since various factors—including above all the spread of nuclear weapons—no longer permit most modern armed forces to fight as they used to, they continue to act *as if* building military force and preparing for war constituted strategy.

The reason why the creation of force is a relatively simple process is, of course, the absence of opposition. This is not to say that those in charge do not have to make choices, sometimes even difficult ones. It takes farsightedness and guts to build an armed force that will only be called to fight in, say, a decade. One has to guess, as best one can, what resources will be available, what kind of opponent the forces will be called on to face, and what kind of environment they will have to operate in. These fundamental questions settled, the time comes to decide how best to meet the challenges ahead. A blueprint is drawn up and resources are allocated. Thousands upon thousands of components, both human and material, are called up or produced, joined together, and meshed with each other. To determine whether the meshing is, in fact, a success, exercises are held and lessons drawn. A feedback mechanism is constructed and oversees the process, making sure it stays on course even as the course itself is monitored for any changes that may become necessary. As the machine is put into gear and starts producing the hoped-for results, inflexibility, friction, and uncertainty make their unwelcome appearance and must be dealt with. All this demands formidable administrative talent, what with priorities to be determined, scarce resources distributed, and deadlines met.

Where one force is matched against another the result is competition. Competition may be defined as a trial of force that is carried out indirectly, so to speak, by means of some medium. The nature of the medium may vary as much as does human life itself. It may consist of the marketplace and find expression in the balance-sheet, as in the case of two industrial firms each of which is trying to increase its own sales at the other's expense. It may be represented by a track in a stadium or by a lane in a swimming pool, as in the case of some athletic events. Competition of this kind can certainly be fierce, even to the point where one firm is driven into bankruptcy and one athlete drops dead of a heart attack. It may also involve much planning, given that resources (be they the firm's finances or the athlete's stamina) are always scarce and must be correctly distributed in time and space. We sometimes speak of economic warfare, nor is it so rare to see an athletic event turned into a battlefield. Nevertheless, competition is not war, nor does it involve strategy, as I understand that term.

The factor that distinguishes competition from conflict is that the rules do not permit the sides to engage each other directly, to obstruct each other, or to engage in mutual destruction even as they try to realize their own ending. On the contrary, the whole idea of "fair" competition depends on this *not* being the case. An athlete who trips up another will, if observed by the referees, be disqualified. An automobile firm that plants microphones in its competitor's offices, or tries to blow up his plant, will be put on trial and, if found guilty, penalized. The dividing line between competition and all-out warfare is admittedly often a little vague. Athletes who specialize in running medium- and long-distance races have been known to so design their race plans as to make the best use of their own talents while neutralizing those of the opposition, and this is not considered unfair. Industrial firms sometimes engage in sharp practices designed to drive the competition off the market. They tailor their products to those of their opponents, engage in aggressive advertising, and undercut the price of rivals. Still, the distinction between the two phenomena does exist. Its importance is cardinal; but for that distinction, "civilized" life would have been impossible.

Thus, neither force-building nor competition involve strategy as such. On the contrary, strategy begins where force-building and competition end—at the point, to repeat, where we are faced with an intelligent opponent who does not passively accept our design, and who actively obstructs them even as he attempts to realize his own. The idea can also be turned around. Activities that do not involve conflict in the above sense, such as force-building and competition, are not "strategic" by nature. This applies regardless of the effort expended, and regardless also of the intellectual effort that it requires. Strategy might therefore be defined as a body of doctrine which both describes the conduct of conflict and prescribes the way this should be done.

Considered as an analytical tool, strategy derives its unique power from the fact that it is independent from the size of the conflict, the medium in which it takes place, the means by which it is fought, and even the amount of violence it involves. For example, strategy is much the same for two squads facing each other across a field as it is for two armies, each numbering a million men, fighting over the possession of a continent. It is also the same regardless of whether the field in question consists of a square mile of land, an ocean comprising millions of square miles, an indefinable and constantly shifting zone of air, or even a chequered board. Strategy does not care a hoot whether the conflict is fought with guided missiles, rifles, spears, or colored beans. Strategy governs war, the most violent of all human activities. However, as is already evident from the fact that they can be described in "strategic" terms such as attack, defense, and all the rest, it also governs football, basketball, chess, and even many innocuous children's games such as ticktacktoe.

In war, the objective of strategy is to overcome force with force— though there comes a point where, one side being much stronger than the other, what is needed is not strategy but a steamroller. Where the disparity in the forces is not too great, the game can begin. Merely to oppose force by force will usually lead to stalemate or, at best, attrition. The art of strategy accordingly consists of employing strength against weakness or, to speak with ancient Chinese military writer Sun Tsu, it consists of throwing rocks at eggs. The opponent, however, is assumed to be intelligent and active. He will, if he can, identify the place where we intend to employ our strength and either bring up forces to oppose it or make his preparations in such a way as to cause our blow to strike empty air. Thus, the primary condition for success is represented by the ability to read the opponent's mind while concealing one's own thoughts. Even as we do this, the process also works in reverse. If the opponent is to be prevented from concentrating his strength against our weakness, we must conceal our mind even as we try to read his. The net result is a complex dynamic interaction between two opposing minds, one that is characteristic of strategy at all levels and, indeed, unique to it. As each side tries to outguess the other, my thought depends on his which in turn depends on mine. As in the case of mirrors that are set to reflect each other, what we get is a self-reinforcing series of mental images whose number, in theory, is infinite.

Whereas images in a mirror reflect each other more or less faithfully, the essence of strategy—whether in war or in football or in chess—consists of the ability to feint, deceive, and mislead. Each side advertises his intention to do one thing and secretly prepares to do another. Each concentrates at place A even as he pretends to be at place B, making out as though he were planning to strike in direction C even while his real objective is D. Nor does the process end at this point. The really artistic touch is to make "truth" and "falsehood" change places at a moment's notice, tailoring their respective roles to the opponent's moves so as to counter his designs and exploit his mistakes. At some point during the process, what was originally intended merely as a feint is transformed into the main thrust. What was originally meant as a main thrust is turned into a mere feint. Over time, truth and falsehood, falsehood and truth, actually *become* each other. Insofar as secrecy often demands that one's real intentions be concealed even from one's own men, the point may come where one of the contending sides, or both, no longer knows, which is which.

It is when we translate this kind of interplay into concrete examples that the paradoxical logic of strategy reveals itself in full. In ordinary life, an action that has succeeded once can be expected to succeed twice—provided circumstances remain the same. If I drop an object once and find that it hits the ground after such and such a time, I can reasonably expect the same thing to happen again, however often the action is repeated. But this elementary fact—on which are based the whole of science and technology—does not apply to war, football, chess, or any other activity that is governed by strategy. Here, an action that has succeeded once will likely fail when it is tried for the second time. It will fail, not *in spite* of having succeeded once but *because* its very success will probably put an intelligent opponent on his guard. The same reasoning also works in reverse. An operation having failed once, the opponent may conclude that it will not be repeated. Once he believes it will not be repeated, the best way to ensure success is precisely to repeat it. A continuous dynamic interaction ensues, capable of turning victory into disaster and disaster into victory.

The logic that operates in time also operates in space. In non-strategic activities the shortest line to an objective is usually a straight line. In war, the shortest line is also the most likely one and, therefore, filled with the carcasses of those who take it. The shortest line is where our opponent will concentrate his forces, thus turning it into the longest one and frustrating our plans. Conversely, the longest line is also the one of least expectation, hence the one that is actually the shortest; other things being equal, an attack taking this line may well stand the greatest chance of success. Nor should the reader be misled into the belief that the problem is merely academic, a game for armchair strategists with leisure on their hands. The advantages of the so-called indirect approach have sometimes been exaggerated to the point of caricature, and the term itself stretched until it became virtually meaningless. Nevertheless, there is no doubt that, historically as well as in theory, it represents one of the fundamental pillars on which all strategy rests.

Equally fundamental to the understanding of strategy is the relationship between concentration and dispersion. Concentration in time and space is perhaps the most important tool in war, given that to successfully attack an opponent usually requires a preponderance of strength. The heavier the concentration of force, however, the less likely it is to be concealed from the enemy. Once discovered, it will be countered, most likely by another concentration being placed directly opposite it. The art of strategy therefore consists not simply of concentrating our own forces but of causing the enemy to disperse his. To bring this about, it will normally be necessary for us to disperse our own forces so as to confuse the enemy and draw him away from our real objective. Thus concentration actually consists of dispersion, whereas dispersion consists of concentration, victory going to him who, retaining control and avoiding confusion, switches rapidly from one to the other. An excellent case in point is provided by the infinitely varied, infinitely complex, operations of the corps comprising the French Grande armeé. Through operations that have never been equalled for the virtuosity with which they combined dispersed marches and concentrated battles, Napoleon was able to overrun most of Europe within the space of only a few years.

Finally, nothing is more characteristic of the world of strategy than the relationship between efficiency and effectiveness. In civilian life, and indeed in any force-creating process of the kind discussed above, efficiency is usually the product of coordination. Every one of a multiplicity of components must be sequenced, dovetailed, geared and meshed with each other. Friction and uncertainty must be eliminated, thus achieving the smooth flow of operations to be found, say, in a well-run automobile factory or a large petrochemical plant. In war, the same principles do not apply, or apply only to a limited extent. The more economical, efficient, and streamlined an organization the greater its vulnerability. If any single component breaks down, the system's very perfection will cause the failure to reverberate and magnify itself. Worse still, an organization that has achieved efficiency by such means as strict central control, tight coupling, economy of scale, and standardization, will probably be inflexible. Being inflexible it may be able to generate tremendous force at a selected point and against a selected objective. However, switching that force from one objective to another, and doing so without the enemy taking notice, may be a different matter altogether.

Thus, the secret of the art consists of finding a correct balance between effectiveness and efficiency, two constituents that, at least as far as the world of strategy is concerned, are not complementary but actually opposed. While it is imperative to create the greatest possible force, the size of the force must be weighed against the ability to use it under conditions of uncertainty. The machine must be made as large as possible, but not so large as to be incapable of being concealed. It must be very strong, but not so strong as to be incapable of rapidly changing the goals against which it operates. It must concentrate all resources at a single spot, but it must also be capable of rapidly dispersing them and switching them from one place to another. It must be sufficiently well rehearsed to carry out the same operation time after time with the minimum of wastage, but training should not be carried to the point where initiative is choked and the force left unable to cope with the unexpected.

Strategy's unique characteristics go some way to dictate the qualities required to find one's way amidst all the deception and feinting; not for nothing did many famous practitioners also develop a reputation as rakes. Julius Caesar was affectionately known as "the bald fornicator." Henry IV of France used to put captured enemy flags at the feet of his mistress, Gabriele d'Este. The young Duke of Marlborough seduced King Charles II's own mistress, Nell Gwynn, and on one occasion had to leap through a window to avoid capture. On another level, Napoleon was as fond of cheating at cards as he was of "stealing" a march. He was also, however, an exceptionally skilled organizer whose powers of reasoning and sheer administrative competence have been seldom if ever equalled. Moltke was an equally great organizer whose memoranda are masterpieces of straightforward lucidity; still, there was a sly streak in his character that made him a master at cards and which he expressed in the form of dry, sardonic jokes directed at himself and at the General Staff that he had created. Eisenhower and his colleague, the British General Archibald Wavell, resembled Moltke in this respect. Both were noted for a certain slyness, even guile, which in both cases hid behind a deceptively open and frank manner.

In the end, neither logic on its own nor its combination with the kind of foxiness common in sharpers and womanizers are sufficient to fight a war. A war involves much more than mustering one's resources to build the most powerful armed forces, concentrating them at a selected spot, and delivering a smashing blow. Nor is it merely a question of combining the employment of force with some crafty game of hide-and-seek. Before strategy even comes into the picture, war is a dance of death. In it, to quote Napoleon, "the fate of the nations, armies, and crowns is decided." At the lower levels it takes a robust nature to cope with the overwhelming mixture of physical hardship, stress, and danger. At the higher level, uncertainty, combined with responsibility for life and death, can easily crush those who are unprepared to deal with it. Often great mental force is required just to keep one's sanity, let alone maintain control and operate effectively. Unless it takes due cognizance of the things that men fight for, as well as the motives that make them fight, no strategic doctrine is worth a fig; conversely, it is from these problems that any attempt at understanding war must proceed.

CHAPTER
V

What War Is Fought For

Political War

We have seen that the two cardinal elements of the Clausewitzian universe are, first, that war is necessarily waged by the state, and second that it necessarily tends towards the use of unrestrained force. It is now time to examine a third cardinal postulate: namely, that war is a means to an end or, to use the master's own highly pregnant formulation, "the continuation of politics with an admixture of other means." No other dictum of Clausewitz's has acquired nearly as much fame, and none is quoted more frequently even by those—some would say, particularly by those—who have never taken the trouble to read his work. So descriptive of much modern armed conflict is the idea that war is the servant of policy, that many people today cannot even imagine an alternative to it. Nevertheless, and if only because its very ubiquity tends to conceal its meaning, it deserves serious analysis.

The end which war is supposed to serve is *Politik,* a German word that may mean either "politics" or "policy." Once again, Clausewitz's thought must be interpreted against the contemporary intellectual background. From Montesquieu to Kant, the majority of enlightenment writers had regarded war as an aberration. It represented an interruption of political intercourse, in fact an interruption of civilized life in general; war was the point where human reason came to an end or, at any rate, where it had not yet triumphed. Nor was this view without effect on the actual conduct of war. Most eighteenth-century commanders were probably influenced by it to some extent, with the result that they tried to make war in a cautious, "civilized" manner while minimizing the damage to the environment. Therefore, when Clausewitz insisted that war was merely one of the forms that political intercourse took, he was making a point that was both new and important. *Vom Kriege* presents war as a language of politics, so to speak, one whose "grammar"—to use its author's own formulation—consisted of shells and bullets rather than words and gestures.

One logical outcome of such a view was that the high conduct of war should be made subject, if not to politicians, then at any rate to political considerations. A second was that war should be fought solely for political reasons; a third, that politics should constitute the most important criterion by which the outcome of war is judged and the next one prepared for. None of these ideas is self-evident. During the nineteenth century they encountered much resistance, particularly on the part of officers who refused to recognize that there might be something higher than war to which, in consequence, they should subordinate themselves. Yet all these ideas have entered modern strategic thought in developed countries, even to the point that they are usually taken for granted.

Whatever the exact meaning of the term "politics," it is not the same as "any kind of relationship involving any kind of government in any kind of society." A more correct interpretation would be that politics are intimately connected with the state; they are, indeed, the characteristic form that power-relationships assume within the kind of organization known as the state. Where there is no state, as was the case during most of human history, politics will be so mixed in with other factors as to leave room neither for the term nor for the reality behind it. Even where the state does exist, only some of its actions are political by nature, whereas the rest are administrative or juridical. Thus, strictly speaking, the dictum that war is the continuation of politics means nothing more or less than that it represents an instrument in the hands of the state, *insofar as the state employs violence for political ends.* It does not mean that war serves any kind of interest in any kind of community; or, if it does mean that, then it is little more than a meaningless cliché.

Though the view of war as the servant of politics fits in well with the "trinity" of government, army, and people, in a sense it antedates the existence of that trinity by many years. Its origins may be found in the early sixteenth century, a time when the major European monarchies were only just being born and before the idea of the "state" was given its modern form in the works of the French thinker, Jean Bodin. In Italy, however, the city-states were in full flower. Most of them—including the one centered on Rome—were despotisms, ruled over by ferocious tyrants who disregarded the law of God and men in an unceasing struggle to maintain their power against their subjects and each other. Against this background, medieval ideas concerning war's religious, chivalric, and legal functions were fast losing ground. Between might and right an absolute gap was opened. Still, to brazenly declare that war was nothing but an instrument of power in the hands of the Prince took courage and invited execration. The man who possessed the first, and was destined to be covered by the second, was the Florentine diplomat and writer, Niccolò Machiavelli.

Here, it is unnecessary to follow the process by which war was taken away from the ruler and entrusted to the state, and in fact to this day the difference is often academic. What is worth pointing out, however, is that the modern strategic interpretation of war is not one that would have recommended itself to most civilizations other than our own. Thus, Sun Tzu—perhaps the greatest writer on military affairs who ever lived—listed "the favor of heaven" as the first condition for success; the idea that war be considered exclusively as a problem in power-politics would have struck him as both impious and stupid. To the eyes of Christian thinkers such as Saint Augustine, or pagan thinkers such as Plato, the same idea would have appeared as abhorrent, cynical, criminal, or all of these. Even as late as the eighteenth century the Marshal de Feuquieres, of whose book Frederick II said that it contained everything worth knowing about war, wrote that the chief qualities required in a commander were honesty and honor.

To sum up, the view of war as a continuation of *Politik,* let alone *Realpolitik,* is in some ways a modern invention. Even if we substitute "rulers" for "state," the view still does not date further back than the Renaissance. Having been invented at a certain point in time, there is no reason to think that it possesses some kind of inherent validity, nor that it necessarily has a great future. Here we will focus on the functions that have been attributed to war by people living in times and places other than our own.

Nonpolitical War: Justice

From Hugo Grotius, if not from Machiavelli, Western political thought has defined war as an instrument in the hands of states; that is, of sovereign political entities recognizing no law and no judge above themselves. That, however, was not the view held by the millenium before about 1500, loosely known as the Middle Ages. It was a period when politics were supposed to be based not on might but on right. Right itself was not understood as man-made but considered as at least partly divine in origin. Hence in some ways it was able to play a greater role, and enjoy greater authority, than is the case today.

Just as medieval science had not yet discovered gravity, so medieval society did not regard itself as consisting of disparate units, each pulling in a different direction and each entitled to pursue its interests with the aid of violence if need be. Instead, the entire *Republica Christiana* was conceived as a single organism made out of many disparate parts. The factor that held all of them together was the law, divine or human as the case might be. Admittedly, much of human law in particular was unwritten and of a customary nature, its origins having long been forgotten. However, in a society that was largely illiterate this very obscurity was often considered a plus. Law was regarded as immanent in the nature of things; the fact that it was unwritten did not weaken, but rather strengthened, the binding force it possessed.

Under such circumstances, the notion of a sovereign political entity admitting neither superior nor peer interference in its "internal" affairs was fundamentally foreign to the spirit of the age. Society was conceived as an organic, living pyramid consisting of many interacting parts and headed by none other than God. Directly under God there came, depending on one's point of view, the Emperor, the Pope, or—according to a doctrine derived from a passage in the New Testament and known as "the two swords"—both of them together. Being responsible to God for running the world in accordance with His decrees, the Emperor and/or the Pope acted as the focus of supreme authority. From them a network of legal or quasi-legal relationships spread outward and downward, reaching throughout the feudal and ecclesiastical hierarchies.

Thus, the typical medieval outlook as represented by Saint Thomas Aquinas in the mid-thirteenth century assigned each component its proper place in the world. In principle only peoples and countries not forming part of the Christian community were considered *hors de loi;* though even in their case certain restrictions, originating in mutual agreement, sometimes applied. Within Christendom, Princes and serfs, lords and priests, townsmen and peasants were supposed to be joined by a network of mutual rights and obligations. Different scholastics expressed different opinions concerning the exact role played by man in the world at large. Still, most scholastics probably considered animate and inanimate nature to be bound by the same set of divine or divinely inspired laws, thus creating a truly organic commonwealth under God.

Had compliance with the law been perfect, and indeed had the system itself been consistent and free of defects, then theoretically there would have been no room left for the conduct of war except, perhaps, in the hands of the Emperor and/or the Pope against heathendom. In practice, however, these conditions did not obtain. There were always wicked men around ready to break the law, both divine and human. Some were heretics, holding and expressing views contrary to accepted religious doctrine, thereby threatening to upset society's entire moral foundation. Others laid claim to things that were not theirs by right; in 1337, to select an extreme example, Edward III of England accused Philip VI of France of stealing an entire Kingdom, thus leading directly to the opening of the Hundred Years' War. Furthermore, although divine law was perfect in principle, opinions concerning its interpretation might differ. The same was even more true of human law, which in addition was often lacking in comprehensiveness.

In the ordinary course of things such problems, being legal by nature, would be left to the courts, secular or ecclesiastical, depending on the status of the disputants and the nature of the business at hand. To the extent that the dispute involved powerful individuals or collectives, however, either the courts might be unable to enforce their authority or else the parties might refuse to submit to them in the first place. Either way, the use of organized violence became necessary, even desirable. War represented the stick in the hands of the law, so to speak. It was the means whereby redress for "grievances" (that central concept of medieval political language) could be obtained, rebellious subjects chastised, and insults of every sort avenged.

Since war was regarded as a continuation of justice, not of politics, any armed conflict necessarily involved a violation of the law on one side if not on both. It thus became vital to distinguish between good and bad belligerents, between war conducted with the authority of the law and that waged without or against it. Either one of two sets of law, the ecclesiastical and the secular, might be consulted. The quest for ecclesiastical opinion led back from Saint Thomas Aquinas all the way to Saint Augustine. While lawyers disagreed over the details, in essence the idea of "just war" could be summed up in three points. First, a war to be considered just had to be waged by public authority rather than by private individuals. Second, it had to be waged with "just intent"; that is, in order to avenge an injury, or inflict punishment, or redress a grievance. Third, the extent of the damage inflicted on the enemy had to stand in rough proportion to the cause for which the war was fought. Thus, in theory at any rate, just war resembled a punishment administered by a benevolent father. The one thing it could not be was a manifestation of naked "interest"; as we shall see, that concept itself had yet to be formulated, let alone declared sacrosanct.

The second tradition that offered a way of distinguishing between just and unjust war was, of course, Roman law as practised during the Republic and set out by Cicero in *de officiis*. Like many primitive societies, the Romans originally regarded justice, or *ius,* as something made by gods rather than by men. War was seen as akin to a lawsuit, a kind of extraordinary legal remedy to be employed if all else failed. As in any court, obtaining justice was largely a matter of pleasing the appropriate judges by following the appropriate procedures. The move towards war usually started when Rome demanded redress for an injury, such as an attack on her allies (as in case of the Hannibalic War) or on her citizens abroad. If that did not work, then a special college of priests known as *fetiales* held a ceremony. Invoking terrible imprecations they would formally declare Rome's enemies' cause to be unjust, that of Rome herself just. The doors to the temple of Mars were thrown open. A delegation was sent out and hurled a spear *(hasta)* into the enemy's territory, thus informing him of the decision. The formalities completed, hostilities could begin. This combination of law and ceremony had obvious application not only to late antiquity, when it tended to become hollow ritual, but to the high and late Middle Ages; a time when lawyers, deeply influenced by the Roman model, were always looking for ways by which to justify the wars waged by their noble masters.

Whether Roman or Christian by origin, the view of war as an act of justice on one side and of injustice on the other had important implications for its conduct. In the case of Rome it meant that, once hostilities were over, the *lex talionis* or law of retaliation went into effect. By refusing to grant what was justly demanded of them, the opponents had turned themselves into criminals. Hence the Romans, provided of course they were victorious, were entitled to exercise justice, extracting an eye for an eye and a tooth for a tooth. It was a right they exercised often enough, razing cities, slaughtering their inhabitants, and enslaving entire populations all over the Mediterranean world.

Perhaps more interesting than these atrocities, which after all have formed the stock-in-trade of war in all ages, is the fate that was reserved for enemy leaders unfortunate enough to be captured. In common with other selected prisoners, they were forced to march in the victorious general's triumph. At the end of the procession they were executed in public, and their corpses subjected to all kinds of indignities so as to secure due punishment not only in this world but in the next. Of course, the victors might choose to exercise *clementia,* and sometimes did. Imprisonment or exile might be substituted for death, nor was it altogether unknown for the defeated leader to be pardoned and restored to his tribe or kingdom. Making a defeated commander beg for his life and obtain a reprieve could be made to serve a useful political purpose. The entire sequence might even be deliberately staged to provide additional proof that war against Rome was a crime and, as such, deserving of punishment; perhaps it was to avoid such a fate that Queen Cleopatra put an asp to her breast and died.

Even more than in antiquity, the idea of just war impacted on its conduct during the Middle Ages. This was because, if war was to serve as a means for enforcing the law, then obviously its conduct had to be reserved only to those who had both the means and the inclination appropriate for that purpose. Just as we today have specially trained and commissioned judges and police officers, so it was necessary to have a group of men versed in the lore of arms and entrusted with its conduct. Again, the existence of such a group chimed in well with the spirit of a legalistically-minded age that insisted that everything had its proper place, and divided society into classes. In principle, and often in practice as well, membership in the various classes was hereditary. Those belonging to each separate class were understood as different kinds of persons, not only economically but in regard to the rights, duties, and social functions that they possessed. Broadly speaking there were three classes, namely those who labored, those who prayed, and those who made war.

During the early Middle Ages, men whose function consisted of enforcing the rules and making war were known as *bellatores* (warriors) or *pugnatores* (fighters). Towards the 11th century their place was taken by the *miles,* a word whose original Latin meaning was soldier but which during the period under consideration was commonly translated as *chevalier, Ritter,* and knight (from the Germanic *Knecht,* meaning page or servant), into French, German, and English respectively. The rise of knights as society's armed representatives, charged with protecting it and setting wrongs right, is thought to have been occasioned by important changes that were taking place in the technology of war: the adoption of the stirrup, the invention of the high saddle, and the technique of couching the lance. Undoubtedly, the military superiority that these changes conferred on mounted warriors was critical in the construction of the social order known as feudalism. Still, nothing would be more erroneous than to assume that it rested on this basis alone. As the dubbing ceremony testifies, a knight before he was anything else was a person whose mission in life was to make war for a just cause. Should he disregard the law and fight for his own "interest," all he could expect was dishonor, punishment, or both.

War, then, was fundamentally a question of knight fighting knight to see who was right. The cause he was defending might be his own; however, it was equally likely to be that of his Lord, or that of the Christian Faith, or—in theory, and sometimes in practice—that of some poor widow or orphan (poor being taken to mean in difficult circumstances, since usually knights did not fight without at least expecting some kind of remuneration). To emphasize the class-character of war, knights sometimes insisted that their opponents be their social equals. They regarded a challenge by a superior as an honor and might refuse to take up arms against one who was socially inferior. As a matter of principle, people who were not knights were not supposed to take up arms and could be punished if they did. The *Chronique des quatre premiers Valois,* a fifteenth-century source, has a story about a French soldier of low social origin who killed the Count of St. Pol in battle; instead of being rewarded by his superiors, he was promptly hanged by them.

Theoretically the reward that the basely born could expect for abstaining from war was to be immune to war's horrors, given that they were regarded as insufficiently important to take part in an exalted activity belonging to the upper classes. The first practical attempts to enforce the rules, limit war, and exempt "innocent" people from its attendant evils got under way towards the end of the tenth century. This was the *Pax dei* (or Peace of God) movement, which started in the south of France and spread northward. Organized by the Church, at first on a local and then on a larger scale, it used the threat of excommunication and refusal of sacraments to try and guarantee the safety of priests, monks, nuns, and ecclesiastical property in general.

As time passed and scholars multiplied, the chivalric code joined forces with the religious, causing the list of people and things that were exempt to grow longer and longer. Those listed in Honoré Bonet's *Arbre de Battailles* (late fourteenth century) could be divided into four classes. First there were ecclesiastics of all sorts such as prelates, chaplains, deacons, and hermits, as well as pilgrims on a sacred journey. The second category comprised heralds and ambassadors engaged on a mission of peace. The third consisted of widows, orphans, and poor people; in short, those considered weak, innocent, and deserving of protection. In view of modern ideas about "total" warfare directed against the enemy's economic infrastructure, Bonet's fourth class is the most interesting of all: it included oxherds, husbandmen, asses and their drivers, persons engaged in agriculture; briefly, anything and anybody performing "useful" economic activities and thus promoting human welfare in general.

Such injunctions were often—perhaps normally—honored in the breach; nor where contemporaries unaware of that fact. Still, this is not to say that they were altogether without influence. The Middle Ages actually had two different words for the two kinds of war, the one waged by knights against knights and the one waged by them against people in general (fights between members of the unfree classes hardly counted as war at all, being regarded as burlesque). The former was known as *guerre*. To quote Honoré Bonet again, it was considered a good and wonderful thing, that unfortunately was often brought into disrepute by the deeds of evil men. So far from rendering those who participated in it guilty of bloodshed, *guerre* (provided of course it was just) was supposed to ennoble them. In particular, single combat between honorable, equally matched opponents was an admirable thing. In its most dangerous form, the one taking place in subterranean mines during sieges, it bonded men, creating links the strength of which was supposed to be second only to those of blood-kinship.

By contrast, war against what we today would call "civilian populations" was not considered war at all; it was a kind of substitute war, known as *guerre guerroyante* or—in extreme cases where the absence of opposition reduced it to mere raiding—*chevauchée*. *Guerres guerroyantes* and *chevauchées* were much more common than *guerre* and also more destructive. They were also distinctly less honorable, appearing in chivalrous literature chiefly as evil activities to be avenged and punished by brave knights. Since *guerres guerroyantes* and *chevauchées* could be highly profitable, they often attracted great noblemen. The Black Prince in 1355 set up a record for this kind of activity, taking time out from the Hundred Years' War in order to ride 900 kilometers across Languedoc while pillaging all the way. Ransoms were extorted, villages ravaged, and entire districts set on fire, all of which was regarded as perfectly normal. Still, even in such cases there were certain limits. A man who committed excesses—particularly when it was a question of robbing churches and raping females belonging to the noble classes—might stand trial. Most likely this would happen if he were captured. However, it was not unknown for a court of chivalry to be set up by a man's own prince, the punishment usually consisting of dishonor, forfeit of property, or even, in extreme cases, death.

A third field where ideas of war as an instrument for obtaining justice between individuals influenced its conduct was the possibility of settling disputes by a duel. The record bristles with instances when opponents challenged each other to battle, this being the logical out-come of a view that regarded war as the proper means by which to determine who was right. In 1056 Emperor Henry III challenged Henry I of France. In 1194 Philip Augustus of France challenged Richard Lionheart of England to a duel of five against five, but, declining to fight in person, was rebuffed. Many other instances are known, including, in 1282, Peter of Aragon against Karl of Anjou; 1346, Kasimir III of Poland against the blind king, John of Bohemia; and 1383, Richard II of England against Charles IV of France. Even as late as 1528 Emperor Charles V challenged Francis I, the stakes being the province of Burgundy. The French King was inclined to accept, or so he announced. However, his Estates forbade it. Using blunt language they told him that "you are not France," thus giving the best possible proof that the transition from the Middle Ages to the modern period was finally on its way.

The professed rationale of these and other challenges was always the same, namely, the desire to "save the blood of Christian people." This laudable goal was to be achieved by limiting the fighting to the principal protagonists, or else to those (either individuals or groups) whom they might name to fight in their stead. Although none of the proposed encounters between kings actually took place, the very fact that they were planned—seriously, as far as we can say—tells us some-thing about the legal character of medieval war. Moreover, collective duels between selected knights on both sides, occasionally *did* take place; for example, the "Combat des Trente" fought between the English and the French in Brittany in 1351, and the "Disfetta di Barletta" of 1503, where 13 Italian knights met 13 from France and defeated them.

Last not least, the view of war as a legal act, and the need to make victory "count," also meant that it was not unknown for belligerents to give up actual tactical advantages in order to fight on equal terms. Such was already the case at the battle of Malledon—the subject of a famous tenth century poem—when the defending Saxons left their fortified position and were soundly defeated for their pains. In 1260, Bela IV of Hungary formally asked Ottokar II of Bohemia for permission to cross the river March so that the battle of Kressenbrun might be fought, and his request was granted. Again, at Najera in Spain in 1367, Henry of Trastamara abandoned his extremely favourable position in order to meet the enemy in the open field. Insofar as most of those who thus voluntarily renounced their advantages ended up by being beaten, some of these tales probably represent *post hoc* justifications for defeat. Still, each age has its own way of reasoning. A modern general who attributes his defeat to bad faith on the enemy's part would merely expose himself to charges of stupidity. By contrast, the very fact that stories such as the above were circulated in the expectation of being believed already shows something about the way medieval people thought.

To conclude, Roman and medieval war—to mention but two outstanding examples of many that could be cited—did not resemble its modern successor and did not stand *hors de loi*. Whatever the differences between them, neither subscribed to Hobbes' view equating right with might. Instead, armed conflict was seen as existing within the framework of the rules and as a means for enforcing them; again, since the rules themselves were at least partly god-mandated, those who violated them could expect to incur the wrath of heaven in addition to the displeasure of men. The Romans tended to look upon their wars as being *ipso facto* just, provided only the appropriate procedures were followed. By contrast, different medieval scholars (and the princes by whom they were employed) often held differing opinions about what constituted a just war, and about which wars were just. Though each side obviously tried to bend the law to suit his needs, this in itself is excellent proof of the law's importance. While the law of war was often violated, equally often it protected those involved or else led to the punishment of those who were caught transgressing it. All this goes far to show that the modern strategic view of war as the continuation of politics is not the only possible one, nor is it necessarily correct.

Nonpolitical War: Religion

To people raised on the Judeo-Christian tradition, the idea of war as an instrument of religion should not come as a surprise. It is already much in evidence in the Old Testament, where wars between peoples were simultaneously conflicts in which the supremacy of their respective gods was proved or disproved. Accordingly, religious criteria were employed in order to distinguish between various kinds of war and establish a different law for each. At the top of the hierarchy came what was later to be called *milchemet mitzvah* (Holy War). Holy war was of two kinds. Either it was waged against peoples especially designated by God as His enemies, such as the Amalekites, or else it served to achieve some sacred end, such as possession of the Land of Israel. Either way it was considered more than a purely human affair; it represented the Lord's own special quarrel, so to speak.

Milchemet mitzvah was a war of extermination in the fullest sense of that term. The Israelites who engaged in it were put under strict obligation to spare nobody and nothing. Men, women, and children, even nonhuman living beings such as asses and cattle, were to be put to the sword. All material possessions were supposed to be burnt, the only exceptions being gold, silver, copper, and iron (this being considered a precious metal), which were to be consecrated to the Lord's use. Divine sanction attended these injunctions. When a miscreant carried away a mantle as well as some gold and silver after the fall of Jericho, he brought down punishment on the Israelites who were defeated at the battle of Ai. In a later passage the Bible tells of King Saul who, having conquered the Amalekites, failed to kill their King and destroy the booty as ordered. Thereupon the prophet Samuel declared his Kingdom forfeit; Saul never recovered from the blow, being henceforward overtaken by what contemporaries called an evil spirit and what we today probably term depression.

A second type of war was the one the Israelites fought against the Midjanites (Numeri 30–32). This time the *casus belli* was revenge of a lesser kind, the Midjanite elders sharing the blame by commissioning the prophet Bil'am to curse the people of Israel. By way of retaliation the Lord ordered Moses to go to war. The Midjanite kings together with all other adult males were defeated and killed, and their cities burnt. At first the Midjanite women and children were spared, though Moses later invoked fear of divine wrath and gave orders that male children, and women other than virgins, share the fate of the menfolk. On this occasion the order to destroy did not apply to the booty, either animate or inanimate. Instead, Moses had it ritually purified and, once this had been done, divided it between the Treasury of the Lord and the warriors themselves.

The various grades of sacred war apart, the Bible also knew secular, or "ordinary" war whose "rules of engagement" differed from the above. Though the Lord was not directly involved in this kind of conflict, His orders for its conduct were strict. Before hostilities were opened, the enemy was to be given an opportunity to surrender, in which case all that could be demanded of them was that they should become "tribute-paying slaves." Should this generous offer be rejected, the Israelites were entitled to proceed with business as usual. All enemy males were to be killed, all females and children captured. The difference consisted in that permission was given to possess and enjoy the booty taken in secular war, including even the late enemy's food. Further, since no religious issues were at stake, mobilization was a semi-voluntary affair. Whereas "even a bridegroom in the midst of his wedding" was obliged to participate in sacred war (Maimonides), in the case of secular war anybody who had just built a house, or planted a vineyard, or taken a wife, or admitted cowardice, was exempt.

This is not the place to make a detailed check on the way these injunctions were carried out in practice. Suffice it to say that, to the extent that war was regarded as an instrument of religion, the right to declare it rested with the ecclesiastical rather than with the secular authorities. Religious criteria also determined who should take part, whether the enemy should be offered quarter, and what was to be done with the booty. They could even affect the actual conduct of operations, as in the case of the Maccabees who refused to fight on the Sabbath, were trounced for their pains, and had to be granted special dispensation by the priests that be. God in His wisdom, moreover, had foreseen the potential clash between religion and what we today would term "interest." This led Him to warn the Israelites that, in the event of sacred war, they were not permitted to take over their defeated enemy's dwellings but obliged to destroy them down to the last stone.

Since the New Testament contains as few references to war as the Old Testament bristles with them, early Christians were caught in a dilemma. Wanting to follow the commandment that "he who lives by the sword also perishes by it" (Mathew 26:52), they were prevented from looking upon leaders such as Moses, Joshua, and David as examples to follow; taking them as examples, they were unable to renounce war. The Fathers of the Church debated the problem among themselves, proposing various ingenious solutions. However, during the first few centuries the idea of renouncing war and turning the other cheek was more in keeping with the practical requirements of a small, powerless community.

This situation changed when Christians became a sizeable fraction of the population, and even more so after Constantine made Christianity into the official religion of the Empire. Eusebius in the first half of the fourth century distinguished between two groups of Christians. The laity was to assume the burden of citizenship and wage war, provided of course it was just. On a higher level, the clergy was to abstain from war and from all other worldly activities, remaining dedicated to God alone. Following this line of reasoning, it did not take long before Ambrose— as much a Roman administrator by training as he was a Saint by voca-

tion—was found praising the courage of Christian soldiers fighting for
Rome against the Barbarians. As Ambrose saw the problem, the barbarians refused to submit to God's appointed representative on earth, who
in this case was the Christian Emperor Gratian. Since they had turned
themselves into His enemies, for Christians to join in fighting against
them was not just permissible but a pious duty. Nor was there any
punishment so terrible that the enemy did not deserve it, at least in
principle.

Ambrose's views were fine for a period when the enemies of
Christendom, now embodied in the Roman Empire, consisted of heathens considered beyond the pale of civilization. In modified form they
continued to do service during much of the middle ages, given that this
period saw many wars that were directed against either heretics or
unbelievers. Both groups being regarded as God's own enemies, fighting them was a sacred obligation; it could result in the extermination of
entire communities, as was to happen during the thirteenth-century
Albigensian Crusade. The Crusades proper were at first governed by
similar ideas, with the result that when the Christians took Jerusalem in
1099 they massacred the population until the streets ran with blood and
the horses waded in gore up to their ankles. Still, even in this case,
warfare in time led to mutual acquaintance between the belligerents.
Acquaintance was followed by a decrease of ferocity and a greater
readiness to limit violence, spare noncombatants, accept ransom, ex-
change prisoners, etc. Though Richard Lionheart had the garrison of
Saint Jean d'Acre massacred in 1191, on the whole the Crusades were
probably neither more nor less bloody than medieval warfare in its
entirety.

Pushed to its logical conclusion, the idea of war on behalf of the
faith inevitably meant that war should be waged only by, or at least on the
behalf of, the Church; an inference that was actually drawn by eleventh-
century Popes such as Gregory VII and Urban II. Though not even
Innocent III early in the thirteenth century was powerful enough to
enforce such a point of view, this was not for lack of trying. The Church
even established several different military orders that attempted to
combine the ideal of the monk with that of the warrior, and were
dedicated to fighting the good fight. Furthermore, the Church sought to
impose limitations on wars other than religious ones. The *pax dei*
movement, mentioned above, represented an attempt to make sure that
the treatment meted out to Christians would not resemble that reserved
for heretics or heathens. Then there was the so-called *treuga dei,* or
truce of God, which sought to limit the duration of the fighting until it

was finally permitted only from Monday to Wednesday. The Church even interested itself in the weapons of war; after all it was the Second Lateran Council, not some court of chivalry, that in 1139 banned the crossbow as suitable for use only against heathens.

As the Middle Ages waned the idea of war for religion was far from dead—on the contrary, some of its greatest triumphs were still to come. Campaigning in South and Central America after 1492, the Spaniards and Portuguese acted in the name of the cross. Fearing God, they always gave the Indians the option of converting to Christianity, exterminating them only when they failed to understand or comply. For almost a century and a half after Luther first nailed his Ninety-Five Theses to the church door at Wittenberg, Catholics and Protestants vied with each other in their calls for Holy War, often slaughtering such populations as happened to disagree with their respective views of Christ's nature. So intensely religious was the Spanish Army of Flanders that it carried the sign of the Madonna even when it mutinied. The troops of Gustavus Adolphus, like Cromwell's Ironsides, went into battle chanting hymns, nor were contemporaries slow to attribute their victories to that fact. The role that religion played in war was reflected in the military textbooks of the period. Many devoted their initial chapters to the religious forms that should be instituted by commanders and observed by the troops; it is as if an analysis of today's American armed forces should open with a description of the military chaplain system.

Thus, on the declaratory level at any rate, religious war remained the most important form of war in Europe until well into the early modern age. Its actual importance, though difficult to determine, is again best brought out by means of a modern analogy. Whatever we think of the American attempt to "save democracy" in Vietnam, probably it was not so different from King Philip II of Spain's attempts to save the souls of his Dutch subjects from the Protestant heresy infecting them. In neither case was idealism unmixed with opportunistic considerations of every kind. Often the admixture made for strange actions (Vietnam veterans will recognize "burning heretics for the good of their souls" as a surprisingly modern phrase) and stranger bedfellows. Still, a strong element of idealism was present in both, especially at the outset; just as Westerners today cannot conceive of a just world that is not democratic, so in early Europe no ordered society could even be imagined that was not based on the right religion. Whatever its guise, there is no question but that idealism contributed to the decision-making process and continued to influence it long after circumstances had altered. As the ideals waned, so did the war.

Beginning with the Treaty of Westphalia—the first one, incidentally, in which God is left out—Westerners mostly abandoned religion in
favor of more enlightened reasons for slaughtering each other. However, in the part of the world subscribing to Islam the same thing only
happened much later, and then to a much more limited extent. The
Koran divides the world into two parts—*dar al Islam* (the House of
Islam), and *dar al Harb* (the House of the Sword), that were supposed
to be perpetually at war. Present-day Islamic sects differ among themselves as to the importance of *Jihad* as compared to other religious
duties; however, by and large every free, adult, able-bodied, male Muslim is considered duty-bound to fight and die for the greater glory of
Allah, the only question being whether the unbelievers are to be
granted even a temporary truce. Among early Koranic scholars, many
were of the opinion that the conquering Arabs had the right to put
inhabitants of occupied countries to death should they fail to convert to
Islam. In practice they were usually given the option of surrender,
whereupon they were made to pay special taxes and regarded as
protected, though inferior, communities.

For the first decades after the birth of Islam it was assumed that the
Muslim world would remain united under its Caliph and that its domain
would keep expanding until the limits of the earth were reached. As a
result, *Jihad* was actually the only kind of relationship that could exist
between the faithful and the unbelievers. However, as time went on
these conditions did not obtain, and other types of war made their
appearance. It was necessary to accommodate to the possibility of
prolonged coexistence with non-Muslim political entities such as Byzan-
tium. It was also necessary to consider the possibility of Muslim territories being lost, as happened for the first time during the eleventh
century when the Normans occupied Sicily. There arose, from the
twelfth century onward, an entire literature, partly religious, partly legal
in character, that sought to define just what Muslims might do to non-
Muslims under what circumstances. Some scholars even went so far as
to invent a third category standing midway between the *dar al Islam* and
the *dar al Harb,* namely the *dar al sulh.* This term was used to designate
states which, though not themselves subscribing to the faith, had entered into treaty-relations with the Muslim world.

The idea of *jihad* faced even greater difficulties when the Muslim
world broke up into warring states which, in turn, often professed
different versions of Islam. It now became necessary to distinguish
between at least two kinds of war, namely against unbelievers on the one
hand and against fellow Muslims on the other. In turn, war against

Muslims was divided into three classes by Al-Mawradi, a tenth-century scholar serving the Baghdad Caliph. There was one kind of *jihad* against apostates *(ahl al ridda)*, another against rebels *(ahl al baghi)*, and another still against those who had renounced the authority of the spiritual leader *(al muharabin)*. Each kind was supposed to be waged by different methods and carried a different set of obligations towards the enemy. For example, *Muharabin* prisoners were not to be executed. Since they were considered as part of the inviolate *dar al Islam,* their houses were not to be burnt, nor their trees cut down.

As was the case in Judaism and Christianity also, Islam laid out detailed procedures for carrying out a *jihad.* Unbelievers were first given the opportunity to convert to Islam; however, such among them as had already refused on an earlier occasion were considered forewarned and could be subjected to a surprise attack. In cases when presenting the demand endangered the Muslim forces themselves, no declaration of war was necessary. Though defeated infidels had no right to life, the Muslims might choose to exercise clemency, sparing women, children, and other defenseless persons, in which case their means of livelihood were not to be taken away or destroyed. Prisoners were considered part of the booty; those who refused to accept Islam could be enslaved or executed, though some opinions had it that they might be put to ransom instead. Of the booty, one-fifth belonged to the commander, one-fifth to the prophet (in practice this was devoted to charity), and the rest to the combatants. Since the rules by which the booty was divided had been laid down by religion they were not subject to arbitrary interference on the part of the commander.

This brief section cannot embrace all known instances of war serving as an instrument of religion. Even a short list would have to include not only the Aztecs—whose entire strategy revolved around the need to capture prisoners for sacrifice—but many so-called primitive societies all over the world. Limiting our gaze to the three great mono-theistic religions, however, it is obvious that historically their attitudes towards war developed along different paths. The Jews' independent existence was interrupted by the destruction of the First Temple. Since then, and until the present century, they only enjoyed statehood during one brief period, from 164 to 57 B.C. As a result, when religious law or *Halacha* began to develop in the second and third centuries A.D., ideas about war were relegated to the sidelines as being of interest only to a handful of scholars far removed from practical affairs. Still, the concept and terminology of *milchemet mitzvah* was never quite forgotten. Though the establishment of modern Israel was mainly the work of atheistic socialists, the smashing victory in the 1967 Six Days' War was seen by many as an act of God and was accompanied by messianic overtones. There is, in Israel today, a resurgence of extremist groups who would like nothing better than to see the entire bloody concept revived and put back into operation.

Though early Christianity professed itself to be opposed to war and bloodshed, as soon as Christians came into power they changed their tune. Throughout the Middle Ages and, even more, the early modern age, Christians fought the heathens and each other. Always in the former case, and often in the latter, they acted in the name of the Cross which they carried before them into battle, following the example set by Constantine and celebrated from then on. The medieval Church even attempted to establish a monopoly over organized violence by founding military orders that combined the ideals of religion and war. True, "the Church Militant" was never quite able to realize its goal of turning secular government into its executive arm. There were always those who waged war in the name of different ideas, be they anchored in feudal law, or else, from the sixteenth century on, such as were derived from *raison d'état*. The Church at most times also contained elements that remained firmly opposed to bloodshed of any kind, Saint Francis of Assisi being but one among many names that could be mentioned.

In Europe, the idea of war as a continuation of religion was never as powerful as during the century or so that followed the Reformation, leading to an uncounted number of wars that were as ferocious as any in history. However, the influence of religious ideas declined after 1648. While rulers might still make use of them to inspire their subjects, from the late seventeenth century on modern states neither went to war in the name of religion nor regulated their conduct of it according to its rules. There was, indeed, a tendency to separate the "actual conduct" of war from everything else. Whereas religion might still sometimes influence such things as the troops' morale or the treatment of the wounded, "strategy" increasingly became the province of the "hard-headed" approach pioneered by Machiavelli and embodied in Clausewitz.

Finally, and precisely because the formation of secular states only began towards the end of the nineteenth century, Islam was much slower than its rivals to shed the idea of religious war. Whereas present-day Egypt, Syria, and the rest profess to be secular states, most still contain a sizeable traditionalist element. These groups' professed goal is a return to the *Shari'a,* or sacred law, and indeed every failure of those states' rulers is attributed to their refusal to do so. As the recent examples of Lebanon, Iran, and Afghanistan show clearly enough, the idea of *Jihad* is still very powerful, indeed so powerful that, unlike most modern states, it has no difficulty finding volunteers ready to commit suicide for its sake. Though in most cases it is directed primarily against the "Westoxicated" ruling elites and only secondarily against unbelievers, throughout the Muslim world today the motivating power of *Jihad* is as great as it as ever been. All of which goes far to show that, even today, the idea of war as the continuation of religion, including specifically its most extremist forms, is anything but dead. Western strategists who are followers of Clausewitz would do well to take this fact into account; or else, failing to understand Holy War, they may well end up as its victim.

Nonpolitical War: Existence

Our analysis so far has assumed that wars are fought *for* something; that is, it has taken for granted the Clausewitzian distinction between war, the means, and whatever its ends might be. Over history, the ends for which people have fought have been extremely diverse. They have included every kind of secular "interest," such as territorial expansion, power, and profit; but they have also comprised abstract ideals such as law, justice, "rights," and the greater glory of God, all served in various combinations with each other and the secular interests. While the above criteria are useful up to a point, paradoxically they leave out what is perhaps the most important single form of war in all ages. This, of course, is war for the community's existence. When faced by such a war, even the most fundamental concepts of strategy tend to break down, thus revealing their own inadequacy as tools for analysis and understanding.

Ironic though the fact may be, it is when the stakes are highest and a community strains every sinew in a life-and-death struggle that the ordinary strategic terminology fails. Under such circumstances, to say that war is an "instrument" serving the "policy" of the community that "wages" it is to stretch all three terms to the point of meaninglessness. Where the distinction between ends and means breaks down, even the idea of war fought "for" something is only barely applicable. The difficulty consists precisely in that a war of this type does not constitute a continuation of policy by other means. Instead, it would be more correct to say—recalling Ludendorff's work on total war—that it merges with policy, becomes policy, *is* policy. Such a war cannot be "used" for this purpose or that, nor does it "serve" anything. On the contrary, the outburst of violence is best understood as the supreme manifestation of existence as well as a celebration of it.

Faced by the question of to be or not to be, war throws off its normal accoutrements and stands forth stark naked. At this stage teleological reasoning—of the kind that is based on terms such as "cause," "goal," and "in order to"—probably does more harm than good. The root of the difficulty lies in the fact that all such terms take for granted a steady, orderly progression from past to present and from present to future. Should a community suffer defeat in its fight for existence and its culture perish—if, quoting the Persian ultimatum to Miletos in 490 B.C., the men are enslaved, the children emasculated, the women exiled, and the country handed over to strangers—then for them this progression will be interrupted, even terminated. With the future abolished and the past erased, even thinking about such a war is fraught with difficulties, forcing the writer to resort to metaphors and examples.

As a case in point, to say that the Algerian people in their eight-year struggle of liberation against France "used" war as an extension of political interests is a gross distortion. It is to confuse policy with the nation's independent identity, even its very existence. The size of the instrument is inflated until it becomes identical with the end that it serves and, therefore, meaningless. In 1954–62 it was the French state that, its safety secured by the Mediterranean, fought for political ends, be they continued dominion, or protection of the European colonists, or possession of Saharan oil, or great-power status (which was still considered to be inextricably linked with the ownership of colonies). By contrast, the Algerian people did *not* fight for their interests, nor did they even have a government capable of formulating them. Had interests in the sense of what is expedient to the Algerians as individuals been the only thing at stake, then surely most of them would have done well to stay at home and look after their own business. Had the *Front de Libération Nationale* impressed its own people as fighting for some kind of "policy," then surely it would never have received a fraction of the support that, in the teeth of everything that the French could do, it got.

What is at issue here is more than mere semantics. To employ strategic language and think of "political goals" as if they applied to French and Algerians indiscriminately is to create a mirror-image that is totally unwarranted and, what is worse, disguises the true causes of defeat and victory. Fighting for what they considered to be their political goals, the French government engaged in a cost-benefit calculation, however rough and however wrong. The calculation made, they "allocated" such and such forces and "used" them for suppressing the rebellion. French casualties were, in fact, quite light: 22,000 military and perhaps 3,000 civilian dead never compared to the numbers being killed in ordinary traffic accidents during the period that the struggle lasted. Nevertheless the French ended up admitting their error, concluding that the price of holding on exceeded any prospective gain. Thus, it is evident that book-keeping rationality actually constituted a prerequisite to surrender: it was precisely *because* the French waged war as a continuation of policy by other means that they lost.

The situation on the Algerian side was entirely different, and indeed the more prolonged the conflict the clearer this became. Spearheaded by the FLN, the population never entered into cost-benefit calculations; had they done so, then most probably their department of "Net Assessment" would have told them not to start the struggle in the first place. Fighting as they did for national existence, the amount of punishment that the Algerians could take was almost unlimited—by the time the conflict ended they had suffered anything between 300,000 and 1 million dead in a population only a third as large as that of France. More important still, cost-benefit calculations, to the extent that they were applicable at all, worked in reverse. The greater the suffering and the destruction, the less the Algerians had to lose. The less they had to lose, the greater their determination that it should not be all in vain. Held captive by conventional strategic thought, the French like other "rational" nations before and after them took a long time to comprehend these facts. When they finally realized what was going on—when it dawned upon them that, on the Algerian side, every additional man or woman killed was turned into another reason to continue the fight— they gave up.

Another very good example of war as a fight for existence is provided by Israel in 1967. Surrounded by numerically superior enemies who never hid their intention of doing away with the Jewish State when the opportunity offered, Israelis had long been on edge. When Nasser in May of that year sent six divisions into the Sinai, dismissed the UN peacekeeping force, and closed the Straits of Tiran, Israel's government and people panicked. When Syria and Jordan aligned themselves with Egypt their panic was reinforced. Rightly or wrongly, it was believed that a second holocaust was imminent. It had long been fashionable—not just in Israel alone—to compare the Egyptian dictator with Adolf Hitler. Now it was thought that he and his allies were aiming at the destruction of the state, to be accompanied by the massacre of at least a sizeable fraction of the Jewish population and the expulsion of the rest.

As the crisis intensified, the need to take political factors into account actually diminished. One by one, ordinary considerations pertaining to the allies to be placated, goals to be attained, and resources to be conserved were peeled off. The moment came when even the expected number of Israeli casualties appeared irrelevant; as the parks of Tel Aviv were being ritually consecrated to serve as cemeteries, "policy" was reduced to the population's raw fear and its determination to sell its life dearly. At this point Israel went to war. For six glorious days war was Israel and Israel was war. The signal given, the country experienced an immense sense of liberation of the kind felt by an athlete at the beginning of a race when every muscle is strained and all constraints cast off. The Israeli Defense Force broke loose and fought magnificently, smashing the Arab armies and winning a victory that was as swift as it was unexpected.

As these and countless other historical examples show, war for existence can be either long or short. In can inspire people to feats of courage and determination far in excess of those that would be called-for if the aim had been merely to "reach" goals, "realize" policy, "extend" or "defend" interests. It can also inspire them to make sacrifices beyond anything imaginable in "ordinary" times, even to the point where cost-benefit calculations are put into reverse and each additional casualty suffered is entered into the "benefit" ledger. Moreover, he who fights for existence has another advantage on his side. Necessity knowing no rules, he feels entitled to violate the war convention and use unlimited force, something that the other side, fighting in the name of policy, cannot do without suffering the consequences described earlier.

Nor should it be thought that war for existence is a marginal phenomenon, representing an unimportant minority among all conflicts. On the contrary, over time any war will tend to turn into a struggle for existence, provided only hostilities are sufficiently intensive and casualties sufficiently heavy. This is because, the longer and more costly the conflict, the more likely it is that the reasons for which it was originally launched will be forgotten. The greater the sacrifices made, the more pressing the need to justify them in the eyes of the world as well as one's own. Given that existence is the supreme goal, the result is that, on the declaratory level and often in practice as well, any prolonged war between equally matched opponents that does not peter out is likely to turn into a life-and-death struggle.

A good example for the way things work is provided by World War I. To judge by the terminology employed by the diplomats in the busy month of July 1914, the conflict broke out over things such as the balance of power, provinces lost and claimed, and alliances which in turn chimed in with something called "honor." Few people's lives in any of the belligerent countries were directly affected by these problems; in each one there must have been plenty who, like the good soldier Schweik, believed that the existing alliance-system obliged Austria to go to war against Turkey, the Germans ("low scum") to attack Austria, and France to come to beleaguered Austria's aid. Though confined to a wheelchair by rheumatism, Schweik energetically cheered the war. Nor did he stop cheering when the misunderstanding was cleared up and it was realized that the war would be fought in alliance with Germany and against France, thus raising a nice question whether the enthusiasm of countless Schweiks in every belligerent country *was*, in fact, based on a misunderstanding.

Time is the greatest enemy of excitement, and war is no exception. Over time enthusiasm tended to wane and was replaced by grim determination. Some 750,000 British Commonwealth dead could not be justified by the need to save poor little Belgium with whom, as a matter of fact, Britain had never even signed a formal treaty. A million and a half French dead could not be justified by the need to recover Alsace-Lorraine, given that for forty-three years France had got along very nicely without those provinces. Two million German dead could not be explained away by pointing to the second Reich's need to assist its Austrian ally, let alone by the desire to maintain some mysterious balance of power. The greater the expenditure of blood and treasure, the more imperative the demand that they should be spent for a vital cause. The original, comparatively modest, war-aims grew and grew. Nations found themselves fighting to create *Mitteleuropa,* or to put down German "militarism," or to make the world safe for democracy, or even to put an end to war itself. All these slogans barely hid the fact that men had stumbled into a life-and-death struggle without really knowing why or what for. The struggle became self-sustaining, and fed on rivers of blood. On and on it went, ending only when one side was so exhausted that social cohesion began to break down and concern for the collective existence of the nation was replaced by fear for the lives of the individuals comprising it.

World World II in some ways provides an even better example of the progression from "political" war to a war for existence. The defeat of 1940 transformed *Mourir pour Danzig* into a fight for the continued independent existence of the French state and, indeed, the French nation. Chamberlain's "honoring our obligations to Poland" became "stopping the Nazi beast" as well as Churchill's "we shall fight on the beaches." On the other side of the hill, a war that started as an attempt to revise the Treaty of Versailles, or region the Polish Corridor, or even to obtain *Lebensraum* for the *Grossdeutsche Reich,* had become passé by the winter of 1941–42. Its place was taken by *"ein Ringen um die Nationale Existenz,"* a battle for the nation's existence that swept along even those Germans who had not originally been happy with the war. Likewise in the Far East, "establishing a greater co-prosperity sphere" only went so far. Later it was replaced by a struggle against "foreign devils" perceived as hell-bent on exterminating every Japanese man and women; a fight which justified any means, including even *kamikaze.* The only major belligerent who, as the war got into stride, did not fight for existence was the United States, a deficiency that, to Göbbels' great delight, was made good when Roosevelt demanded "unconditional surrender."

That the process can also work in reverse is shown by America's agony in Vietnam. Such was the disparity in the size and power of the belligerents, and so large the distances separating them, that any attempt to represent the war as a struggle for existence was bound to founder on its own absurdity. Hence the original goals for which the US went to war included stopping Communism and preserving democracy in South Vietnam, both of which comprised a fair share of idealism even if the idealism was never pure. As the war escalated, the demand that it should be fought not for some kind of starry-eyed idealistic goal but for "hard-headed" interests became more strident. "Interests" were used to justify an ever-increasing expenditure of treasure and blood, but the greater the expenditure the greater also the difficulty of pointing out what interests could justify it. Finally, when Henry Kissinger entered office as head of the National Security Council, he published an article saying that the United States was in Vietnam because it was there; this being tantamount to an admission that it had gone to war for no reason at all.

Nor is the American experience in Vietnam all that atypical. It has been shared by many other countries, including even Israel, which at one time had given its enemies (and the world) an object-lesson in what war for existence can do. In the late 1970s, according to available reports, Israel's nuclear arsenal was growing even as some Arab countries were showing signs of being ready to make peace. At the same time the Israeli Defense Force was perfected, quantitatively and qualitatively, to the point that it became the mightiest army ever fielded by a country of such size. By 1982 it appeared as if existence was no longer at stake, enabling the government under prime minister Begin to proceed along more conventional lines and invade Lebanon. An "instrumental" war par excellence, the Lebanese adventure never commanded a political consensus. The longer it lasted, the less clear it was why it had to be fought at all. Years later it remains controversial to the point that the political leadership has been publicly accused of murder, much in the way that the anti-war opposition in the United States at one time blamed Lyndon B. Johnson for killing American kids.

The situation is tinged with irony, since of all Israel's wars this was the one that was waged most carefully and with the greatest regard for saving lives. The Israeli Defense Force in Lebanon weighed expected benefits against incurred costs—not just in terms of Israeli casualties but also the political cost that would result from killing too many "innocent" Arabs. Partly as a result, its advance was uncharacteristically slow and heavy-handed. The Air Force in its private feud against the Syrian SAM defenses performed magnificently, gaining a victory whose spectacular nature was matched only by its irrelevance to the war's ultimate outcome. Meanwhile, conscious of the need to keep casualties down, the ground forces advanced ponderously. The armoured columns were the most modern ever fielded, but they halted at the slightest sign of opposition and called for artillery support to open the way. Against an opponent inferior in both quality and—for the first time in any Arab-Israeli War—quantity, their performance was nowhere as tempestuous as it had been in the past.

To sum up, Clausewitzian war as the continuation of policy only goes so far in explaining the historical facts. A very important form of conflict, namely war for existence, fits into the framework with difficulty if at all; a war of this kind defies the laws of gravity, so to speak, causing cost-benefit calculations to be stood on their head. When this happens strategic rationality, far from assisting in the attainment of victory, can become a prerequisite for defeat. From the Americans in Vietnam to the Soviets in Afghanistan, the number of those who found their calculations upset and their plans confounded by the enemy's determination to suffer and endure is legion. It would be a travesty of the truth to say that the mere fact that a community is fighting for its existence suffices to guarantee victory against any odds. However, it is true to say that, in such a struggle, the odds are not seldom reversed.

Insofar as there have always been struggles for existence, doctrines that derive from the Clausewitzian Universe, and that emphasize rationality, the primacy of politics, and cost-benefit calculations have always been wrong. Insofar as some such struggles will undoubtedly continue to take place, those theories cannot form a sound basis for thinking about them, and hence for planning a war, waging it, and winning against them. Nor are these points of theoretical import only. Policymakers and others who think that they can make rational use of their countries' military forces to attain political goals have a lesson to learn: the power of interest-type war is limited by definition, and pitting it against noninstrumental war, in many cases, does little more than invite defeat.

The Metamorphoses of Interest

"Have you noticed how inexpressible is the individuality of one man, how difficult it is to know distinctly what distinguishes him, how he feels and lives, how differently his eyes see, his soul measures, his heart experiences, everything? What depth there is in the character of a single people which, even after repeated and probing observation, manages to evade the world that would capture it and render it recognizable enough for general comprehension and empathy. If this is so, how then can one survey an ocean of entire peoples, times, and countries, comprehend them in one glance, one sentiment, or one word, a weak, incomplete silhouette of a world? A whole *tableau vivant* of manners, customs, necessities, particularities of earth and heaven must be added to it, or precede it; you must enter the spirit of a people before you can share even one of its thoughts or deeds. You would indeed have to discover that single word which would contain everything that it is to express; else one simply reads—a word."

From Machiavelli to Kissinger, the term which more than any other sums up the purpose for which war has been waged is "interest." "Interest" is the Ark of the Covenant in the temple of policy, the stock-in-trade of decision markers at all levels. So deeply entrenched has the concept become that it is treated as if it were equivalent to rationality; often to provide an explanation as to why somebody acted in this way or that means the establishment of a link, real or imagined, between the action and his or her "interest." It is therefore not trivial to point out that "interest" in the political sense of the term, that is, something that a state has or claims or intends to take or defend *regardless of reason or right,* is a modern expression. Rooted in a world-view where law and morality are considered to be man-made and entirely separate from power, it only entered the English language in the sixteenth century; that is, just at the time when the foundations of the first modern states were being laid. Presumably the members of earlier generations based their strategy on a different kind of reasoning and waged their wars for different ends, it being unlikely that people who were not even familiar with the term got themselves killed on its behalf.

An attempt to draw up a list of all the different goals for which past people went to war would be tantamount to writing a history of civilization. Here I can do no more than provide the briefest of outlines. To start at the beginning, among tribal societies the objective of war was less the "interest" of society as a whole than the grievances, objectives, and glory of individuals. As the expression "brave" already indicates, adult males in these societies derived their status chiefly from their prowess as warriors. A man of acknowledged bravery could expect to make his voice heard in the tribe's affairs, including decision-making on questions of war and peace. Military prowess could also be translated into concrete advantages of every kind. Often the outstanding warrior did not even need to "own" property, given that he enjoyed privileged access to the necessities of life, sexual favors, and marital partners.

As was also to happen during the feudal Middle Ages, paradoxically this emphasis on personal prowess resulted in a rather ineffective form of waging war. For example, since each warrior was intent only on counting *coups* (pieces of the enemy's body or of his equipment) and collecting objects (human scalps) that were otherwise entirely useless, North-American Indian methods of warfare gave little scope to discipline and less to organized tactical formations. For this and other reasons, their typical tactics were the ambush, the skirmish, and the raid; when risking an open confrontation with regular troops, even such as did not enjoy the advantage of superior technology, they did not stand a chance and were usually easily defeated. Thus one might almost say that, in such societies, the relationship between the community and its "interest" was inverted. War, far from being waged as an instrument of the tribe's overall "policy," was actually conducted in such a way that the policy lost out in favor of other goals considered higher or more important.

In some primitive societies the principal objective of war was to obtain live prisoners for the pot. Cases where extreme scarcity forced people to resort to eating human flesh are not entirely unknown; however, they have nothing to do with war. Historically, most societies which practised cannibalism on a regular basis did not do so because they were hungry, and indeed the very idea was often met with derision when it was raised by anthropologists. Wherever we look—be it at pre-Columbian Brazil, eighteenth-century Dahomey, or the Fiji Islands during the nineteenth century—slain warriors were not immediately eaten, nor were prisoners consumed on the spot. Instead, their role was to act as the *pièce de résistance* in the subsequent victory celebrations. To the extent that celebration requires any rationale at all, it often consisted of the desire to acquire the qualities of a late brave opponent. In both Dahomey and Fiji, this line of reasoning was carried to the point where, in case the captive was not actually brave, elaborate ceremonies were staged to make it appear as if he were.

The principal objective for which the highly advanced MesoAmerican civilizations, later destroyed by Cortez, went to war was also to procure prisoners, who were taken in very large numbers. However, in this case the captives' destination was not the roasting fire. Instead they were used—if that is the term, since apparently it was not done entirely without cooperation on their part—as sacrificial victims who would fructify and renew the universe with their heart's blood. The braver a prisoner the more valuable he was. Outstanding ones were kept alive for up to a year and well treated, all the while undergoing elaborate rituals designated to prepare them for their role. The sacrificial occasions themselves bore a ceremonial character and were graded by the importance of the god in question; the principal sacrifices were carried out amidst immense public gatherings, attended by all the pomp and circumstance that these societies could muster. So vital was the act of sacrifice for the survival of society that, in case no ordinary conflict was taking place, special "flower wars" were held during which Aztec nobles fought each other by way of selecting those who would be offered. Even when confronted by Europeans, the Indians continued to aim less at killing their opponents than at taking them prisoner, a fact that is said to have played a role in their downfall.

Nor should it be thought that it is only faraway, exotic peoples that have gone to war for objectives that appear incomprehensible to us. The Biblical Book of *Judges* carries the story of how the People of Israel went to war to avenge an outraged woman (the concubine at Gib'ah), the outcome being the death of tens of thousands and the near extinction of the Tribe of Benjamin. Western civilization opens at the moment when, to recover a woman who had followed her lover out of her own free will, a thousand ships were launched and a war started that lasted ten years and ended with the sack of a royal city. It is not so very long ago since good Europeans, unable to agree whether or not wine and bread could be metamorphosed into God (or the other way around), sought to settle the question by cutting each other's throats. Now one may certainly enter all these different goals, and many more besides, under the rubric of "interest." One should, however, recall the words of the eighteenth century German sage, Johann Gottfried Herder that headed this section. When a term's meaning is inflated to mean everything, the point comes where it no longer means anything.

Today we take it for granted that territorial control is a major objective for which wars are fought. Yet anthropologists have often noted that nomadic and semi-nomadic tribes, such as those who used to live in deserts and jungles, normally had no concept of territoriality. If anything, the prevailing attitude was the opposite of our own: it was not a certain territory that belonged to the people but the people who belonged to a certain territory. Since the ancestral spirits that gave meaning to the life of the tribe were limited to certain areas, conquest was out of the question. Then again, had the tribe suddenly decided to expand, the kind of institutionalized government and permanent military organization needed to take over and hold a district did not exist. To the extent that it had any territorial basis at all, armed conflict therefore tended to revolve around access to pasturing grounds, watering places, and the like. Whatever the interests for which the members of these societies killed each other, they could not and did not include conquest in our sense of the term. From the Australian aborigines through the Amazonian tribes to the West Guinean headhunters, seen from this point of view the activity on which they engaged was not war at all but merely a succession of armed raids.

A similar attitude prevailed in classical Greece, where the *polis* was a religious as well as a political unit. Each of the autochthonic city states—that is, those located in the Hellenic homeland not known to be colonies sent out by other cities—was supposed to have received its territory directly from some god. Such being the case, usually the "excuses" (to quote Thucydides) for which the city-states fought each other consisted of the need to assist an ally or avenge an injury. True, there were cases when areas lying on the border between two cities were disputed and became the object of even repeated armed conflicts. Particularly between 431 and 404 B.C., wars between Greek and Greek could also lead to the destruction of entire cities and the massacre or enslavement of their populations. However, even in such extreme cases there was no question of conquering or annexing the newly vacant territories. Even Messene, home of the Helots and the most abject of all city-states, was never annexed by the Spartans but merely subjugated. When the Athenians sacked and razed the city-state of Melos they did not join the land to their "national territory," but formed a new *polis* consisting of colonists (*kleruchoi*) who were sent to take the original inhabitant's place. Plato in *The Republic* compares relations between cities and their colonies to those between parents and children. As time passed, the ties between "mother" and "daughter" tended to weaken until the latter became almost entirely independent.

Nor should the modern reader be misled into thinking that the city-states' reluctance to conquer and take over each other's land was merely an odd quirk of no great practical importance. In fact, the entire history of classical Greece and its failure to join forces even in face of an overwhelming external threat can be understood solely against a way of thought which regarded the *polis* and the territory on which it stood as inviolate. Since each of the original city-states claimed to have been founded by a special divine act, it was not just men but gods who stood in the way; to give up one's political independence meant surrendering one's religion, and vice versa. Thus, the most that Greek city-states could do by way of establishing larger political units was to set up alliances such as the Peloponnesian League, the Delian League, and (later) the Aetolian and Achaean Leagues. Many such leagues started out as multi-polar defense organizations and ended up dominated by a single powerful city. Often the passage of time brought about a situation where membership became compulsory and attempts at secession were treated as rebellion. Still, they never evolved into states or empires as we understand those terms.

The process whereby secular political ideas replaced those that were based on religion got under way during the Peloponnesian War. Later, towards the end of the fourth century B.C., Alexander and his Macedonian successors engaged on the large-scale conquest of territories that, however, were non-Hellenic. Next they assumed divine powers, founding new cities by the dozen. The outcome was that any lingering ideas concerning the heavenly protection enjoyed by cities and their territories were soon discarded. Force having been used to establish the new empires and determine their frontiers, force might be used to alter them again. It thus took the demise of one age—the classical—and the inauguration of another—the Hellenistic—to give birth to the concept of war for territorial expansion. The new concept in turn gave rise to the instrument for its realization, standing armies, or perhaps things worked the other way around. To the extent that both the concept and the instrument now existed, Hellenistic wars were fought for reasons closely resembling those of our own day.

In Roman times, and during much of the Middle Ages, the things for which people claimed to fight and, to a large extent, did fight were mostly of a religious or legal nature; *dieu et mon droit*. Conversely, nothing was more characteristic of the modern age than the fact that political considerations were separated from those that were legal and, in particular, religious, causing the latter two to be regarded as irrelevant to war. From 1648 on, the concerns for which states went to war were purely secular and rested almost exclusively on power-calculations. The idea of the territorial state—"territorial" meaning, at first, simply contiguous—was invented between 1600 and 1650, coinciding with the appearance of the first modern maps. From Louis XIV through Napoleon and right down to Adolf Hitler, geographical expansion and consolidation became the most important objective of armed conflict by far; as Frederick II once put it, a village on one's borders was worth more than a province a hundred miles away. Had these worthies been alive today, no doubt they would have rubbed their eyes in disbelief. Since mankind's most subscribed-to document—the United Nations Charter—expressly forbids the use of force for altering national boundaries, very probably they would have asked why we post-World War II people bother to fight at all.

Nor is the question all that easy to answer, at any rate as far as war between states is concerned. The Charter and the weight of public opinion on which it rests have brought about a situation where states are decreasingly able to declare openly that their goal is conquest, let alone the elimination of another state. Perhaps more important, even if physical conquest is achieved, the chances of its being recognized by the international community have become very slight. Usually what follows is not a peace treaty but a cease-fire or armistice, creating a juridical twilight zone that can last for years or even decades. Such has been the case in the Middle East since 1948; in the Far East a somewhat similar situation has prevailed ever since the USSR occupied northern Sakhalin in 1945. From then on, the number of instances in which war has led to the alteration of state borders—let alone to international recognition of the changes—can easily be counted on the fingers of one hand. Even in Africa, where many frontiers were originally the result of lines drawn with a ruler upon a blank map, borders are usually regarded as sacrosanct, no matter how illogical they might be.

Three and a half centuries after the end of the Thirty Years' War, nobody goes to war in order to prove that God is on one's side—or so most of us thought until the Ayatollah Khomeini's advent to power in Iran taught us otherwise. Certainly, the fact that objectives that have been historically very important—such as booty, slaves, or women—are considered out of bounds at this moment constitutes no guarantee that they will not return. Concerning the future, each of us is welcome to let his or her imagination run wild. The one thing that seems reasonably certain is that, as the nature of the warmaking organization changes, so will that of the ends for which it goes to war. The things people will fight for tomorrow will not be identical to those they fight for today, and the way they are related to religious and legal considerations may also be different from our own.

No doubt cynics will argue that goals such as justice and religion are mere pious smokescreens, since, once the verbiage is stripped away, always and everywhere selfish considerations pertaining to the community's interest raise their ugly head. This charge is neither original nor unfounded: all too often right merely serves as a cover for might. However, it can also be put upside down. If modern strategic thought views rationality in terms of reducing justice and religion to the underlying interests, then the same intellectual meat-grinder is capable of reducing interest to underlying religious or legal principles. For example, was it American economic and political interests that led to "Manifest Destiny" and the subjugation of a continent? Or was it the quasi-religious idea of "Manifest Destiny" that translated itself into economic and political interests? We may turn the question over and over, sprinkling it with footnotes as we go along; any answer that does not take both sides into account will do an injustice to human nature.

To conclude, the contemporary strategic premise that sees wars as making sense only when they are fought for reasons of policy or interest represents a point of view that is both Eurocentric and modern. At best it is applicable only to the period since 1648, when war was conducted predominately by sovereign states that in turn were supposed to base their relations on power rather than on religion, or law, or—as in numerous primitive societies—kinship. As an explanation of the more remote past, the premise is either meaningless or much too narrow. As a guide to the future, it is almost certainly misleading. To apply it to the wrong conflict can be positively dangerous. As recent events have shown time and again, to believe that justice and religion are less capable of inspiring people to fight and die than is interest is not realism but stupidity.

Worse still, ordinary Clausewitzian thought is incapable of coming to grips with what in some ways is the most important form of war, namely, one whose purpose is existence. Confronted with such a war the entire strategic structure begins to show cracks. The very idea of policy, implying as it does calculations of the cost-benefit type, becomes inappropriate, the proof being any number of cases when modern states, from the Americans in Vietnam to the Israelis in Lebanon, lost heavily *because* they went to war with strategic considerations in mind.

All of which boils down to saying that policy and interest, even rationality itself, change from place to place and from time to time. They themselves form part of the war convention: neither eternal nor to be taken for granted, and far from capable of providing self-evident clues for the conduct of war.

CHAPTER
VI

Why War Is Fought

The Will to Fight

Though war for existence has already stretched the framework to the breaking point, this volume so far has proceeded within the strategic tradition. It is assumed that war consists essentially of the members of one community engaging in mortal violence against those of another; and that the killing is—or should be—a rational means for achieving some rational end. Proceeding in reverse order, I shall argue the above fundamental pillars of the Clausewitzian universe are wrong; being wrong, they also constitute a recipe for defeat.

War by definition is a social activity resting upon some kind of organization. Hence the idea that it is a means for extending or defending some kind of interests—be they political, legal, religious, or whatever—may apply to the community as a whole. As many commentators have pointed out, however, even in this case the strategic approach probably overstates the degree of rationality involved. In any kind of regime the people who comprise the decision-making body are made of flesh and blood. Nothing would be more preposterous than to think that, just because some people wield power, they act like calculating machines that are unswayed by passions. In fact, they are no more rational than the rest of us—and indeed, since power presumably means that they are less subject to constraint, they may be less. A person whose life is governed solely by rational considerations pertaining to utility is, in any case, an inhuman monster. Now most decision-makers are not monsters; whereas those who are, such as Adolf Hitler or the ex-Ugandan dictator Idi Amin, can scarcely be described as rational.

Let us leave the place where the decisions are made, be it the *agora* of some Greek city state where the gesticulating crowd has gathered or the air-conditioned office of some modern prime minister with its multicolored telephones and hot lines. The farther down the line of command we proceed, the more the ordinary world is left behind. Approaching the fighting, we listen to the thunder of cannon and the howl of shot. Soon we discover ourselves trying to guess which one has our number on it. Our senses are strained, sharpened, focused, until they become impervious to anything else. Our head empties, our mouth dries. Both past and future melt away; at the point of impact the very notions of "because of" and "in order to" vanish as body and mind struggle to achieve the absolute concentration that is essential for survival.

At bottom, the reason why fighting can never be a question of interest is—to put it bluntly—that dead men have no interests. A person may well lay down his life in the name of God, king, country, and family, or even for all four at once. However, to say that he does so because he has some kind of posthumous "interest" in the survival even of his nearest and dearest is to invert the meaning of the term and turn it into a caricature of itself. Thus considered, warfare constitutes the great proof that man is *not* motivated by selfish interest; as the original meaning of the term *berserker* (holy fighter) testifies, in some ways it represents the most altruistic of all human activities, akin to the sacred and merging into it. It is the *absence* of interest on the part of those who brave death or die bravely that explains why society so often confers the highest honors on them, even to the point where, like Greek or Norse heroes, they are taken into the pantheon and themselves become gods.

The motives which make men willing to lay down their lives are, therefore, by no means always the same as the goals for which the community goes to war, nor is it rare for the individual to be altogether ignorant of the community goal. The relationship between the two is perhaps best illustrated by the analogy of a heavy train climbing up an incline while propelled by two locomotives, one in front and one at the rear. A person watching might well ask how the train moves, since the first locomotive strains at the links whereas the second causes them to slacken. In practice, the workload is always found to be distributed between the two. A few wagons are pushed all the time, others are pulled. Most are in between, pushed at one moment and pulled in the next. The number of wagons being pushed will be greatest when the leading locomotive has already reached a plateau whereas the rest of the train is still climbing. In the same way, the role instrumental considerations play in war is inversely related to the severity of combat. For a man to die for his own interest is absurd; to die for those of somebody or something else, more absurd still.

The other point where conventional strategic thought goes astray concerns the premise that war consists essentially of members of one group killing those of another. In fact, war does not begin when some people kill others; instead, it starts at the point where they themselves risk being killed in return. Those, and there are always some, who engage in the former but not in the latter are not called warriors but butchers, murderers, assassins, or any number of even less complimentary epithets. Given the existence of crime, that is, transgressions against the social norms, most societies do have laws or customs that allow, even oblige, unopposed killing to take place under certain circumstances. However, killing people who do not or cannot resist does not count as war. Nor are those responsible for such killing likely to earn the respect reserved for warriors.

Thus, in modern countries that have the death penalty, the identity of those who administer the electric shock or open the valves of the gas-chamber is always carefully concealed. Since previous societies were more intimate and carried out their executions in public they were unable to preserve anonymity, though masks were often used. The solution was to entrust the job to the members of certain families. They were considered unclean and lived in seclusion; in London, for example, their house was located on the south bank, away from "good" society and downriver from everybody else. In some cases they required a special license to enter the towns where they worked, risking assault if they showed themselves on other occasions. The hangmen themselves before proceeding to their gruesome business used to beg for the victim's forgiveness. Often they found it hard to get married, with the result that in sixteenth-century England, for example, they received permission to cohabit with the dead.

The problematic nature of unopposed killing can also be seen from the way that modern military execution-squads are set up and perform their task. To prevent any one man being accused—and accusing himself—of committing murder, the members of such squads are usually selected at random and their number made to vary from six to twelve. Of those, one (in some countries, more than one) is issued with a blank cartridge without his knowledge. The condemned person is granted a last wish and his eyes are bound, both of these rituals intended as much for the executioners' protection as for his own. Sometimes he is admonished to die bravely so as not to create difficulties for others and, it is claimed, for himself. Should the procedure misfire and the victim fail to die, then again the notion of the *coup de grâce* is specifically meant to imply that, under such circumstances, to shoot a defenseless person in the back of the neck does not amount to murder.

Finally, Himmler on several occasions went out of his way to convince his subordinates that their grisly work of gassing defenseless Jews was, in fact, part of a sublime task. Still, not even in Germany during the Nazi era did serving in the extermination camps count as a great honor. The holocaust had to be carried out in secret, or else presumably it could not have been carried out at all. Interviewed in his Nuremberg cell, the colonel in charge of Auschwitz—Rudolf Höss—said that his marriage went to pieces as his wife became reluctant to sleep with him. Höss' subordinates, the members of the death-head units, were mostly recruited from the lowest social strata. Some were petty criminals, released from the jails on condition that they agree to serve. When these people realized the nature of their assignment they often asked for a transfer, and when that was refused took to alcohol. The nickname they were called by regular troops, *Judenhelden,* "Jew-heroes," speaks for itself.

Thus, war does not consist simply of a situation where one person or group puts the other to death, even if the killing is organized, done for a purpose, and considered legal; rather, it begins at that point where inflicting mortal injury becomes reciprocal, an activity known as fighting. This is not to deny Patton's quip that the whole point of war is to make the other poor bastard die for *his* country; it is, however, to say that the only way in which this worthy goal can be achieved is by putting one's own life at risk. In any war, the readiness to suffer and die, as well as to kill, represents the single most important factor. Take it away, and even the most numerous, best organized, best trained, best equipped army in the world will turn out to be a brittle instrument. This applies to all wars regardless of time, place, and circumstance. It also applies regardless of the degree of technological sophistication involved, whether it is with the aid of sticks or tanks that the actual fighting is done. Nor is the problem merely academic. Much of the history of armed conflict—specifically including that of post-1945 low-intensity conflict and the defeats suffered by some of the world's mightiest armed forces—can be read as a demonstration of the fact that, where there is a will, there is usually a way.

The whole of late–twentieth-century strategic thought rests on the idea that war is an instrument of policy; and indeed Clausewitz's main claim to fame comes from his being the first to base the theory of war on that proposition. Yet it is precisely *because* it assumes that war consists of killing for a purpose that *vom Kriege* and its derivatives cannot, and will not, tell us what makes men willing to risk their lives. Since, in any war, the reasons that cause troops to fight constitute the most decisive factor of all, the time has now come to take our leave of strategy, looking into the human soul instead.

Means and Ends

The essence of war is fighting. Everything else that takes place in war—the gathering of intelligence, the planning, the maneuvering, the supplying—either acts as a prelude to fighting or exploits its results. To use Clausewitz's own metaphor, fighting and bloodshed are to war what cash-payment is to business. However rarely they may take place in practice, they alone give meaning to all the rest.

Fighting is best understood as a reciprocal activity. It gets under way, not when some people take the lives of others but at the point where they risk their own. Beginning already in the eighteenth century, there is a tradition that requires officers to enter the battlefield armed with symbolic weapons such as demi-pikes, pistols, or swagger sticks; to this extent it might even be said that, for those picked members of the armed forces, war can consist *only* of being killed. Though time will cause us to become habituated to danger, there is no such thing as becoming indifferent to it. The closer to battle we get, the greater the emptiness by which we are surrounded, and the less the power of the military organization to make us obey its commands. History has often seen troops pressed in the back by sergeant-majors with pikes or pistols at the ready; however, there are obvious limits to the amount of coercion that can be applied. No reward however great can be more valuable than life, no penalty however terrible worse than death. At the point of impact the Roman gladiators' call, *ave Caesar, morituri te salutant,* still echoes. Those who stare death in the face have entered a realm where they are beyond human ability to influence them, and where they are no longer subject to anything but their own free will.

Just as it makes no sense to ask "why people eat" or "what they sleep for," so fighting in many ways is not a means but an end. Throughout history, for every person who has expressed his horror of war there is another who found in it the most marvelous of all the experiences that are vouchsafed to man, even to the point that he later spent a lifetime boring his descendants by recounting his exploits. To select a few examples only, all of them recent and all of them belonging to our own Western civilization, Robert E. Lee is reported to have said that "it is good that war is so terrible or else we would love it too much." Theodore Roosevelt loved nothing better than a good fight (a subject about which he wrote at great length) and, when the opportunity presented itself, put himself at the head of the Rough Riders and went a-hunting Spaniards. Winston Churchill spent his youth chasing from one war to the next and, on the eve of World War I, wrote a lady friend to tell her how excited, geared-up, thrilled it made him feel; in 1945 the approaching end of World War II made him feel like committing suicide. For his part, George S. Patton on one occasion told his diary how much he "loved" war.

Nor should it be thought that these were just the personal oddities of great men—bizarre, perhaps, but ultimately insignificant. On the contrary, it stands to reason that people who do not enjoy combat (or can pretend to do so, which in the end boils down to the same thing) will be unable to lead others into it. One reason why Patton, Churchill, Theodore Roosevelt, and Lee were considered such great leaders was because, for them, fighting represented the medium in which they came to life. Enjoying themselves, they and their counterparts at all times and places were able to inspire countless followers who, as they went into combat, came to know the meaning of excitement, exhilaration, ecstasy, and delirium. Few among us are immune to these sensations, nor perhaps are those who *are* immune to them deserving of admiration. The list of those who have put their enjoyment of war on record is endless. It even includes some who, like the World War I British poet Siegfried Sassoon, later became most vociferous in describing its horror and futility.

To pass from fact to fiction, the *Illiad,* the *Chanson de Roland,* and the *Nibelungenlied* are but three out of countless literary masterpieces whose subject is war. All of them owe their fame to the fact that they constitute a paean to those who risked their lives in it as well as a description of their deeds. From the reliefs in Assurbanipal's place through the friezes of the Parthenon all the way to Rubens' paintings, again some of the greatest visual art of all times has depicted people and armies in the act of fighting. Had it not been for war, or rather strife, the shelves devoted to history in most bookstores would have been largely empty. Already Herodotus, the "father of history," justifies his decision to write by the need to put on record "the great and famous deeds" of men, by which he did not mean their achievements in the raising of poultry. His example was later followed by Thucydides and Livy, to mention but two of the greatest. From their time to ours there has never been any doubt but that war, real or imagined, not only makes rattling good history but that history is exciting mainly to the extent that it deals with wars.

The fact that war is or can be supremely enjoyable is equally evident from the history of games. From the contests of the Germanic tribes described by Tacitus all the way to modern football, the most popular games have always been those that either imitated fighting or provided a substitute for it; paradoxically this even applies to the handful of societies, such as the Eskimos of Alaska, who for various reasons were not familiar with war as such. The phrase used by Avner, servant of Ish Boshet, "let the boys rise and play in front of us," (Samuel II, 2, 13) sounds as if it referred to some innocuous game. In fact, however, it initiated a round of murderous hand-to-hand combat where all twenty-four participants were killed. The penultimate and most exciting contest held by Achilles on Patroclus' grave consisted of an armed duel between the two greatest Achaean heroes, Diomedes and Ajax; it was distinguishable from the real thing only by the fact that it was stopped at the last moment when a glittering spear threatened to pierce Ajax's throat. Again, the reader should not commit the fashionable error of looking down upon such games as suitable merely for bloodthirsty degenerates. Augustine was as Christian a person as has ever lived; in his *Confessions* he gives a vivid account of the way the Roman *ludi* were capable of turning spectators into raving maniacs, even against their will.

Nor should it be overlooked that combat itself has very often been treated not just as a spectacle but as the greatest spectacle of all. From the time that the Trojan women crowded the walls to watch the single combat between Achilles and Hector, countless have been the cases when battles were attended by excited onlookers. During the early Middle Ages, a period that thought of war in semi-juridical terms, there were even cases when their location was selected in advance, usually on a meadow near some river bank, specifically in order that people should be able to gather and watch; after all, justice should be seen and not just carried out. Just as any pair of street fighters will soon attract a crowd, so in Froissart it is possible to find many an occasion when knightly armies ceased fighting, leant on their swords, and watched duels taking place between individuals or groups. Coming late in the Middle Ages, the battle of Agincourt was as ferocious as any and, what is more, destined to end in an infamous massacre. Yet it was typical of the period in that, even as the opponents slaughtered each other, their respective heralds assembled on a nearby hill and watched the proceedings.

The advent of firearms caused troops to spread out and fronts to lengthen. It also exposed spectators to stray bullets, thereby making battle-watching more difficult and increasing the risks involved. Still, Vandervelde the Younger was only the most celebrated among numerous artists who, beginning in the late seventeenth century, attended battles both on land and at sea. Working by commission or on their own initiative, they painted the action and sold the results. As late as 1861 thousands of smartly-dressed Washingtonians turned out to watch the battle of First Bull Run, behaving as if they were on a picnic and ending up running for their lives when the Confederates gained an unexpected victory. Nor did this experience deter them for long: when the ironclads *Virginia* and *Monitor* clashed at Hampton Roads in March 1863, the shores on both sides of the Bay were again crowded with spectators. To this day, anyone who has ever witnessed air combat can testify to the hushed silence, the rasping breath, and the cheers or groans which escape the onlookers' throats every time a plume of smoke indicates that a plane has been shot down. For every person who has seen such things in reality, moreover, there are a thousand who pay for the privilege of reading about them in the papers or watching them on the screen.

Thus, conventional strategic thought has put the cart in front of the horse. Danger is much more than simply the medium in which war takes place; from the point of view of participants and spectators alike, it is among the principal attractions, one would almost say its *raison d'être*. Had war not involved braving danger, coping with it, and overcoming it, then not only would there have been no point in fighting but the activity itself would have become impossible. Coping with danger calls forth qualities such as boldness, pride, loyalty, and determination. It is thus able to cause people to transcend themselves, become more than they are. Conversely, it is only in the face of danger that determination, loyalty, pride, and boldness make sense and manifest themselves. In short, danger is what makes war go round. As in any sport, the greater the danger the greater both the challenge of braving it and the honor associated with doing so.

Danger—even vicarious or make-believe danger—accounts for the popularity of any number of amusements from roller-coasting to dangerous but senseless escapades, such as cliff-jumping, that figures so largely in the *Guinness Book of Records*. Strenuous sports such as skiing, surfing, white-water rafting, and mountain climbing owe their fascination to the same factors: nor, once again, is it by accident that the latter's vocabulary in particular includes many terms borrowed directly from war. What sets war apart, what makes it unique, is precisely the fact that it is the most dangerous activity of all, one that makes the remainder pale and for which no other can offer an adequate substitute. Wherever else we care to look, we find the opposition to be second-rate. In some cases it is inanimate and incapable of thought, in which case it is scarcely justifiable to speak of opposition at all (however much climbers like to talk of mountains "resisting" an assault). In other cases it is represented by animals, as in hunting. Some animals are big and dangerous, others small and inoffensive. Insofar as they only have a limited ability to engage in an intelligent response, however, there are limits to what may be gained by coping with them.

Contests between humans that fall short of war are known as games. All games owe their existence to their being surrounded by rules and, indeed, are defined by them. Whatever the kind of game we are talking about, the function of the rules is to limit the kind of equipment that may be used, the human qualities that may be thrown into the fray and, most important, the amount of violence that may be brought to bear. All such restrictions are artificial, hence in a certain sense absurd. War's unique nature consists precisely in this: it has always been, and still remains, the only creative activity that both permits and demands the unrestricted commitment of all man's faculties against an opponent who is as strong as oneself. This explains why, throughout history, war has often been taken as the ultimate test of a person's worth; or, to speak with the terminology of previous ages, the judgment of God.

What makes coping with danger so supremely enjoyable is the unique sense of freedom it is capable of inspiring. As Tolstoy notes of Prince Andrej on the eve of the Battle of Austerlitz, he who has no future before him is free of care; which is why the very terror of fighting is capable of inducing excitement, exhilaration, even vertigo. Fighting demands the utmost concentration. By compelling the senses to focus themselves on the here and now, it can cause a man to take his leave of them. In this way it is granted to the warrior to approach, even cross, the thin dividing line between life and death. In the whole of human experience the only thing that even comes close is the act of sex, as is also evident from the fact that the same terms are often used to describe both activities. However, the thrills of war and fighting are probably more intense than those of the boudoir. War causes human qualities, the best as well as the worst, to realize their full potential. From the time of Homer on, there has always been a sense in which it is only those who risk their lives willingly, even joyfully, who can be completely themselves, completely human.

It is true that other factors—including rewards and coercion—are mixed up with the will to fight, but, since it is the ultimate meeting of men with death that we are speaking of, that is beside the point. So is the fact that passage of time will usually cause the appeal of danger to be adulterated or lost. The most intense delights, like the most intense agonies, would be unbearable if they had not been limited in duration. Furthermore, the opposing experiences of pain and delight are actually interdependent; neither can exist without the other, and provided only they are sufficiently intense they are capable of turning into each other. The breathless tension, the pounding blood, that precede the most intense exhilaration themselves form part of it, as do the panting breath and leaden fatigue by which it is followed. Nor is the intrusion of cause and consequence into pure delight unique to war. From boxing and football down, not even the most exciting spectator-sports are able to sustain the tension indefinitely, and indeed one reason why a time limit is imposed is to ensure that the game remains exciting. The essence of the game consists in that, as long as it lasts, reality is suspended, abolished, lost. The joy of fighting consists precisely in that it permits participants and spectators alike to forget themselves and transcend reality, however incompletely and however momentarily.

Since he who fights puts everything at risk, whatever he fights for must be deemed more precious than his own blood. Not even Machiavelli, the high priest of "interest," thought he could make his fellow Italians fight for the liberation of their country by pointing out the profits that such an exercise might bring to each of them; accordingly *The Prince* concludes with a passionate appeal to their *antico valor*. God, country, nation, race, class, justice, honor, freedom, equality, fraternity come under the same category of myths for which men are prepared to give their lives and for which, in fact, they have always given their lives. More remarkably still, the equation also works the other way around. The more blood has been shed in the name of a myth—mostly our own blood, but sometimes that of the enemy as well—the more hallowed it becomes. The more hallowed it becomes, the less prepared are we to consider it in rational, instrumental, terms. So elemental is the human need to endow the shedding of blood with some great and even sublime significance that it renders the intellect almost entirely helpless. As inscriptions on monuments erected to the German dead of World War II prove, when no cause exists it has to be invented.

For something to be fought over, it does not have to be intrinsically valuable. On the contrary: objects that are otherwise entirely useless can acquire the highest value for no other reason than that they originate in war, thus serving as reminders of dangers met, withstood, and overcome. The North-American Indian system of taking *coups* as proof of valor is a case in point. So are the trophies that often decorate the homes of modern soldiers. Legend has it that Ghengis Khan on one occasion was asked to name the one thing most enjoyable in life. His answer was that it consisted of pressing the wives and daughters of the defeated enemy to one's breast; by which he surely did not mean to say that he was short of women to take to bed. From Alsace-Lorraine to Danzig, and from Kashmir to the Gaza strip, many are the otherwise godforsaken regions that would never have acquired anything like the significance attributed to them were it not for the fact that they had been repeatedly fought and bled over. Conversely, subsequent generations that have not themselves been involved in the fighting are often at a loss to understand what their predecessors got so excited about and shed their blood for.

The same mental processes that cause the value of the objectives of war to be enhanced are also responsible for embellishing the means used in it. Throughout history weapons and equipment have been cherished, even worshipped, for no other reason than that they related to armed conflict. One way this phenomenon manifested itself was the custom of giving them names: in the *Chanson de Roland* swords like *Durendal, Joyeuse,* and *Precieuse* are so highly regarded as to be treated almost like animate beings. Moreover, weapons are not just utilitarian devices but symbols of might. Hence the paradoxical fact that, though of all kinds of tools they are the most likely to be lost or damaged in battle, more than any other they have been subject to decoration even to the point where they turned into vastly expensive works of art. The rabbis who wrote the Talmud already argued among themselves whether weapons might or might not be carried on the sabbath, the idea being that their decorative value was considered to be as great as their functional one. While the passage of time has caused the decorative aspect of weapons to assume different forms, it has not been lost. Just as the Greeks and Romans in their time dedicated weapons to the gods and hung them in their temples, so we today put them at the center of our squares and parade them on suitable occasions.

What makes the process by which weapons are enhanced into symbols of might so remarkable is the fact that, far from being motivated by utilitarian considerations, the process is capable of being carried to the point where it first undermines, then negates, the purpose of those weapons. Display and propaganda can render a weapon too precious to risk, particularly if it is powerful and, for that reason, probably expensive and limited in number. This, for example, was what happened to World War I battleships. First they had their significance inflated by years of naval propaganda and reviews. When war came they for the most part remained in harbor, content to let the smaller, cheaper, more expendable submarines, destroyers, and torpedo boats fight it out among themselves. Present-day aircraft carriers find themselves caught in a similar trap. In their case, too, we find power, expense, small numbers, and symbolism reinforcing each other in a vicious circle. Materially as well as symbolically, so precious are these vessels that it is difficult to think of a target against which they may be usefully put at risk. Hence their official mission of "projecting force" sounds like a contradiction in terms. Should war in fact break out, then in all likelihood they will share their predecessors' fate.

What applies to the weapons of war applies equally well to the dress worn in it. Tribal braves always saw war as the one great occasion to put on whatever finery they possessed, including feathers, plumes, masks, and tattoos. If there is one thing that the great warrior-epics never tire of, surely it is singing the praise of their heroes' splendid appearance. Though Augustus was a much greater politician than he was a general, the statue that he placed in the Forum that is named after him shows him attired in armor, an example later followed by Marcus Aurelius who, to judge by his celebrated *Meditationes,* was by temperament one of the most peaceful rulers who ever lived. As existing specimens show, medieval armor was often valued as much for decorative reasons as for practical ones. As late as 1799 the Mamluks carried their choice possessions with them onto the battlefield, with the result that the French after their victory found themselves fishing in the Nile for their opponents' bodies. A visit to any military museum will show what fortunes have been lavished on golden helmets; on etched, inlaid, and fluted suits of armor; on lacquered body cover, and the like; so that even today equipping one of the Queen of England's Horse Guards costs about as much as a small car.

As armor lost its function and was replaced by uniforms, a late–seventeenth-century invention, again it was not long before the taste for decoration took over. Eighteenth-century rulers such as Louis XIV, Peter the Great, and Charles XII, as well as lesser princelings, often took to designing uniforms as a hobby. Unsurprisingly, many of the costumes they produced were, militarily speaking, as useless as they were gorgeous. Nor should it be thought that stiff collars, shining buttons, tall hats, tight pants, multicolored straps, and powdered perukes were intended for parades and nothing else. On the contrary, during much of history and as late as the Napoleonic period, battle themselves represented the greatest parades of all. Then as now, armies that marched, engaged on foraging operations, or dug trenches during siege warfare often looked like a bunch of scarecrows. However, the eve of every large engagement would find the troops hard at work polishing their weapons and bringing their uniforms up to par. The modern archeologists' penchant for attributing a "ceremonial" function to any expensive, highly decorated, objects that they find both rests on a misunderstanding of the past and reflects that misunderstanding. As Plato says, battle is the time when it behooves a man to look smart.

Over the last century and a half, the growing range and lethality of weapons have rendered martial displays problematic; one by one, and usually much against their will, armies were forced to shed their splendid uniforms and replace them by drab, utilitarian "fatigues" blending into the landscape. Still, as late as World War I uniform was the normal attire for heads of state other than the presidents of republics, who for this reason often cut a poor figure among their resplendent colleagues. To this day the predilection for uniforms is common among certain social groups who dress themselves in "tiger suits," jump shoes, and berets. The rulers of many developing countries, as well as guerrilla leaders from, Jonas Sawimbi to Yasser Arafat, like nothing better than to strut around in martial apparel. While for the most part this is no longer the custom in the developed world, here too there is a sense in which military dress has remained ceremonial dress par excellence. From Beijing to the White House, whenever rulers want to impress, they surround themselves with guards of honor whose uniforms are often as useless as they are theatrical.

In addition, every military possesses a whole class of objects that have been created specifically to serve a symbolic function and be considered more precious than blood. Standards, flags, and similar embodiments of military tradition are as ancient as war and, under ordinary circumstances, indispensable to the military spirit. Often in history they possessed a religious significance; among these were the Biblical Ark of the Covenant and the medieval French *oriflamme*. Napolean personally presented each regiment with its eagle. In Nazi Germany flags were supposed to be "consecrated" by Hitler and by the blood of fallen comrades. Whatever the mythology by which they are surrounded, such symbols are supposed to derive their significance from the highest values of the society in question. More important to our purpose, that significance is deemed to increase in proportion as they had been carried in battle, fought over, and bled for. From the day of Caesar's veterans to those of the Grande Armée, countless are the cases when troops gave their lives for their standards, not because they were useful or intrinsically valuable but because they and honor had become fused into one. When rewards become meaningless and punishment ceases to deter, honor alone retains the power to make men march into the muzzles of cannon trained at them. It is also the one thing a man can take with him to the grave, even if—as has often been the case—it is not his own grave.

A profound paradox surrounds these and other objects of military ritual and symbolism. They are, without exception, "real" and "unreal" at the same time. A flag is but a colored rag, an eagle a gilded piece of bronze made to resemble a rather nasty bird and carried on top of a wooden pole. The goat being marched in front of the regiment is nothing but a hairy quadruped; however, he is also a treasured mascot. Ditto for the fanciful uniforms, the burnished armor, the heavily decorated weapons, and the cherished trophies, to say nothing of the dancing and the prancing and the marching and the strutting by which they are surrounded. To suppose that the troops who carry out the ritual, wear the armor, and march behind the goat are unaware of their objective nature is to insult their intelligence. It is, however, true that the successful conduct of war requires a certain boyish enthusiasm. This enthusiasm, in turn, can cause those who engage in it to retain their boyishness; war has always been the business of the young.

What applies to rituals of every sort is equally true of fraternity, equality, freedom, honor, justice, class, race, nation, country, God. As rationalistically-minded critics from Socrates down have often pointed out, in one sense these are merely empty words; they exist, if at all, solely in the minds of men. Hence there is a sense in which shedding one's blood for them is ultimately based on an act of make-believe, one that is not so very different from that of a child who plays at "being" a train. War has a unique ability to make the profoundest myths, the strongest beliefs, and the most impressive rituals stand up stark naked. Only if they are experienced as great and marvelous things, in other words as ends in themselves, will they be able to inspire devotion. Morale-raisers that are deliberately presented as such—"we present you with this flag in order that you may daily salute it and, by so doing, become more willing to fight and die"—are merely humbug. They will fail in their purpose and invite ridicule besides.

War, in short, is grand theater. Theater changes place with life, becomes life; life in turn becomes theater. We hard-headed strategists are free to deride the theatrical aspects of war as irrelevant and silly, and indeed to do so is easy and somewhat cheap. Still, we have the entire history of war as testimony to the fact that—provided only they are experienced deeply enough—it is just such silly baubles that make people willing to brave danger, act heroically, and put their lives at risk. After all, putting one's life at risk, acting heroically, and braving danger are just what war is all about. In the words of an Israeli armored commander after the Six Day War, "we have looked death in the face and *he* cast down his eyes"; no army will be capable of serving as an instrument for attaining or defending political or other objectives, unless it is prepared and even eager to do just this. Far from being a Clausewitzian means to an end, war can inspire people to fight because, and to the extent that, it is the one activity most capable of causing the difference between the two to disappear; the highest form of seriousness is, precisely, play.

Tension and Rest

Danger is the *raison d'être* of war, opposition its indispensable prerequisite; conversely, unopposed killing does not count as fighting but as murder or, in case it takes place under legal auspices, as execution. The absence of opposition makes military strategy impossible, and for an army to fight under such conditions would be both unnecessary and foolish. All this is to say that, by describing uncertainty as a characteristic of war, Clausewitz and his modern followers have put reality upside down. Uncertainty is not just the medium in which war moves and which helps govern the opponents' moves; above all, it is a condition for the existence of armed conflict.

Where the outcome of a struggle is a foregone conclusion the fighting will tend to cease, as much because one side gives up as because the other becomes bored. Throughout history, individuals and armies who felt that their situation was hopeless have asked for quarter. The victors, so long as they remained in possession of their senses and were not carried away by such emotions as rage or the lust for revenge, usually accepted. Whatever unpleasantness followed later—and sometimes what did follow later was even more unpleasant than the war itself—was not considered part of the fighting but, to use the Roman phrase, retaliation. Such retaliation may be more or less necessary, more or less justifiable, more or less in accord with the prevailing war convention. Since the outcome is not in doubt, however, it does not involve the tension that constitutes the essence of fighting. Nor are those who engage in it or profit from it usually regarded as deserving special honors; on the contrary.

The perfect illustration of the effect that certainty can have on war is provided by early–eighteenth-century sieges. This kind of warfare, it will be remembered, consisted of scientifically bringing the fire of cannon to bear against brick ramparts. A combination of practical experience and theoretical reflection had perfected military operations to the point that they were reduced almost entirely to applying the laws of physics as developed by Galileo and Newton. Taking into account the size of a fortress, the number of cannon, and the amount of ammunition available to both sides, the outcome of the siege and even its duration could be calculated in advance. Under these circumstances it is scant wonder that such warfare became less the art of defending fortresses than of surrendering them with honor, as the saying went.

Nor should the reader think that this is merely an interesting but irrelevant historical episode. On the contrary, the lack of a defense—the fact that war can be reduced to physics, and its outcome rendered certain—presents perhaps the most critical single element governing the contemporary world. It constitutes the principal reason why nuclear war is impossible; and why, in spite of forty-five years of intensive confrontation between the superpowers that by the logic of all previous history should have come to blows long ago, no conflict has taken place so far. Now this is not necessarily to say that nuclear weapons will never be used by anyone. They may be, and in fact some would argue that the chances of this happening are increasing daily because of the proliferation that is taking place. The point is that if they are used, whatever takes place will be not war in the historical sense of that term, but a massacre, an act of suicide, or a combination of both.

For the same reason, visions of automated warfare as expounded by members of the Artificial Intelligence community and their followers in the military are destined to remain unfulfilled. At present, and as far into the future as we can look, computers operate by working their way through long strings of yes/no, either/or, questions at a speed no human can match. While recent developments allow parts of the strings to be worked on simultaneously (parallel processing), this still does not enable them to tolerate ambiguity. Thus their performance depends on the attainment of certainty concerning all the relevant factors in the field to which they are applied. Now this does not exclude computers from being used in certain well-defined types of military operations, particularly those that take place in highly structured, yet simple, environments. However, it does mean that, should information ever become perfect—should a complete mathematical model of the battlefield become available—then that model itself will already spell the end of the fighting. As in any game, where the outcome of a war can be calculated in advance, fighting does not make sense since it can neither serve as a test nor be experienced as fun. Such a situation permits armed conflict to be replaced by a computer; and indeed this volume has already argued that one reason why low-intensity conflict is taking over from war and pushing the latter into complex environments is precisely because simpler ones are beginning to be dominated by computers.

Full-scale computerized warfare is still far away, whereas nuclear war will hopefully never take place at all. Under actual historical circumstances, the principal factor affecting the question of certainty has not been perfect information, nor the lack of a credible defense, but the relationship of strength to weakness. Now, armed forces represent large, complex, and multifaceted systems, and so, to a much greater extent, do the societies on which they rest. Their power is always made up of many elements, some of them operating in different and even conflicting directions. It is quite possible, and even normal, for an army to be strong in some ways and weak in others. What is more, perception and reality are seldom entirely consistent; very often what appears powerful on the surface is rotten underneath, and vice versa. Yet, despite all these reservations, there is no doubt that strength and weakness also represent absolute, tangible, realities. Some forces have numbers, leadership, organization, equipment, training, experience, and morale on their side and are consequently strong, whereas others that do not have those factors, or have them to a lesser extent, are correspondingly weak.

Here we are concerned with a situation where the relationship between strength and weakness is skewed; in other words, where one belligerent is *much* stronger than the other. Under such circumstances, the conduct of war can become problematic even as a matter of definition. Imagine a grown man who purposely kills a small child, even such a one as came at him knife in hand; such a man is almost certain to stand trial and be convicted, if not of murder then of some lesser crime. In the same way, legally speaking, the very existence of belligerence, war, and fighting already implies that the opponents should be of a broadly comparable nature. Not by accident is the word *bellum* itself said to come from *due-lum,* a combat of two. Where no symmetry exists, violence may still take place, even violence that is organized, purposeful, politically-motivated, and on a fairly large scale. However, usually the name such violence is given is not war but disturbance, uprising, or crime. These are accompanied by their opposite numbers, namely, repression, counterinsurgency, and police work.

In the world of strategy, several possibilities present themselves when one side is much stronger than the other. The weak party may declare *nolo contendere* and refuse to take up arms at all, as the Indian resistance movement under Mahatma Gandhi did. If the weak party does opt for violence, then logically two courses are open to him. Either he will take cover behind some natural or artificial obstacle, or else he will rely on surprise, cunning, ambush, and hit-and-run tactics. The one thing he almost certainly will not do is stand up in an open fight; then again, if he does fight—either out of his own free will, having miscalculated, or else because he is forced to—the outcome is not so much a battle as a massacre. Thus, in practice as well as in law, the very fact that fighting takes place almost always implies a degree of equality, real or perceived, between the forces available to both sides. Where no such equality exists war itself becomes ultimately impossible.

A war waged by the weak against the strong is dangerous by definition. Therefore, so long as the differential in force is not such as to render the situation altogether hopeless, it presents few difficulties beyond the tactical question, namely, how to inflict the maximum amount of damage on the enemy without exposing oneself in open fighting. By contrast, a war waged by the strong against the weak is problematic for that very reason. Given time, the fighting itself will cause the two sides to become more like each other, even to the point where opposites converge, merge, and change places. Weakness turns into strength, strength into weakness. The principal reason behind this phenomenon is that war represents perhaps the most imitative activity known to man. The whole secret of victory consists of trying to understand the enemy in order to outwit him. A mutual learning process ensues. Even as the struggle proceeds, both sides adapt their tactical methods, the means that they employ, and—most important of all— their morale to fit the opponent. Doing so, sooner or later the point will come where they are no longer distinguishable.

A small, weak force confronting a large, strong one will need very high fighting spirit to make up for its deficiencies in other fields. Still, since survival itself counts as no mean feat, that fighting spirit will feed on every victory, however minor. Conversely, a strong force fighting a weak one for any length of time is almost certain to suffer from a drop in morale, the reason being that nothing is more futile than a string of victories endlessly repeated. Conscious of the problem, such armies have often sought to compensate the troops by providing them with creature-comforts; one is reminded of the iced beer that was helicoptered to American units operating in the Vietnamese jungle and, a more absurd example still, the mobile banks that accompanied the Israelis into Lebanon. However, over the long run no amount of pampering can make up for the fact that fighting the weak demeans those who engage in it and, therefore, undermines its own purpose. He who loses out to the weak loses; he who triumphs over the weak also loses. In such an enterprise there can be neither profit nor honor. Provided only the exercise is repeated often enough, as surely as night follows day the point will come when enterprise collapses.

Another very important reason why, over time, the strong and the weak will come to resemble each other even to the point of changing places is rooted in the different ethical circumstances under which they operate. Necessity knows no bounds; hence he who is weak can afford to go to the greatest lengths, resort to the most underhand means, and commit every kind of atrocity without compromising his political support and, more important still, his own moral principles. Conversely, almost *anything* that the strong does or does not do is, in one sense, unnecessary and, therefore, cruel. For him, the only road to salvation is to win quickly in order to escape the worst consequences of his own cruelty; swift, ruthless brutality may well prove to be more merciful than prolonged restraint. A terrible end is better than endless terror and is certainly more effective. By way of an analogy, suppose a cat-and-mouse situation. Its very size precludes the mouse from tormenting the cat, though it *is* capable of driving him crazy—a different matter altogether. The cat, however, must kill the mouse at once. Should it fail to do so, then its very size and strength will cause its actions to be perceived as unnecessary; hence—had it been human—as cruel.

Since neither cat nor mouse can be said to have a moral consciousness, all this applies regardless of which side has objective justice on its side. More significant to our purpose, the question of right and wrong itself turns out to depend in large part on the balance of forces. From the Trojan War on, the legends which have been woven around historical fighting organizations such as the Army of Northern Virginia and the Afrika Korps provide eloquent testimony to the truth: it is not a just cause that makes for a good war but a good war that makes for a just cause, especially in retrospect. If Hector is the most humane and most attractive among the main Homeric characters—the only one, perhaps, who is never called by a harsh epithet—this is because, commanding the weak and foredoomed to defeat, he has to be so. In our own time, for every work written about Montgomery or Grant there are several about Rommel and Lee. A good war, like a good game, almost by definition is one fought against forces that are at least as strong as, or preferably stronger than, oneself.

Troops who do not believe their cause to be good will end up by refusing to fight. Since fighting the weak is sordid by definition, over time the effect of such a struggle is to put the strong into an intolerable position. Constantly provoked, they are damned if they do and damned if they don't. Should they fail to respond to persistent provocation, then their morale will probably break down, passive waiting being the most difficult game of all to play. Should they hit back, then the opponent's very weakness means that they will descend into cruelty and, since most people are not cut out to be sadists for very long, end up hating themselves. Self-hatred will easily lead to disintegration, mutiny, and surrender. People will burn their draft cards, flee the country, go to prison, take to drugs, even "frag" their own officers or commit suicide, anything to avoid the indignity that fighting the weak implies. Nor is the fate of those who *do* fight likely to be much better; returning from the "battlefield," they will find themselves treated as outcasts rather than as heroes. The results are inevitable. Often, as in Vietnam, to evacuate the field will be the sole alternative to complete collapse.

Since the very act of fighting the weak invites excess, in fact, *is* excess, it obliges the strong to impose controls in the form of laws, regulations, and rules of engagement. For example, Westmoreland's own headquarters drew up rules of engagement regarding tactical air strikes, artillery fire, and ground fire, that were issued to the troops upon their arrival in the country and then updated every six months. Operating in complex urban terrain, Israeli troops combating the *Intifada* have been subjected to even more complicated regulations. Arms may not be used except by explicit order under certain circumstances and against certain kinds of targets. Standing orders determine who may be hit, at what distance, and by what kind of bullet; theoretically, to react to a molotov cocktail thrown at one it is first necessary to open the book and consult the relevant paragraph. The net effect of such regulations is to demoralize the troops who are prevented from operating freely and using their initiative. They are contrary to sound command practice if they are observed and subversive of discipline if they are not. Hence the truth of Clausewitz's dictum, plainly observable in every low-intensity conflict fought since World War II, that regular troops combating a *Volkskrieg* are like robots to men.

A sword, plunged into salt water, will rust. How long it will take to do so depends on circumstances. A professional force, isolated from the rest of society, carefully trained and habituated to fighting as its life-blood, will probably stand up better than one that is made up of conscripts, particularly if the conscripts are changed every twelve months. Discipline, itself an attribute of professionalism, counts for a lot. Control over the channels of information, both internal and external, may also be useful up to a point. By carefully managing the news and exercising selective censorship it is possible to prevent the worst atroci-ties—to repeat, almost anything committed by the strong against the weak counts as an atrocity—from reaching the public at home. The time when that public will turn against the war and those responsible for it can be postponed, though not indefinitely. In the long run such controls will prove counterproductive as troops, civilians, and neutrals cease to believe what they are told. At that point, either they look for alternative information or start inventing it.

Perhaps the most important quality that a strong force engaged against a weaker one needs is self-control; and indeed the ability to withstand provocation without losing one's head, without overreacting and thereby playing into the enemy's hands, is itself the best possible measure of self-control. There must be a voluntary weakening, even disarming, of one's own forces in order to meet the opponent on approximately equal terms, much as the sporting fisherman uses rod and hook rather than relying on dynamite. A good case in point is provided by the British who have been fighting and taking casualties in Northern Ireland for the last twenty years. Now the war against the Irish Republican Army is very hard on the British troops and has not been without occasional excesses. Still, strict discipline and careful training—the characteristics of professionalism par excellence—have enabled the Royal Army to hold on quite well. Never at any point has it engaged in indiscriminate violence or meted out collective punishments, nor has it brought in heavy weapons. As a result, it has not alienated the bulk of the population. Since they are operating in a country that in one way or another has been experiencing trouble for eight centuries, the British may not be able to win, but at any rate they need not lose.

Where iron self-control is lacking, a strong force made to confront the weak for any length of time will violate its own regulations and commit crimes, some inadvertent and others not. Forced to lie in order to conceal its crimes, it will find the system of military justice under-mined, the process of command distorted, and a credibility gap open-ing up at its feet. In such a process there are neither heroes nor villains, but only victims: whom the gods want to destroy they first strike blind. So difficult to counteract are the processes just described that those caught in them may well *never* recover. In the end, the only way to revive a country's ability to wage war may be to tear down the existing armed forces and set up new ones in their stead, which in turn will probably require a political revolution of some kind.

An army that has suffered defeat at the hands of the strong may nourish its vengeance and wait for another opportunity. This is what the Prussians did after 1806, the French after 1871, and the Germans after 1918. However, once a force has been vanquished by the weak it will grow timid and wary of repeating its experience; and it will forever look for reasons why it should not fight again. Confronted by a real enemy—one who is as strong as, or stronger than, itself—a force grown accus-tomed to "fighting" the weak is almost certain to break and run, as the Argentinian Army did in the Falklands. Thus, it is probably no exagger-ation to say that, until the Gulf Crisis finally presented them with an opportunity that was too good to miss, the U.S. Armed Forces still had not put Vietnam behind them. Meanwhile, whether the armed forces of the Soviet State—following their failure in Afghanistan—will ever be able to fight another war outside their own borders is also doubt-ful. For the moment, it looks as if they are going to have their hands full trying to prevent their own society from disintegrating.

We have been dealing with "squishy" factors such as good and evil because, far from being divorced from warfare, ethics constitute its central core. On the whole, the relationship between strength and weakness and the moral dilemmas to which it gives rise probably represents the best explanation why, over the last few decades, modern armies on both sides of the ex-Iron Curtain have been so singularly ineffective combating low-intensity conflict. After all, colonial uprisings by definition were the business of the downtrodden and the weak. Often the insurgents were scarcely even considered human, being called by such names as gook (Vietnam), kafir (Rhodesia), or Arabush (Israel). Conversely, low-intensity conflict may well be regarded as the coming revenge of those people. Refusing to play the game according to the rules that "civilized" countries have established for their conve-nience, they developed their own form of war and began exporting it. Since the rules exist mainly in the mind, once broken they will not easily be restored. Though hardly a day passes anywhere in the world without some act of terrorism taking place, it appears that the process has only just begun, and the prospects for combating or even containing it are bleak.

Aside: Women

The best way to get at the heart of a problem is often indirect. To understand the nature of armed conflict, consider the part played—or not played—in it by the females of the species. Were war simply a rational instrument for the attainment of rational social ends, then the role of women should have been just as great as that of the men; after all they comprise half of humanity, and by no means its least important half. To the extent that war is indeed an instrument for increasing or safeguarding society's welfare, women's stake in it is no smaller than that of men. This is true in general, and also because defeat is likely to create a situation in which they, and their children, will be among the first victims.

Today and for some time past, the reason most often given for the nonparticipation of women in war is the fear that capture would lead to rape in addition to other kinds of maltreatment. This argument rests on a misunderstanding; it takes present-day distinctions between combatants and noncombatants for granted and projects them back into a past where they do not belong. During most of history, the opportunity to engage in wholesale rape was not just among the rewards of successful war but, from the soldier's point of view, one of the cardinal objectives for which he fought. For example, Homer in the *Illiad* narrates how the one thing that prevented the Achaeans from giving up and returning home was the prospect of "bedding one of the Trojan men's women." Already during antiquity, the fact that Alexander did not abuse Darius' captured womenfolk led people to suspect that he might be sexually abnormal. When Scipio Africanus refused to take a pretty captive who had been set aside for him the action was regarded as praiseworthy, slightly eccentric, and wholly exceptional. Most of their troops were less fastidious. As late as the fall of Magdeburg in 1631, "shrill shrieks" would rise from a captured city as a matter of course and regardless of whether the women had, or had not, participated in the actual fighting. The only way to prevent such a calamity was by timely surrender, but even then immunity was by no means certain.

The desire to spare women from being violated by the enemy did not, in any case, prevent them from participating in rebellions and insurrections of every kind. Now rebels differ from warriors in that they are criminals by definition; not coming under the war convention, they cannot expect mercy. As Argentinian women imprisoned by the military junta had reason to know, those who are labeled rebellious or subversive do not enjoy even the measure of protection, however restricted and however theoretical, normally afforded to prisoners of war. Yet from the Old Testament all the way down to the Spanish rebellion against Napoleon, rare has been the uprising in which women did not play a prominent, sometimes even a decisive, part. Nor did taking part cause them to put their sexuality aside; the story of Judith killing Holophernes after spending the night with him may be apocryphal, but it is also archetypical. Recent cases such as Algeria, Vietnam, and the Palestinian *Intifada* even suggest that the extent to which women are carried along by a popular uprising presents one very good indication of its prospective success. As they fought, suffered, and bled, the fortitude displayed by women was as great as, or greater than, that of the men.

The real or imagined differences between men and women have been the subject of a vast literature. Women have been accused of frivolity, garrulousness, quarrelsomeness, and jealousy, of having insatiable sexual appetites, and of "inner emptiness." From Seneca to Freud, and from Saint Paul to Erik Erikson, all these charges have found their way into whatever passed for serious literature at various times and places. During the last few decades, attempts have been made to put these allegations on a scientific basis. Numerous experiments have been made to demonstrate that women are less or more intelligent, less or more brave, less or more endowed with special qualities such as a propensity for mathematics, technical aptitude, spatial perception, or whatever seemed important at the moment. By and large, these attempts have failed. Looking back, one finds that most of the studies that did discover differences date from the fifties and sixties, whereas those that denied them were usually published in the seventies and eighties. Hence their results may owe more to prevailing social attitudes than to inherent validity.

The one point where the difference between the sexes is evident even without resort to scientific testing concerns average physical strength, especially in the upper body. Now war, before it is anything else, is the province of physical discomfort, deprivation, and danger; the sheer wear and tear is inconceivable to those who have not experienced it firsthand. Accordingly, the first qualities required by the combatant are strength and stamina, nor is it in vain that physical development forms a cardinal goal of any basic training program. It is true that some men are weaker than most women and a few women stronger than most men; still, no army in history has proceeded to match women with men in regard to bodily strength, using the results as a way to determine whom to enlist and whom to reject. When Socrates in *The Republic* suggested something of the kind, his ideas were met with incredulous ridicule. Had it been tried in practice, then no doubt it would have caused the men to rebel.

Women's relative physical weakness has not, in any case, prevented many societies from using them as beasts of burden in activities that are not war, and that do not involve them in competition with men. The Arab Middle East is not the only place where, even today, the wife can be seen carrying a heavy jar of water on her head while walking behind her husband who is riding a donkey. A standard accusation often made by Western propagandists during Cold War days was that, in Communist countries, women are allotted the most back-breaking physical labor such as agricultural planting, sweeping the streets, or—since these are shortage economies—shopping. The Communists' equally standard retort—one already found in Marx's own writings—was that, in the capitalist West, the money-masters are wont to treat women as commercial property, wage-slaves, or a combination of both. Nevertheless, the women of developed societies are considered lucky when compared to those of many developing ones, where they are made to do some of the heaviest work in addition to carrying their babies on their backs. On second thought, *are* they lucky?

Thus, neither the desire to exempt woman from heavy physical labor nor the need to protect her from rape can explain why, with a few esoteric exceptions to be discussed in a moment, they have seldom taken part in war. Apparently the real reason why women are excluded is not military but cultural and social. There are many animal species among whom the males—especially young males—are superfluous once the act of procreation has been performed; reflecting the hopes of women and the fears of men, there are numerous myths, both ancient and modern, suggesting that such might be the case among humans as well. Following this line of reasoning, it may not be an exaggeration to say—and indeed it has often been said—that much of human civilization is best understood as an attempt on the part of the males to sublimate their inability to produce the one most marvelous thing on earth. This interpretation may explain why, in every society known to us and as far back as we can look, most human achievements in religion, art, science, technology, etc. have been the product of men. By this I emphatically do *not* mean to say that women have contributed nothing important; rather that, as Margaret Mead points out, in most societies things are considered important because, and to the extent that, they are the province of men.

Conversely, the very fact that any given type of activity is done by women always causes it to be placed lower on the ladder of social prestige; as the famous double standard shows, this applies even to sex. In particular, woman's work hardly counts as work at all, with the result that it remains unpaid and does not figure in economic statistics. Thus, housekeeping is a function that is essential to any society and one that by reason of its variety and unpredictability requires much skill. Yet to call somebody a housewife almost amounts to an insult; in recent years the term has become so derogatory that it had to be replaced by euphemisms such as "homemaker." Similarly throughout history fields that were dominated by women, such as midwifery and the manufacture of cloth, were for that reason considered inferior. For example, in ancient Greece "carding wool" was synonymous with contemptible work. It was something that no self-respecting man would do except by way of punishment, and doing it was actually assigned to Heracles as one of the Twelve Labors undertaken to atone for a murder he had committed. Today the same still applies to professions such as nursing, teaching, and secretarial work; the last two used to be dominated by men and, so long as they were, enjoyed much higher status than they do today. In the Soviet Union, where 60 percent of all physicians are female, it also applies to medicine.

A field that is dominated by women by definition does not allow men to realize themselves as men—and indeed in any society the worst insult that can be directed at men is to call them "women." The entry of a few women into a field can act as an incentive; it may spur the men to work all the harder and perform all the better. However, there exists a critical point—say, 15 percent—beyond which a growing number of women present will cause the men to desert a field, any field, in favor of greener pastures. Men become bank executives whereas women, through no fault of their own, stay behind as tellers; women remain social workers while men become public welfare administrators. Discrimination starts the process, yet once it gets under way a vicious circle ensues. Since in any society women's work is ipso facto considered to be less valuable, over time the field in question will no longer be able to attract high-quality personnel. Unable to attract high quality personnel, the economic rewards that the field commands will decline. Declining economic rewards will cause social prestige to drop, and so on. Though in all circles of this kind cause and effect are notoriously difficult to separate, usually the direction in which they lead is clear enough. What is more, all this applies regardless of the work's intrinsic dignity; that is, whether it consists of sweeping the streets, operating typewriters, or teaching at a postgraduate school.

What applies to economic activities of any kind is even more true of war. In every human society that has practiced it, war has been the field in which sexual differences are most pronounced. Throughout history war has stood out as the most important male preserve by far; the one great occasion in which a display of manliness was considered absolutely essential for success and, accordingly, not just permitted but required and desired. The association between "man" and "warrior" is, indeed, so close that in many languages the two terms are interchangeable. For good or ill, to have women take part in war would have greatly diminished its social prestige, taken away its purpose, and destroyed its *raison d'être*. Had men been made to fight side by side with women, or else to confront them as enemies, then for them armed conflict would have lost its meaning and might well have come to an end.

Thus, the real reason why women do not participate in war is the same one that usually prevents mixed football teams from being formed. We are prepared to watch, even applaud, women's sports provided they are kept separate from those of the men and do not interfere with them. However, suppose some feminist-inspired, legislative assembly had pushed through a law obliging all professional football teams to reconstruct themselves on sexually integrated lines; the effect would have been to put the male players into an impossible dilemma, damning them if they hit the women and damning them if they did not. Rather than suffer the field to be littered with female bodies—or submitting to the even greater indignity of being beaten by a woman— most men would probably cease playing. Integration would it have led to the eclipse of the game. Nor, probably, would it have been long before another, still more violent, substitute was found.

Even the exceptions, the insurrections mentioned above, prove the rule. Where insurgents face a powerful, well-armed, military or police apparatus, the discrepancy in force is such that women can be allowed to participate in the insurgency without threatening the significance of what the men are doing. Once victory causes the relationship between strength and weakness to become less lopsided, however, the laws of ordinary life reassert themselves and women—again through no fault of their own—can expect to be cast out into the cold. A perfect case in point is provided by Palmach, the elite unit of volunteer youths that later formed the core of the Israel Defense Forces. Starting as a semi-clandestine organization under British rule, and backed by an egalitarian socialist ideology, Palmach was sexually integrated to an extent rarely attained by any other armed force before or since. Men and women worked together, trained together, lived together in adjacent tents, and even shared the same showers with only a sheet of galvanized iron to separate them. It was normal for women to accompany the men on missions, particularly on undercover missions that involved obtaining intelligence, transmitting messages, smuggling arms, and the like.

As the British left and Israel's War of Independence broke out, the forces emerged out of the underground and went into overt action. No sooner had the IDF been formally established than the winnowing-out process got under way, and any women fighters that remained existed almost entirely in Arab imagination. After the 1948 War, Israeli women, though still subject to the draft, were confined to traditional occupations as secretaries, telephone operators, social workers, and—as IDF folklore has it—brewers of tea; officers alone excepted, their highest aspiration was supposedly to be allowed to wear a red beret, fold parachutes, and be kissed by paratroopers as their reward. The impression given by press photographs of beautiful girls cleaning their weapons is, in this respect, misleading. The weapons-training that Israeli women are given in the army is almost entirely symbolic. Furthermore, a historical examination of the arms they *did* train with will show that they consisted either of weapons that had previously been discarded by the men, or were so plentiful as to be available even to females.

The October 1973 Arab-Israeli War was followed by a very great expansion in the size of the IDF, qualitative as well as quantitative, straining the available manpower pool and creating a demand for skilled operators in particular. Against this background, a renewed attempt was made to employ women in additional capacities. At first some women commanded men during basic training, or else instructed them in driving heavy self-propelled howitzers; later it was realized that they were better used as technicians, communicators, and operators of sophisticated equipment from computers to radar. On the whole they have done an excellent job, with the result that the increased presence of women at all ranks up to brigadier-general became evident from about 1980. However, the experiment has not been without its social cost. Not only were women given some of the worst jobs, but jobs have come to be considered undesirable because they are being done by women. The damage has been done. To be sure, only a combination of many different factors can account for the decline in the Israeli Army's social prestige and its growing difficulties in attracting first class manpower. However, the increased presence of women at all ranks is probably one of them.

Throughout history, there have been a few occasions when women disguised themselves as men and campaigned for months or even years. While on active service they proved themselves as brave as any men; yet discovery always led to dismissal at the hands of a male establishment that, for reasons that had nothing to do with the quality of the women's performance, felt embarrassed by their presence. These cases aside, apparently the only time women took part in combat overtly—during struggles other than insurrections—and on any scale, was in myth. The story of the Amazons (literally, "without breasts") is instructive. Supposedly, the Amazons were a nation of women-warriors who lived near the Black Sea on the fringes of civilization. Various legends tried to account for the way they perpetuated themselves from one generation to the next. The offspring were captured in battle, or else the women met with men once every year for the purpose of procreation; either way, the fate of young males was to be killed. Their characteristic weapon was the bow, which was considered the coward's arm. Amazons, moreover, by definition could not have courage, which in Greek is called *andreia* and which is derived from *aner,* man. It is thus clear that, legendary or not, the Amazons' status was in question. The one quality that is most essential to the warrior they could never have. As if to add offense to injury, to become warriors they had to give up sex and—according to one version—cut off their breasts, the organ marking them as women.

Women employed by the modern military are made to wear ties and cut their hair short. Jewelry, strong makeup, miniskirts, and deep necklines are forbidden as likely to cause tension among the male troops. In such armies whole volumes of regulations exist concerning all the things one may not do to one's female co-soldiers; reading this material, one might think rape is the one thing uppermost in every man's mind. For example, in the IDF it is (theoretically) a punishable offense for male and female soldiers to spend the night together. A commander must not subject his female subordinates to sexual harassment, which, strictly interpreted, means that he is expected to ignore the most prominent things about them. Women are provided with separate quarters that are out of bounds to men. A military physician may not examine female soldiers, nor a military policeman lay hands on them, unless precautions to eliminate potential sexual abuse are taken first. Other armies have sought to solve the problem in comparable ways, often to the detriment of military effectiveness; for example, by forbidding male enlisted men to date female officers (to avoid the appearance of sexual discrimination, *all* unofficial contact between officers and other ranks had to be prohibited). At the time when the U.S. Army first formed "mixed companies," there was even talk of providing the women with disposable cardboard penises to enable them to urinate standing in the field.

What makes all these precautions necessary is the fact that the military are social organizations. As with other organizations, but to a much greater extent, their ability to function depends on their cohesion. The best armed forces have ever been those which, even as they were staring death in the face, have known how to obliterate the distinction between "thou" and "I" in favor of "we." The imperative requirement that pleasure and pain be shared by the troops in common cuts right across the relationship between men and women, a relationship which, whether for biological or social reasons, is always private by nature. Many tribal societies have marriage arrangements that seem strange and complicated to us, including not just polygyny but polyandry and even limited wife-swapping within the extended family or clan. Moreover, polygyny has been carried over into many societies that are not primitive. Still, no human group ever appears to have practiced complete promiscuity nor to have treated men and women exactly alike. So fundamental is the clash between public requirements and private attachment that armies have often sought to turn their troops into quasi-eunuchs, forbidding them to marry and shaving off their most characteristic male attributes. Conversely, women's presence in the military can be tolerated only to the extent that they are dewomanized. Either they are turned into public property, that is, prostitutes, or else they must be treated like substitute men. This is a choice many of them find degrading, and no wonder.

To conclude, the treatment that women have always received and still receive at the hands of the military constitutes one powerful argument against the Clausewitzian view of war as a means to an end. Conversely, the fact that women *have* been able to enter numerous Western armed forces from the mid-seventies on should not be taken as a sign that relations between the sexes have changed or are changing. Only in Israel, a small nation that for many years struggled against far more numerous opponents, did the armed forces welcome extensive female participation, and even so that participation has been problematic in many ways. In every other case, it was not the requirements of national defense but feminist pressures that inspired legislation and forced women's entry into the military. Thus the forces themselves seem dimly aware that their own role as real-life fighting machines is coming to an end. At a time when their usefulness is being undermined by nuclear weapons on the one hand and low-intensity conflicts on the other, going to war is the last thing that most state-run armies can plan to do. Under such circumstances, the fact that they have been able, or compelled, to find a niche for women is best understood as both cause—albeit a relatively minor one—and symptom of their approaching demise.

The Strategic Straitjacket

In *Thirteen Pipes,* the Soviet writer Ilya Ehrenburg has a story ("Pipe Number Four") about two soldiers in World War I who are sent by their respective commanders to patrol no-man's land. Pierre, the Frenchman, is a smallish, sunburnt winegrower whose home is in Provence. Peter, the German, is a strapping, pale, potato-eating farmer originating in East Prussia. Pierre fights for "freedom, or iron, or coal, or the devil knows what." Peter also fights for "freedom, or iron, or coal, or the devil knows what." As they prepare to engage in hand-to-hand combat and kill each other, both think of their wives' breasts.

Seen from the point of view of the decision makers at the top, war may indeed be an instrument for attaining or defending political objectives, though close inquiry will almost certainly reveal that their supposed rationality is merely a thin veneer covering other, less conscious, motives. However this may be, probably in most wars ever waged the vast majority of combatants were not even aware of the exact nature of the political considerations for which they were supposed to be fighting. Had those considerations been understood; then again the link between them and whatever factors constitute an army's fighting power is never simple. The policy of an organized community is by no means always identical with the goals of the individuals comprising it. Only in the extreme case of war for existence do the interests of the community translate themselves directly into the lives of the individuals; even then, the overlap is not always absolute.

Other things being equal, the larger and more complex any war-making entity is, the less likely are the interests of the individual to coincide with those of the state; which is why writers such as Plato and Rousseau wanted to limit their ideal societies to the dimensions of a city-state. For example, at the time when the United States went to war in Vietnam, no Viet-Cong or North Vietnamese soldier had destroyed

American private property or injured any American person. Most G.I.'s probably did not understand the complicated chain of reasoning that led to the decision to intervene, even supposing—and this is not at all certain in retrospect—that there was something to understand. The state is a cold monster. Sending men to die in the interests of somebody or something else is not war but murder of the most obscene kind. The assumption that men will fight at the push of a button, merely because such is the state's "policy," represents the first seam in the straitjacket created by modern strategic thought.

Even if people initially do know what they are supposed to fight for, a drawn-out conflict all but guarantees that the original goals will be forgotten, and that means will take the place of ends. A perfect illustration of the way things work is provided by Alexander's campaigns. As they were setting out, the Macedonian peasants who made up his Army may have wondered what they were doing; in fact most non-Macedonian Greeks, apparently concluding that they were not doing anything in particular, chose to stay home. By the time the Army had crossed the Hellespont and was operating in enemy territory the question no longer mattered. Following their commander to the edges of the civilized world and beyond, the troops marched and fought not for this end or that but because fighting and marching had become the stuff of which their lives was made.

To judge by Arrian's narrative, Alexander himself was well aware that his efforts were, at bottom, divorced from any kind of "realistic" policy, and the further away from Macedonia he got the more true this became. Having smashed the Persian Empire and deposed Darius, time after time he is found attacking remote barbarian tribes, not because doing so was part of whatever plans he may have had but merely because they and their strongholds were reputed to be too strong to conquer. On reaching India, he was confronted with the fact that the troops had finally had enough and were clamoring to return home. He used every kind of argument to dissuade them, reeling off past accomplishments and promising future rewards in addition to those already given. Nothing worked, so he mustered his final plea: "Work," he argued, "so long as it is noble, is an end in itself." From Alexander's day to ours, the ten-year campaign of uninterrupted victories was destined to remain without parallel in history; yet once the question "what for" had been asked, it took only a few days for the campaign to end.

From this, the second seam in the strategic straitjacket ought to be evident. It consists of the belief that, since men supposedly fight in order to attain this end or that, whatever human feelings they may have are irrelevant to the business of war. Now Clausewitz himself went to great lengths to emphasize the importance of the emotional side of conflict; usually, however, the more "serious" any piece of modern strategic literature, the less it has to say about the most elemental human feelings. It is as if people by the mere act of donning uniform become calculating machines that are incapable of experiencing fun, love, sexual desire, comradeship, fear, anger, hatred, lust for revenge, or thirst for glory. For all-too-long the normal method has been to leave such things to psychology, sociology, anthropology, and a host of other disciplines. To the extent that their existence was acknowledged at all, they were gathered into a separate compartment that was then labeled "irrational" and put aside. One is reminded of the physicians in Molière's *Malade imaginaire* who were content if they could call a disease by some long latinate name.

Among the issues which the strategic view of war cannot encompass, perhaps the most important one is the role of women and everything pertaining to them. Throughout the 863 pages of the modern German edition of *vom Kriege,* women are not mentioned even once; reading it, one would never guess either that 50 percent of humanity consists of females, or that the author himself was happily married. From Clausewitz's day to ours, the strategic literature largely fails to mention women except as inferior substitutes for men. Yet in fact no interpretation of war—least of all future low-intensity war—can be even nearly complete unless it takes into account the various roles played by women, be it as instigators, cult-objects, cherished protégées, objectives, victims, workers, and fighters.

However, the significance of war to the relationship between the sexes goes even further than this. Just as men are unable to give birth, so armed conflict has always been the one field from which women have been most rigidly excluded. Just as men's need for women is at its greatest when the time comes to produce children, so women's need for men peaks when they require to be defended against other men; it is no accident that so many wars witness the lowering of ordinary standards of morality and are followed by baby-booms. Moreover, the words "in order to" distort the issue. Had war not existed, separating the sexes and making them attractive to each other, then probably it would have to be invented. Whatever one's view of the role women play in armed conflict, surely such matters are not unimportant. If, as seems to be the case, strategy cannot encompass them, then so much the worse for strategy.

The third major seam in the strategic straitjacket is the belief that, since war represents the use of the utmost violence to attain a social end, concepts such as morality, law, and justice only enter into it barely if at all. Now it is ancient wisdom that one person's poison is another person's meat; the ability to decide what does and does not constitute "objective" justice is vouchsafed to gods, not men. Still, it would be cynical as well as incorrect to assert that all causes are born equal. Some causes are undoubtedly more just than others, both in regard to their own nature and to the methods that are used to fight for them. Nor is it true that, provided only one has sufficient divisions at one's command, such considerations may be ignored with impunity. This is because most soldiers are not criminals; and indeed never in history have criminals made good soldiers.

When everything is said and done, troops will only be prepared to risk their lives if they feel, not merely in their brains but in the marrow of their bones, that their cause is just. Propaganda and terror can help determine what any one society at any one moment will consider to be just; propaganda and terror cannot sustain this feeling indefinitely, however, nor can they act as a substitute for it. An army that violates its own sense of justice for too long and in too flagrant a manner will end up by finding its fabric weakened even to the point of complete collapse. A war whose conduct fails to make a clear distinction between what is and is not permitted will degenerate into chaos and, ultimately, cease to be war at all. Perhaps more significant still, war itself provides as good a clue to justice as any that may be found. Whatever the goals for which it is fought, and whatever the methods it employs, no war can be just that does not rest on a rough balance of forces between the belligerents. Now it is true that such balances are complicated, and difficult to measure, and up to a certain point subjective; there are even cases when the true balance of forces can only be known after the struggle and as a result of it. Still, the fact that something is hard to define and to foresee does not mean that it does not exist or does not matter.

Since matching strength against weakness is unnecessary by definition, it is also wrong. As the ancient Chinese sage Lao Tsu points out, he who is *really* strong should be wise enough to avoid being caught in such a situation; and indeed the ability to do so constitutes the supreme test of excellence. Should circumstances beyond one's control (the wording itself already suggests weakness) cause a mismatch to arise nevertheless, then a swift, brutal solution may well be the best. Failing this, the longer the struggle the more doubtful its morality and the greater the problems it causes. Merely because an armed force finds itself in the false position of fighting the weak—or, more correctly, putting him down—it will commit crimes. If enough crimes have been committed, its entire structure will begin to disintegrate as excuses, accusations, and counteraccusations poison the public atmosphere. Though the process can be slowed down it cannot be stopped, nor can its outcome be avoided. That outcome, once again, consists of the troops refusing to fight.

The above discussion does not exhaust the list of modern strategic follies. One and all, they go back to the original sin: namely the idea that war consists of the members of one group killing those of another "in order to" achieve this objective or that. As I have pointed out, however, war does not begin where some people take the lives of others but at the point where they themselves are prepared to risk their own. Since it is absurd for a person to die for the interests of somebody or something else, the entire modern "professional" model of armed forces fighting for their "clients" is little better than a prescription for defeat. Since to die for one's own interests is almost equally absurd, there is a sense in which people will fight *only* to the extent that they experience war itself and everything pertaining to it as an end. Insofar as war, before it is anything else, consists of fighting—in other words, a voluntary coping with danger—it is the continuation not of politics but of sport. Precisely because it is instrumental by nature, strategic thought not only fails to tell us why people fight but prevents the question from being asked in the first place. Yet I can only repeat that, in any war whatsoever, this is the most important question of all. However strong an army may be in other respects, where fighting-spirit is lacking everything else is just a waste of time.

CHAPTER
VII

Future War

By Whom War Will Be Fought

As the second millennium A.D. is coming to an end, the state's attempt to monopolize violence in its own hands is faltering. Brought face to face with the threat of terrorism, the largest and mightiest empires that the world has ever known have suddenly begun falling into each other's arms. Should present trends continue, then the kind of war that is based on the division between government, army, and people seems to be on its way out. The rise of low-intensity conflict may, unless it can be quickly contained, end up destroying the state. Over the long run, the place of the state will be taken by warmaking organizations of a different type.

To understand the future, study the past. The state is a comparatively recent invention, and indeed its rise to dominance is one very good reason for calling ours the "modern" age. As the opening line of *The Prince* shows, even as late as Machiavelli's time the concept of the state was still sufficiently nebulous to require explanation. Throughout the sixteenth century wars continued to be made by principalities, republics, cities and coalitions of cities, religious leagues, and independent noblemen, to say nothing of robbers—both official and unofficial—operating on their own behalf. Hindsight allows us to perceive that this was a period when states were in the ascendant; yet it was not before the Treaty of Westphalia that they were able to exercise anything like a legal monopoly on the use of organized violence (the ideal of a de facto monopoly was, perhaps fortunately, never quite attained). Even so, the state was a purely Western conception whose writ initially ran across

192

no more than the approximately 3 percent of the earth's surface between Gibraltar and the Vistula. European colonies apart, in most parts of the world states only began making their appearance in the twentieth century.

The process by which states were created was part cause, part symptom, of the threefold distinction between government, army, and people. Over time it led to war being redefined as the province of the former two to the exclusion of the latter; between 1648 and 1939 written international law displayed a growing tendency to forbid persons who were not members of armed forces from participating in war (whatever the provocation), threatening them with dire punishment if they did. By the nineteenth century these distinctions had become so firmly established that adherence to them was being used as a touchstone for non-European countries that aspired to "civilized" status. Such were the Ottoman Empire, Persia, Thailand, China, and Japan, which in 1905 expressed its maturity by scrupulously adhering to the law of war as it then stood. Over time, of course, there have been innumerable cases of armies violating civilian rights and of civilians taking up arms against armies. Still, the use of the term "reprisal" in the one case and "uprising" in the other shows that the distinctions were usually honored even in the breach. They served as the foundation on which the whole of Western military practice, as well as Clausewitzian military thought codifying it, were built.

Just as the rise of civilians, armies, governments, and states was the result of specific historical circumstances, so another set of circumstances seems to have weakened those entities in the decades since 1945. A detailed discussion of those factors would require a separate book, but a few salient ones will be mentioned here. Most elementary is the fact that, over time, any kind of rivalry tends to play itself out. The "thirty years" war of 1914–1945 came at the end of three centuries of more or less intense interstate conflict. It seems to have convinced many people in the developed world that armed force can no more resolve differences between national states than the original Thirty Years' War was capable of resolving those between religious communities; and indeed this proposition has since been written into formal international law. After 1648 it was widely recognized that religious disputes could not be settled by force, causing Catholic Leagues and Protestant Alliances to cease fighting and disappear. Likewise, the state that has taken their place may be on its way to oblivion, both because its ability to fight organizations similar to itself is increasingly in doubt, and because there is not much point in being loyal to an organization that does not, cannot, and will not fight.

The outstanding factor responsible for this situation is, of course, the spread of nuclear weapons. From Central Europe to Kashmir, and from the Middle East to Korea, nuclear weapons are making it impossible for large sovereign territorial units, or states, to fight each other in earnest without running the risk of mutual suicide. This point is not new. The first to suggest that "close intermingling with the enemy" represented the best hope conventional forces had of avoiding nuclear destruction were the "tactical nuclear warfighting" theorists of the late 1950s who were concerned with the use of atomic artillery and short-range missiles. Their analysis was correct but, seen in retrospect, did not go far enough. The unlimited range of modern delivery vehicles; their ability to reach any point in enemy territory; the sheer power of the nuclear warheads that they carry; and the absence of an effective defense—all of these are well on the way to rendering national frontiers meaningless. If fighting is to take place at all, then not only the armed forces but the political communities on whose behalf they operate will have to become intermingled. If and when such intermingling takes place, it is very likely that the forces fielded by these communities will no longer be of the conventional kind. Under such circumstances the distinction between armed forces and civilians (both those at the bottom and those at the top) will probably break down in the same way as it did, say, during many of the wars between 1338 and 1648.

If states are decreasingly able to fight each other, then the concept of intermingling already points to the rise of low-intensity conflict as an alternative. The very essence of such conflict consists in that it circumvents and undermines the trinitarian structure of the modern state, which is why that state in many ways is singularly ill-suited for dealing with this kind of war. On the whole, the best that developed countries—from Britain in Northern Ireland to Italy, (and, most recently, the Eastern Bloc from Yugoslavia to Uzbekistan)—have been able to do is to contain terrorism. A degree of violent activity that even as late as the 1960s would have been considered outrageous is now accepted as an inevitable hazard of modern life, so much so that the casualty rate is often compared to that caused by traffic accidents. Moreover, low-intensity conflict is fast becoming a first-class export commodity of developing countries with little else to sell. Throughout the Third World, numerous new states have never been able to establish themselves vis-à-vis other kinds of social entities, including ethnic tribes in particular. In the face of their quarrels, the distinction between government, army, and people began to fall apart before it had even been properly established.

The fact that makes this scenario all the more credible is, once again, that war represents perhaps the most imitative activity known to man. Strategy is interactive by definition; any attempt to defeat the enemy that involves outwitting and deceiving him must be preceded by an endeavor to understand him. From the time that the Romans took to the sea and Hannibal equipped his men with captured Roman weapons, the outcome of any drawn-out conflict has always been a mutual learning process. Belligerents who were originally very dissimilar will come to resemble each other first in point of the methods that they use and then, gradually, other respects. As this happens, provided only the struggle lasts long enough, the point will come where the reasons for which they originally went to war are forgotten. One need not share Hegel's view concerning the primacy of war in human affairs to agree that one important way by which human societies of any kind develop their internal structure has always been through fighting other societies. After all, no community illustrates this fact better than the modern nation-state itself, an organization that acquired its characteristic institutions—including specifically the armed forces and their separation from government and people—partly through the need to fight similar organizations.

Doubtless the process by which the state will lose its monopoly over armed violence in favor of a different kind of organization will be gradual, uneven, and spasmodic. Things will happen at a different pace in different parts of the world. Most likely, disintegration will be accompanied by violent upheavals similar to those which, in Europe, began during the Reformation and culminated in the Thirty Years' War. Probably the first to be affected will be states in Asia, Africa, the Caribbean, and Latin America, and indeed some would say that in many of them the process is already well under way. Next on the list are large, heterogeneous empires such as the Soviet Union (including some of the other Warsaw Pact members), in which, once again, the process has already begun. China and India are also likely candidates. Both countries are afflicted by an expanding population that makes it almost impossible for them to solve their economic problems. Both contain powerful centrifugal forces that are making their influence felt, as well as entire peoples whose memories of former political independence, even greatness, have by no means been erased. Given a suitable opportunity, they are increasingly certain to have a go at breaking away.

The United States is another large, multiracial society where weapons are widely available and that has a tradition of internal violence second to none. During most of its history, abundant natural resources, an open frontier, and—later—global expansion enabled Americans to raise their standards of living. As they did so, from time to time they fought a war in which their aggressions found an outlet. However, none of the three factors any longer exists. The frontier was closed long ago. America's economic viability has been on the decline since about 1970. Partly as a result, so has its ability to dominate the rest of the world, a process that not even the victory over Iraq is likely to halt. As Americans found it took running faster and faster just to stay in place, social tensions have mounted and so has escapism—the use of drugs; President Reagan described it as "our number one war." America's current economic decline must be halted; or else one day the crime that is rampant in the streets of New York and Washington, D.C., may develop into low-intensity conflict by coalescing along racial, religious, social, and political lines, and run completely out of control.

If only because they have strong traditions to fall back on, some of the oldest states, particularly Japan and those of Western Europe, may be able to hold out the longest. Japan is particularly fortunate because it is isolated, exceptionally homogeneous, and presently rich; yet even today Japanese politicians shudder at the possibility that "huddled, teeming, masses" from poor countries in the region may start arriving on their shores. West European states are likely to see their sovereignty undermined as much from above, at the hands of international organizations, as from below. Should Europe be united, then whatever form its organization assumes almost certainly will not resemble a "state" as the term is understood today. A continent-wide community whose sole purpose in life is to increase per-capita income and the Gross National Product will hardly be able to count on people's undivided loyalty. Integration will probably strengthen regional pressures for independence on the part of Basques, Corsicans, Scots, and a host of other peoples; the first to succeed will act as a battering-ram for the rest. Not all these movements will employ violence to gain their ends. Still, and also in view of the growing numbers of resident, non-European, non-Christian people, in the long run the possibility exists that low-intensity conflict will break out and sweep over at least part of the continent.

What will the community be like that may one day take the place of the state as the principal warmaking entity? Considering our knowledge of mankind's history, there are plenty of candidates to choose from. In the past, war has been made by tribal societies such as existed from prehistoric times until recently; city states of the kind that were common in the ancient world and also in late-medieval and early modern Europe;

royal despotisms such as the ancient Assyrian, Persian, Hellenistic, and Roman Empires; feudal social structures such as were at one time dominant in both Europe and Japan; religious associations seeking to establish the glory of this god or that; private mercenary bands commanded by warlords; and even commercial organizations such as the British East India Company and its opposite numbers in other countries. Many of these entities were neither "political" (politics being inextricably mixed up with a host of other factors) nor in possession of "sovereignty" (a sixteenth-century term). They did not have armed forces or, by implication, governments and peoples in our sense of those terms. Nevertheless they *did* engage in purposeful, organized, large-scale violence, or war.

No more than Froissart could foresee the end of the feudal political system and its replacement by the modern one that is based on states, can we today foresee what kind of new order will arise after the latter's collapse. However, since *none* of perhaps two dozen armed conflicts now being fought all over the world involves a state on both sides we may offer an educated guess. In most of Africa the entities by which the wars in question are waged resemble tribes—indeed they *are* tribes, or whatever is left of them under the corrosive influence of modern civilization. In parts of Asia and Latin America the best analogy may be the robber barons who infested Europe during the early modern period, or else the vast feudal organizations that warred against each other in sixteenth-century Japan. In North America and Western Europe future warmaking entities will probably resemble the Assassins, the group which, motivated by religious and allegedly supporting itself on drugs, terrorized the medieval Middle East for two centuries.

In the future, war will not be waged by armies but by groups whom we today call terrorists, guerrillas, bandits, and robbers, but who will undoubtedly hit on more formal titles to describe themselves. Their organizations are likely to be constructed on charismatic lines rather than institutional ones, and to be motivated less by "professionalism" than by fanatical, ideologically-based, loyalties. While clearly subject to some kind of leadership with coercive powers at its disposal, that leadership will be hardly distinguishable from the organization as a whole; hence it will bear greater similarity to "The Old Man of the Mountains" than to institutionalized government as the modern world has come to understand that term. While rooted in a "population base" of some sort, that population probably will not be clearly separable either from its immediate neighbors or from those, always the minority, by whom most of the active fighting is done. A warmaking entity of any size will have to be "in control" of a territorial base of some sort. However, that base is unlikely to be either continuous, impenetrable, or very large. Probably its frontiers—itself a modern term—will not be marked by a clear line on a map. Instead there will be the occasional roadblock cropping up at unexpected places, manned by ruffians out to line their own pockets as well as those of their bosses.

The most important single demand that any political community must meet is the demand for protection. A community which cannot safeguard the lives of its members, subjects, citizens, comrades, brothers, or whatever they are called is unlikely either to command their loyalty or to survive for very long. The opposite is also correct: any community able and, more importantly, willing to exert itself to protect its members will be able to call on those members' loyalty even to the point where they are prepared to die for it. The rise of the modern state is explicable largely in terms of its military effectiveness vis-à-vis other warmaking organizations. If, as seems to be the case, that state cannot defend itself effectively against internal or external low-intensity conflict, then clearly it does not have a future in front of it. If the state does take on such conflict in earnest then it will have to win quickly and decisively. Alternatively, the process of fighting itself will undermine the state's foundations—and indeed the fear of initiating this process has been a major factor behind the reluctance of many Western countries in particular to come to grips with terrorism. This is certainly not an imaginary scenario; even today in many places around the world, the dice are on the table and the game is already well under way.

What War Will Be All About

To understand the future, study the past. People are often prepared to violate the law or else bend it to suit their purposes, nor is this phenomenon limited to the military. However, the very fact that the law can be bent itself entails the existence of the law—in our case, of fairly clear ideas as to who may use violence against whom, for what ends, under what circumstances, in what ways, and by what means. Thus there is no doubt that the war convention represents a tangible reality. Like all human creations it is rooted in history, and hence liable to change. While no one can foresee the future, it is at least possible to indicate a few of the directions that change is likely to take.

As the conduct of war is taken over by organizations other than the state, the military-political leaders responsible for its conduct will lose their privileged position. Our present-day separation between the warmaking political entity and its ruler or rulers did not always apply in the same form. Among tribal societies, and indeed throughout ancient and medieval times, killing the enemy leader represented the best possible method of winning a war. For example, the Persians after the battle of Cunaxa first invited the Greek leaders to a banquet and then cut them down in the hope of obtaining the surrender of the Ten Thousand. Alexander at Gaugemela went straight for Darius (the fact that the "Great King," as the Greeks called him, also acted as commander in chief of his field army and fought in the front ranks merely confirms our point) in the well-founded hope that on him alone depended the cohesion of the Persian forces. In Rome, a soldier who killed the enemy commander was rewarded with the *spolia opima*. King Harald's death at Hastings was accidental but brought about the disintegration of his army. As late as Machiavelli's time, killing enemy leaders in battle or by treachery constituted a normal method in the conduct of international affairs. If Lucretia Borgia became notorious for poisoning her enemies, then probably this was less because the methods she used were exceptional than because she was a woman.

The decisive moment when "state" and "government" became separated from each other took place during the second half of the sixteenth century. The demise of feudalism and the incipient rise of the modern bureaucratic state led to a situation where most rulers ceased to exercise direct command over their armies, and also ceased fighting in person. Though there were always exceptions to the rule—Napoleon being the greatest and also one of the last—the majority now waged war without ever leaving their palaces, choosing to transmit their authority by means of ministers of war, commanders in chief, and field commanders. Unlike their medieval predecessors, these subordinate figures were merely servants of the state. They were not supposed to be fighting on their own personal interest and were, in any case, capable of being replaced at the sovereign's whim. Over time they developed a set of common interests and also a code of behavior that spread across nationalities, frontiers, and even fronts. Making war *ad hominem* no longer made sense.

This, too, was the age when the principle of legitimate rule was becoming widely recognized. With continuity assured, killing, imprisoning, or otherwise molesting those responsible for the conduct of war at the top no longer served a useful purpose. Consequently it was abandoned, and its abandonment enshrined in the war convention; that is, in international law and the public ideas concerning morality on which it rests. Vattel regarded it as a sign of progressing civilization that, by the mid-eighteenth century, the sovereigns of belligerent states were addressing each other as *monsieur mon frère*. Ferdinand of Brunswick, commanding the Hanoverian Army during the Seven Years' War, on one occasion had a captured telescope returned to its owner, the French commander Saint Germain. When Napoleon besieged Vienna in 1809, his artillerymen directed their fire away from Schonbrunn Palace where Princess Marie-Louise (the future Empress) was known to be lying ill; his own subsequent exile to Saint Helena was much criticized at the time. By the late nineteenth century, rulers such as Napoleon III who did become prisoners were considered a political embarrassment, to be got rid off as soon as possible.

Even during the period of total war from 1914 to 1945 apparently only two operations were mounted whose goal was to kill a specific enemy general, and both were launched in World War II. One was aimed at Erwin Rommel, the Afrika Korps commander whose reputation in 1942 had risen so high that his very name had a demoralizing effect on the British in the Western Desert. The other was organized by the Germans during the Battle of the Bulge and targeted Eisenhower, who for a week or two was accompanied by bodyguards even when he went to wash his hands. Both operations miscarried. Had they succeeded, then they would have been a clear violation of the war convention as it then stood; the members of Colonel Skorzeny's Brandenburger Regiment who had the misfortune to be captured while wearing American uniforms were, in fact, executed. Meanwhile there is no evidence that Hitler and Stalin, by common consent two of the worst scoundrels who ever lived, attempted to assassinate each other or their colleagues in other countries.

As the twentieth century draws to a close, the process seems about to switch into reverse gear. If low-intensity conflict continues to spread, then the place of bureaucratic warmaking organizations will be taken by such groups as are constructed on personal and charismatic lines. This will cause present-day distinctions between leaders and the political entities that they head to disappear or become blurred. Reflecting the new realities, the war convention will change. Over the last three centuries or so attempts to assassinate or otherwise incapacitate leaders were not regarded as part of the game of war. In the future there will be a tendency to regard such leaders as criminals who richly deserve the worst fate that can be inflicted on them. With political and personal factors becoming intermingled in the new forms of organization, neither the leaders' families nor their private property can expect to enjoy immunity. Instead they will be subject to attack, or the threat of attack, as a means of bringing pressure to bear. Hence, many leaders will probably decide to remain unattached and lead a semi-nomadic, semi-underground life, as Yasser Arafat already does.

As a matter of cold fact, leaders *are* increasingly being targeted. As long ago as 1956 the French captured a Moroccan passenger plane carrying the entire FLN leadership. This was the sort of coup that would have been inconceivable in any kind of war except counterinsurgency. At the time it was considered so contrary to the prevailing war convention that the orders to carry it out are said to have been destroyed. Since then such things have become almost commonplace, particularly in places like Lebanon, Afghanistan, and Latin America, where assassinating or kidnapping the opposing leader is as much a normal method of war today as it was during the Italian Renaissance. Nor is the method confined to "uncivilized" countries. The Israelis in 1981 tried to repeat the French operation, but against the PLO leadership, forcing down a Syrian passenger aircraft in mid-route but failing to find the persons they were after. The Americans in 1986 bombed Tripoli in an apparent attempt to get a Muamar Ghadafi; they missed him, but some members of his family were killed. Again, in 1989 the Israelis successfully kidnapped three leaders of the Pro-Iranian Hizbulla organization in Lebanon, thus proving that he who fights terrorists for any period of time is likely to become one himself.

From the White House to 10 Downing Street, even the most casual tourist cannot fail to notice the change in attitudes that has taken place. Presidents and prime ministers who not so long ago used to live almost without protection now admit to difficulty in protecting their own lives, let alone those of the citizens for whom they are responsible. They are surrounding themselves with elaborate barricades and turning their residences into fortresses. Those who man the defenses are not military personnel, nor do they even look like soldiers. They do not necessarily wear uniform, let alone skirts. The weapons that they carry are not openly displayed. Many of the most visible defenses are, in fact, little but a facade designed to warn the curious and deter the amateur terrorist. Meanwhile the real work of affording protection is carried out unobtrusively by members of the various secret services, another indication of far-reaching changes in trinitarian organization to come.

The switch from established to emerging forms is equally likely to affect the war convention in regard to the treatment of rank-and-file prisoners, wounded, and the like. Conventional international law as it developed from Hugo Grotius on looked at soldiers as the "instruments" of the state. Insofar as they served the interests of the state rather than their own, there was a growing tendency to regard wounded, prisoners, and other types of personnel rendered temporarily helpless as victims of war; whatever the victors' practical behavior, in law the problem was to afford protection against "unnecessary" evil. However, modern organizations responsible for waging low-intensity conflict are usually incapable of coercing their members in the same way states do. To the extent that they do employ coercion, the state does not regard it as legitimate. Hence it is difficult to sustain the idea that enemy troops are merely doing their "duty" (to quote Vattel again) as obedient tools in the hands of the organization to which they belong.

Whereas enemy leaders who fight for an ideological cause presumably cannot be influenced in their loyalties and must be imprisoned or killed, future rank and file prisoners are likely to be treated as minor criminals. A good indication of things to come was the so-called "chieu hoi" program in Vietnam, by which captured Viet Cong were offered the opportunity to "rally" and switch sides. A practice that was considered perfectly normal during much of history will thus be revived. Prisoners who accept the offer will be classified "innocent" or "misled" and trusted within limits. Refusal will be taken as proof of guilt and followed by harsh reprisals, including death. No doubt one factor that will determine the outcome in individual cases will be the amount of duress applied. Once again, there is nothing here that has not already happened a thousand times in countless low-intensity conflicts since 1945. Such conflict is indeed the wave of the future, if present events are any indication.

A third area where significant changes are likely concerns the distinction between soldiers and civilians. Apart from the "total war" that was waged in World War II, most conventional wars over the last three centuries have been directed against soldiers. Even in World War II the distinction was preserved to the extent that the most important Axis leaders held responsible for violating it were brought to justice. On the Allied side, while there were no comparable trials, the men who through strategic bombing incinerated hundreds of thousands of Axis civilians—Marshal Harris' Bomber Command—were not considered fit to receive a campaign medal as most others did. As the spread of low-intensity conflict causes trinitarian structures to come tumbling down, however, strategy will focus on obliterating the existing line between those who fight and those who watch, pay, and suffer. Hence probably the existing war convention will go by the board in this respect as well.

Organizations waging low-intensity conflict will, almost by definition, be unable to control large, contiguous pieces of territory any more
than medieval and early modern governments did. The difference
between "front" and "rear"—both of them comparatively recent terms
inseparable from the modern state—will progressively break down.
Under such circumstances war will become a much more direct experience for most civilians, even to the point where the term itself may be
abolished, or its meaning altered. War will affect people of all ages and
both sexes. They will be affected not just accidentally or incidentally or
anonymously from afar, as in the case of strategic bombing, but as
immediate participants, targets, and victims. Practices that for three
centuries have been considered uncivilized, such as capturing civilians
and even entire communities for ransom, are almost certain to make a
comeback. Indeed in many countries infested with low-intensity conflict they already *have* made a comeback, and in some they had never
really been abandoned.

A seldom-asked question concerns the war conventions' attitude to
cultural monuments, works of art, churches, and the like. The existing
belief-system, enshrined in international law, regards them as deserving
protection as far as military necessity permits. However, future low-
intensity conflict is likely to take a different attitude. Cultural monuments and works of art are irrelevant to war only insofar as they are
produced by politically insignificant individuals and groups inside the
state. It is the essence of low-intensity conflict that it drives down the
threshold of "political significance," so to speak, from the level of the
state to that of the organizations, groups, and individuals that comprise
the state. Where people as people are politically significant, their scientific and artistic productions are unlikely to be accorded even the
limited amount of respect they now receive. To recall a historical
precedent, when Lord Cumberland "pacified" Scotland in the mid-
eighteenth century he made a point of killing pipers and destroying
their bagpipes, arguing that they were weapons of war.

Again, the sanctity of churches and other religious shrines is easily
observed when the prevailing secular system of belief indicates that they
are of no political significance, indeed that religion itself insofar as its
effect on war is concerned is mere superstition. Such, however, may not
be the view of future generations. One has only to consult the Bible to
discover that during much of history religious institutions not only
failed to enjoy immunity but were considered to be prime targets.
Capturing the enemy's religious symbols constituted the high road to
victory, whereas their loss was considered both cause and proof of

defeat. It is not so long ago since, even in the enlightened West, the first thing a Protestant force did to a captured city was to drive out the bishops, smash the statues, cleanse the churches (also of their plate), and hold a thanksgiving service to the Lord in whose name all these praiseworthy acts had been committed. Low-intensity conflict being less institutionalized than conventional war, probably the emphasis it puts on symbolic objectives will be greater. The true, the beautiful, and the sacred will be its first victims.

Additional developments are on the horizon. Most people tend to take the distinction between private and public property for granted; in fact, however, it is in many ways a product of the modern trinitarian state, even to the point that Jean Bodin in the sixteenth century conceived of the state specifically in order that it should distinguish between the two. A future dominated by low-intensity conflict is unlikely to observe the distinction, even in theory, any more than the medieval *guerre guerroyante* did. Future low-intensity conflict is also likely to make increased use of weapons that are prohibited today, such as gas, the reason being that they are cheap, easy to manufacture, and well-suited for use in closed, urban spaces. All this is closely linked up with the central point that has been made before but will bear repetition. Once the legal monopoly of armed force, long claimed by the state, is wrested out of its hands, existing distinctions between war and crime will break down much as is already the case today in places such as Lebanon, Sri Lanka, El Salvador, Peru, or Colombia. Often, crime will be disguised as war, whereas in other cases war itself will be treated as if waging it were a crime.

This is not to say that, as low-intensity conflict replaces conventional war, all restraints will go by the board. Previously I have argued that the conduct of war without a war convention, in other words without a set of clear and widely shared ideas as to what it is all about, is impossible in the long run. Terrorists have the strongest possible motive to distinguish themselves from mere murderers; after all, in the not unlikely case of capture, their fate depends on it. Nor is it necessarily true that terrorists, or even criminals, are less scrupulous than most of us. Few groups spent as much time agonizing over who might and might not be killed "for the cause" than the well-educated young people who formed terrorist movements in turn-of-the-century Tsarist Russia. Though relations among Mafia *padroni* often bore an uncanny similarity to international warfare, they made a point of not targeting each other's wives and children. Practical experience as well as theoretical considerations point to the conclusion that the demise of the old distinctions will not result in complete anarchy. Over time a different war convention will emerge, possibly one that is based on distinctions between the "guilty" and the "innocent." Though errors, differences in interpretation, and deliberate transgressions will cause the new convention to be as leaky as the old, this is not the same as saying that it will not exist or will not matter.

At any given time and place, prevailing ideas concerning who may do what in war, to whom, for what purposes, under what circumstances, and by what means constitute a broad reflection of that society's culture, structure, and warmaking institutions. The really important point is less trying to guess what the future will be like than trying to grasp the vital role played by the war convention even at present. An armed force that violates the war convention for very long will disintegrate. This will be all the more the case if it is powerful, hence unable to convince others— and itself—of the imperative need for it to break the rules. On the other hand, the convention is subject to change through time and space. Therefore, nothing is less conducive to the successful waging of armed conflict than to take the existing convention for granted. A system of thought that ignores the war convention altogether, like *vom Kriege* and its successors, cannot fail to misrepresent the nature of armed conflict.

How War Will Be Fought

Like a man who has been shot in the head but still manages to stagger forward a few paces, conventional war may be at its last gasp. As low-intensity conflict rises to dominance, much of what has passed for strategy during the last two centuries will be proven useless. The shift from conventional war to low-intensity conflict will cause many of today's weapons systems, including specifically those that are most most powerful and most advanced, to be assigned to the scrap-heap. Very likely it also will put an end to large-scale military-technological research and development as we understand it today.

Strategy as defined in this volume is eternal, applicable wherever and whenever wars are fought and not just deterred. For war to be waged, armed force has to be created. Once created, uncertainty, friction, and inflexibility will appear and must be coped with. Meanwhile, decisions also have to be made regarding the use of force not only in the abstract but against a living, reacting enemy. All this is true regardless of the scale of the conflict and also of the medium in which it takes place, whether land, sea, air, or outer space. It is also true regardless of the weapons used, unless we have a situation where uncertainty can be eliminated, the enemy's reaction ignored, and a war won by means of a single mighty blow. That is why nuclear strategy is not strategy at all. This case apart, nothing is more characteristic of strategy than its mutual, interactive character. In this respect it is one and the same regardless of location, means, and purpose, even of whether it is war or some competitive game that we are talking about.

By contrast, classical strategy, as understood by Jomini, Clausewitz, and most later prophets of conventional war, is the product of specific periods and circumstances. The art of "using battles in order to achieve the objectives of the war" presumes that the two sides have considerable armed forces and that those forces are distinguishable from each other, separated by geography, and at least potentially mobile. It also implies that the range of their weapons is not unlimited, another assumption that is being rendered increasingly questionable. In addition, there is a whole series of actors and concepts that conventional strategy takes for granted and that form the tools of its trade. They include large territorial units, battles as distinct from campaigns on the one hand and skirmishes on the other, fronts, rear areas, "strategic depth," bases, objectives, and lines of communication, to mention but a few. Now it does not take more than a cursory reading of military history—preferably in the original language and not in some modern translation—to discover that neither the concepts nor the factors are self-evident or eternal. Which of course is precisely why the term strategy itself, though derived from ancient Greek, only came into use late in the eighteenth century.

As a matter of fact, the application of strategy in its classical sense to low-intensity conflict has always been problematic. Even as Jomini wrote his *Précis des grandes operations de guerre,* Spanish guerrillas were showing that it was perfectly possible to wage war—and a very savage war at that—on a small scale. Many of those involved were illiterate peasants as well as women, children, and priests. Probably they had never even heard of strategy, which, as Tolstoy points out in *War and Peace,* was a newfangled notion with a sophisticated ring to it. Confronted by the most powerful conventional armed forces that the world had ever seen, the insurgents made do without "armies," campaigns, battles, bases, objectives, external and internal lines, *points d'appui,* or even territorial units clearly separated by a line on a map.

Though guerrilla warfare has not always been successful, from that day to ours the lesson that strategy is irrelevant to it has been repeated a thousand times. Mao spoke of guerrillas as fish swimming in the "sea" of the surrounding population, the point of the analogy being precisely that the sea does not have features that distinguish one part from another. Similarly in Vietnam, the Americans discovered that strategy, as taught at staff and war colleges, was inadequate for understanding "a war without fronts," let alone for successfully waging it. Seen in this light, the geographical bias of strategy, as understood from Jomini through Moltke to Liddell Hart, stands out clearly; which also explains why the latter in particular does not cite a single example from the Middle Ages, when warfare in many ways resembled modern low-intensity conflict. In short, such conflict is to conventional warfare what the Einsteinian world-view is to the Newtonian.

If low-intensity conflict is indeed the wave of the future, then strategy in the classical sense will disappear—indeed many would say that already today it is little more than an exercise in make-believe whose relevance is limited to the war games played by general staffs. Like the domain to which it belongs—conventional war—strategy has been caught in a vise between nuclear weapons on the one hand and low-intensity conflict on the other. Nuclear weapons work against geographical distinctions of any kind: in the future, if armed forces—and, most probably, the political units by whom they are fielded—are to survive and fight in earnest, they will have to become intermingled with each other and with the civilian population. Low-intensity conflict will ensure that, once they are intermingled, battles will be replaced by skirmishes, bombings, and massacres. The place of lines of communications will be taken by short, convert approaches of a temporary nature. Bases will be replaced by hideouts and dumps, large geographical objectives by the kind of population-control that is achieved by a mixture of propaganda and terror.

The spread of sporadic small-scale war will cause regular armed forces themselves to change form, shrink in size, and wither away. As they do, much of the day-to-day burden of defending society against he threat of low-intensity conflict will be transferred to the booming security business; and indeed the time may come when the organizations that comprise that business will, like the *condottieri* of old, take over the state. Meanwhile, and as has already happened in Lebanon and in many other countries, the need to combat low-intensity conflict will cause regular forces to degenerate into police forces or, in case the struggle lasts for very long, mere armed gangs. Though most present-day militia still put on something resembling a uniform when it suits their purpose, over time uniforms will probably be replaced by mere insignia in the shape of sashes, armbands, and the like. Their wearers will not amount to armies as we understand the term.

Again, a special chapter in the conduct of future war is formed by the weapons it will employ. The invention of strategy late in the eighteenth century took place at the very time when the crew-operated weapons that had long dominated siege-warfare were also beginning to govern operations in the field. Though this coincidence is seldom noted, it is probably not accidental. From the mid-nineteenth century on, the trend away from individual weapons and toward large, crew-operated ones has been one of the dominant themes of modern warfare. The majority were designed principally for use against each other *en rase campagne,* as the saying went. Many of the most powerful, such as tanks, are really unsuitable for anything else; where people and their dwellings are present—in other words, where there is something to fight *about*—they only become entangled. Alternatively, the purpose of many of the most powerful weapons has been to attack objectives deep in the rear. In the case of heavy bombers and ballistic missiles, their inability to pinpoint targets meant that they could only be used when no friendly forces were expected to be within a radius of many miles.

Today, even third-rate powers are acquiring weapons whose reach is practically unlimited, and that are able to reach any point in the territory of any conceivable enemy. Based on recent advances in electronics, other weapons are sufficiently powerful to drench the battlefield in fire and also to blast a concentrated opposition to smithereens. However, most systems—including in particular heavy artillery, missiles, and aircraft—still are not sufficiently accurate to make much of an impression on any enemy who is extremely dispersed, or indistinguishable from the civilian environment, or intermingled with friendly forces. Because of this fact, intermingling with enemy forces, mixing with the civilian population, and extreme dispersion have become the normal practice in low-intensity conflicts. If countless instances from Vietnam to Nicaragua and from Lebanon to Afghanistan have any lesson to offer, surely it is that the most advanced weapons have simply not been relevant to them. This is because, as experience shows, any good they can do is more than balanced by the damage inflicted on the environment, and their own insatiable demands for supply and maintenance.

By this interpretation, most modern crew-operated weapons— including specifically the most powerful and sophisticated among them—are dinosaurs. Like them, they are doomed to disappear, and, the process is already well underway. During World War II the United States produced up to 100,000 aircraft in a single year. Today the USAF, despite being the richest organization of its kind anywhere, can scarcely afford

to buy more than 100 fighters annually. At up to $500 million apiece—
the price of a single "Stealth" bomber—so rare are modern weapons
systems that, like some fake antiques, they have to be virtually hand-
crafted. Since new major systems seldom reach operational status at
planned cost, there is always a tendency to pare numbers and stretch
programs, causing per-unit price to escalate. Once the weapons exist
they are too expensive to be tested or trained with, so that simulators
have to be used. Finally, when low-intensity conflict does break out and
the opportunity to use the hardware presents itself, it seems wasteful to
employ such expensive systems against persons who are often an
illiterate rabble, and who are not even regular soldiers. As a result, in
Lebanon for example, the US Navy's first air-strike (leading to the loss of
two aircraft, total value perhaps $60 million) was also the last. *Summa
summarum,* already today only one country can afford to own more
than a handful of these systems; nor does even the US intend to
replace those lost in the Gulf.

   An excellent index of the extent to which any military technology is
taken seriously is the secrecy by which it is surrounded. The turn of the
century 75 mm. cannon (French); the World War I giant howitzers
(German) and tank (British); the World War II ballistic missiles (German) and proximity fuse (British); such was the secrecy with which
these devices were surrounded that it sometimes interfered with development, deployment, and operations. When Harry Truman succeeded
Roosevelt as president of the United States in April 1945, he had to be
broken in on the news of the atomic bomb and, taken unawares, could
only stammer that it was "the greatest thing in the world." By contrast,
since 1945 secrecy in the West has all but disappeared. It has become
common for plastic models of the most advanced tactical aircraft to
appear in toy shops before they are officially unveiled, and nobody cares
enough to sue the manufacturers. A flourishing literature has come into
being whose main business is to advertise new weapons systems in
great detail, even to the point where Israeli pilots refer to *Aviation Week*
as *Spy Technology.*

   The phenomenon is most evident in the United States, where the
need to sell new weapons to Congress leads to extensive publicity
campaigns. In Washington, D.C., a meeting devoted to a highly technical
subject such as active armor for tanks can draw an audience of hundreds
from among the "defense community." Those who attend include
congressmen, government officials, military officers, defense contractors, representatives of the media, and so on. Furthermore, during the
last few years there have been indications that countries that tradi-

tionally took war seriously, such as Israel and the Soviet Union, are following suit. The Soviets now permit Western officers to visit their bases and have begun putting some of their most advanced weapons systems, such as the Mig-29 fighter, on show in international fairs. A worsening economic situation has forced Israel's Weapons Development Authority (RAFAEL) to cut the period during which newly developed systems cannot be exported; in other words, to accelerate their declassification. Meanwhile, the few things that *do* matter remain as secret as ever. This includes, at one end of the scale, the nuclear capability of countries such as Taiwan, the two Koreas, Pakistan, India, Israel, and South Africa; and, at the other, the inner workings of monitoring devices, night-vision equipment, and the like.

In the not too distant future, major military-technological research and development as we have known it since the industrial revolution will grind to a halt. Even today, for every new weapons systems actually fielded there are perhaps a score that never get beyond the drawing board; the research and development process is in large part an empty game whose main purpose is to provide employment and serve as a welfare system for engineers. Toys, particularly those that look powerful and dangerous, may have their attractions for generals in and out of uniform. However, from the point of view of society at large it simply makes no sense to produce weapons that are too expensive, too fast, too indiscriminate, too big, too unmaneuverable and too powerful to use in real-life war. It makes even less sense to design weapons whose development costs are such that they can only be produced on condition that they are sold to others; particularly since lead times are now so long—ten to fifteen years—as to make it likely that some of the buyers will have become enemies. The vast quantities of arms which Britain, France, Italy, and many other countries sold Saddam Hussein between 1980 and 1990 (and which were subsequently used by him against their own armies) are a case in point. Much of the modern heavy weapons industry is, militarily speaking, a house of cards. It supports itself through exporting its own uselessness.

This does not mean that new technology has no role to play in the military future. What it does mean is a move away from today's large, expensive, powerful machines toward small, cheap gadgets capable of being manufactured in large numbers and used almost everywhere, much as, in the past, firearms replaced the knight and his cumbersome armor. Already magnetic identification cards are widely used to allow their owners to enter and leave buildings. Once the technology matures, cards will be provided with transmitters and linked to computers, permitting their wearers to be continually traced as they move through secure zones, bases, or installations. Similar equipment, only slightly modified, may be applicable to the license-plates of vehicles. Surveillance cameras and closed circuit-television currently being used to monitor the inside of buildings as well as city-traffic may be adapted for wider purposes; the Israel Defense Forces in connection with the *Intifada* have experimented with cameras mounted on balloons. The race between scramblers and listening devices is on. So is the one between monitoring machines and the odorless, signature-less, explosives used by terrorists, together with poisoned umbrellas and booby-traps of every kind. All these gadgets have more in common with George Orwell's telescreen—itself a real technical possibility—than with today's tanks, missiles, and aircraft.

The technology of surveillance may be useful up to a point, as was proved in China when automatic cameras originally installed to monitor traffic were used to identify individual demonstrators following the 1989 Tiananmen disturbances. Still, Orwell was probably wrong in his belief that technical equipment is capable of completely suppressing low-intensity war, and can thus lead to the establishment of permanent totalitarian dictatorships. Experience shows that the information-recording and transmitting equipment used to bolster a regime can be equally handy in subverting it. Devices declared tamper-proof by their manufacturers will nevertheless be tampered with. The more perfect and ubiquitous the technology, moreover, the greater the sheer workload involved in watching everybody all the time. Though the use of artificial intelligence and networked supercomputers may alleviate this problem to some extent, the personnel involved in the security-system is likely to remain a weak spot. Surveillance is the most boring type of work and not the most highly paid. Over time, even the best-motivated personnel are likely to become inattentive. People are also capable of being outwitted, bribed, or subverted.

The problem of subversion is likely to be serious. In the recent past, military establishments, so long as they fought each other, were able to take national loyalties more or less for granted. However, this will be decreasingly the case. Nor, probably, will the establishments of the future be able to control their members in the same way, and to the same extent, as do state-run armed forces with their uniforms, regular pay, extensive welfare systems, and powerful counterintelligence services. Tomorrow's warmaking organizations will not recognize the kind of distinctions that, in the past, allowed governments but not individuals to profit from war. They will probably allow their members more room to satisfy their personal needs directly at the expenses of the enemy. Once satisfying personal needs and making a private profit are considered important and legitimate motives, subversion, treachery and shifting allegiances by individuals and entire units will become as commonplace as they have often been in the past. To quote Philip II, father of Alexander the Great: where an army cannot pass, a donkey laden with gold often will. Such is likely to be the stuff of which future strategy is made.

Judging by the experience of the last two decades, the visions of long-range, computerized, high-tech warfare so dear to the military-industrial complex will never come to pass. Armed conflict will be waged by men on earth, not robots in space. It will have more in common with the struggles of primitive tribes than with large scale conventional war of the kind that the world may have seen for the last time in 1973 (the Arab-Israeli War), 1982 (the Falklands), 1980-88 (the Iran-Iraq War), and 1991 (the Gulf Crisis). Since the belligerents will be intermingled with each other and the civilian population, Clausewitizian strategy will not apply. Weapons will become less, rather than more, sophisticated. War will not be waged at one remove by neatly uniformed men in air conditioned rooms sitting behind screens, manipulating symbols, and pushing buttons: indeed the "troops" may well have more in common with policemen (or with pirates) than with defense analysts. War will not take place in the open field, if only because in many places around the world there no longer *is* an open field. Its normal *mise en scene* will be complex environments, either those provided by nature or else the even more complex ones created by man. It will be a war of listening devices and of car-bombs, of men killing each other at close quarters, and of women using their purses to carry explosives and the drugs to pay for them. It will be protracted, bloody, and horrible.

What War Will Be Fought For

As marriage has not always been concluded for love, so war has not always been waged for "interest." In fact, the term "interest" as herein used is a sixteenth-century neologism; even so, the examples provided by the *Oxford English Dictionary* suggest that it was applied first to individuals and only then to states. Its very introduction forms part and parcel of the rise of the modern world-view. "Realism" is what we call the school that bases itself, not without pride, less on justice and religion and more on power. After Newton, the positions of the planets could no longer be explained by their proper or rightful place but only by the forces linking them; and the same is true of the relations among states.

From the time of Joshua to that of Cromwell's Ironsides—who indeed saw themselves as the Israelites reincarnated—the main reason for which men slaughtered each other was not "interest" but the greater glory of God. From the time of Cicero to that of Thomas Aquinas and beyond, the most prominent thinkers until about 1500 A.D. did not even consider the use of armed force for "interest" as legitimate in itself. Instead, such use was considered a crime against the laws of gods and men, a crime that was punishable, and was punished when opportunity arose. On this view was based the idea of "just war" which in one form or another governed Western civilization for well over a thousand years. The first to attain fame by setting up an absolute distinction between private and public morality was Machiavelli in the sixteenth century. He thereby fired the opening-shot in a debate concerning the relationship between the two, a debate that was destined to last for centuries; and it led up to the Italian statesman Cavour saying—around 1860–that "had we done for ourselves what we are doing for our country, what scoundrels would we be." Thus, the rise of the state and its "reason" is best understood as a figleaf. It allowed the notion of justice to be discarded and "interest" to be put in its place, all without compromising the decency of individuals.

At present, so strongly entrenched is the notion of interest that even genes, mere pieces of protein, are credited with having them and with developing strategies for their realization. Attempts to explain men's actions in other terms tend to be greeted with suspicion even to the point where they are not regarded as an explanation at all; whenever an important action takes place we assume that there *has* to be a utilitarian reason behind it and that this reason is the "real" one. For example, modern biographies of Alexander the Great typically refuse to take his grand gestures at face value. This causes the biographers to find—or invent—"sound" politico-military reasons as to why the defeated Porus was restored to his kingdom and why the Macedonian commander refused to "steal a victory" and fight Darius at night. The trouble with all such explanations is that they turn history upside down. The very disparity between Macedonia, a small and poor country, and the giant Persian Empire it set out to conquer should put to rest any notion that the decision was based on "interest." So should the fact that, according to our sources, Alexander determined on his course while still a boy in his father's court.

Considered in this way, explanations working in terms of interest are anything but realistic—in fact they are the reverse of realistic because they explain the past by assuming the validity of patterns of thought with which that past was not necessarily familiar. Now of course this is not to say that interest did not play a part, even a prominent part, in wars for which reasons of justice, religion, or vainglory were cited; for example, the Romans when they declared themselves to be the injured party, and embarked on a *bellum iustum,* did aim also (some would say mainly) at expanding their "dominion" and acquiring a fresh supply of booty and slaves. It is to say, however, that the Roman admixture of interest with vainglory, religion, justice, and many other factors itself reflected their social structure, and differed from ours by as much as their type of political organization did. Such being the case, there is no reason to assume that the existing amalgam is in any way self-evident or permanent. Instead it is the product of specific historical circumstances, liable to change.

There is enormous difficulty in predicting the direction in which change will proceed. One's position is comparable to that of a late fifth-century B.C. Athenian trying to divine the shape of the Hellenistic World; or else of a citizen in the late Roman Empire guesstimating the shape of the Middle Ages. From the vantage point of the present, there appears every prospect that religious attitudes, beliefs, and fanaticisms will play a larger role in the motivation of armed conflict than it has, in the West at any rate, for the last 300 years. Already as these lines are being written the fastest growing religion in the world is Islam. While there are many reasons for this, perhaps it would not be so far fetched to say that its very militancy is one factor behind its spread. By this I do not mean to say merely that Islam strives to achieve its aims by fighting; rather, that people in many parts of the world—including downtrodden groups in the developed world—are finding Islam attractive precisely because it is prepared to fight. Obviously, the resurgence of religion as a cause of armed conflict will cause the war convention to change in other ways as well.

If the growing militancy of one religion continues, it almost certainly will compel others to follow suit. People will be driven to defend their ideals and way of life, and their physical existence, and this they will be able to do only under the banner of some great and powerful idea. That idea may be secular by origin; however, the very fact that it is fought for will cause it to acquire religious overtones and be adhered to with something like religious fervor. Thus Muhammed's recent revival may yet bring on that of the Christian Lord, and He will be not the Lord of love but of battles.

If, in the future, war will be waged for the souls of men, then the importance of extending territorial control will go down. Long past are the days when provinces, even entire countries, were regarded simply as items of real estate to be exchanged among rulers by means of inheritance, agreement, or force. The triumph of nationalism has brought about a situation where people do not occupy a piece of land because it is valuable; on the contrary, a piece of land however remote or desolate is considered valuable because it is occupied by this people or that. To adduce but two examples out of many, since at least 1965 India and Pakistan have been at loggerheads over a glacier so remote that it can hardly even be located on a map. Between 1979 and 1988, Egypt spent nine years of diplomatic effort in order to recover Taba. Now Taba, south of Elath, is a half-mile stretch of worthless desert beach whose very existence had gone unnoticed by both Egyptians and Israelis prior to the Camp David Peace Agreements; all of a sudden it became part of each side's "sacred" patrimony and coffee-houses in Cairo were named after it.

By way of an analogy, consider the period from the Treaty of Westphalia to the French Revolution. Through any number of wars, some of them so ferocious as to claim the lives of tens upon tens of thousands, the principle of "legitimate rule" helped create a situation where hardly a single dynasty was overthrown or a new one established; not even when the Russians occupied Berlin in 1760 was there any question of deposing Frederick the Great, let alone abolishing the Prussian State. Then, 1789 marked the beginning of a period when it became possible, even fashionable, to overthrow kings wholesale. As the process took hold, the sanctity that had attached to dynasties was gradually transferred to national borders, and for one state to grant right of passage to the forces of another became tantamount to sacrilege. The new belief system solidified after the First World War and grew into dogma after the Second when it was also enshrined in international law. This made it extraordinarily difficult to use war as an instrument for altering borders; where the territorial integrity of one state is violated, all others feel themselves threatened. Now this should certainly *not* be taken to mean that present-day boundaries are fixed for all eternity or that future low-intensity war will be content to leave them as they are. To judge by the way both Syrians and Israelis have acted in Lebanon, the goal will be not so much to abolish frontiers as to render them meaningless; and indeed the concept itself may end up by taking on a new significance.

Another effect of the postulated breakdown of conventional war will probably be a greater emphasis on the interests of the men at the head of the organization, as opposed to the interest, of the organization as such. As the world stands today, rulers are supposed to keep their own personal interests separate from those of their political organization; even in the eighteenth century, before the French Revolution, Horace Walpole in a private letter wrote that statesmen who took their countries to war for personal reasons were "detestable knaves and gamblers." Common wisdom has it that the two sets of considerations must on no account be mixed, and indeed much of a modern state's politico-legal apparatus is specifically designed to prevent corruption from raising its head. However, the future is likely to differ in this respect as well. The spread of low-intensity conflict will cause the "private lives" of leaders to be abolished and the medieval situation to be restored whereby "privy" stood for the only place where the king went alone. As states start to collapse, leaders and warmaking organizations will merge into each other. Very probably this will not be without effect on the goals they pursue in war, nor on the kind of rewards they offer to those engaging in it.

It stands to reason that an admixture of coercion will always be needed to make men fight; however, there is no need to assume that future warriors will necessarily continue to regard themselves simply as professionals performing their duty towards some abstract political entity. Should the organization of warmaking entities change—should the personal interests of leaders become more prominent-then the same will happen to those of their followers. As used to be the case until at least 1648, military and economic functions will be reunited. Individual glory, profit, and booty gained directly at the expense of the civilian population will once again become important, not simply as incidental rewards but as the legitimate objectives of war. Nor is it improbable that the quest for women and sexual gratification will re-enter the picture. As the distinctions between combatants and noncombatants break down, the least we can expect is that such things will be tolerated to a greater extent than is supposed to be the case under the rules of so-called civilized warfare. In many of the low-intensity conflicts currently being waged in developing countries this is already true, and has, indeed, always been true.

Even today, one reason behind the dismal record of regular forces fighting irregulars may well be the reward system; in other words, the goals for which troops fight and for which they are allowed to fight. If only because their members have to make a living, organizations engaged in low-intensity conflict often permit, even encourage, them to take their rewards directly from the enemy. By contrast, the livelihood of modern soldiers is assured by the organization to which they belong. Any other rewards they may seek—such as promotion, or honor in the form of decorations—are supposed to come exclusively from that organization, which in turn uses them as its prime instrument for maintaining control. So long as armies primarily confronted each other this constituted no problem, though as a matter of fact some of the greatest commanders from Napoleon down knew when to turn a blind eye to their troops' depredations. However, a modern armed forces may have demotivated their troops by applying the same rules in a low-intensity conflict. Perhaps it is too much to expect a man to fight if, theoretically, taking a watch from a dead terrorist for one's personal use (instead of handing it over to the authorities) counts as a misdemeanor. Those who plan on using regular armed forces to combat drug-traffickers need to pay heed.

In sum, to say that peoples go to war for their "interests," and that "interest" comprises whatever any society considers good and useful for itself, is as self-evident as it is trite. Saying so means that we regard our particular modern combination of might and right as eternally valid instead of taking it for what it really is, a historical phenomenon with a clear beginning and presumably an end. Even if we do assume that men are always motivated by their interests, there are no good grounds for assuming that the things that are bundled together under this rubric will necessarily be the same in the future as they are today; it being obvious that the things that are considered "good" for society (and even the meaning of "society" itself) are at least partly the product of that society's nature, organization, and belief-system. Nor is this merely a point of philosophical concern. The logic of strategy itself requires that the opponent's motives be understood, since on this rests any prospect of success in war. If, in the process, the notion of interest has to be thrown overboard, then so be it.

Moreover, in the future there will undoubtedly be many cases in which the whole idea of fighting a war "for" something will be largely inapplicable. Organized communities of whatever type will sometimes go to war for no other "reason" than that they absolutely have to, as has happened in the past. There will also be cases, when wars originally started "in order to" realize this or that objective will degenerate into life-and-death struggles for existence. The more equally balanced the opponents, the longer, the more intensive and more bloody any war, the more likely this is to happen. The more true this becomes, the less applicable the Clausewitzian Universe and, even more, those modern interpretations of it that insist on regarding war merely as the tame tool of policy. Which leads us to the last cardinal question we have to consider.

Why War Will Be Fought

In this volume war has been somewhat arbitrarily taken, as a given. One by one, the phenomena that surround war—including the organizations by which it is waged, the conventions to which it is subjected, and the aims for which it is fought—have been shown to be the product of historical circumstance. Even as they changed, war stood up as the eternal, unchanging axis around which revolves the whole of human existence and which gives meaning to all the rest. In the words of Heraclitus, *polemos panton men pater esti*—strife is the origin of everything.

The above notwithstanding, this volume does not argue that war is biologically predetermined—no more, say, than are religion, science, productive work, or art. However, it does argue that war, far from being merely a means, has very often been considered an end—a highly attractive activity for which no other can provide an adequate substitute. The reason why other activities do not provide a substitute is precisely because they are "civilized"; in other words, bound by artificial rules. Compared to war, *der Ernstfall* as the Germans used to say, every one of the many other activities in which men play with their lives is merely a game, and a trivial one at that. Though war too is in one sense an artificial activity, it differs from all the rest in that it offers complete freedom, including paradoxically freedom from death. War alone presents man with the opportunity of employing all his faculties, putting everything at risk, and testing his ultimate worth against an opponent as strong as himself. It is the stakes that can make a game serious, even noble. While war's usefulness as a servant of power, interest, and profit may be questioned, the inherent fascination it has held for men at all times and places is a matter of historical fact. When all is said and done, the only way to account for this fascination is to regard war as the game with the highest stakes of all.

Thus, to explain the occurrence of war, there is no need to see it as having been programmed into human nature; on the other hand, there is no proof that this is not so. In recent decades numerous experiments, some of them bizarre, have been carried out to determine whether the brain has a center where aggression is concentrated. The results have been ambiguous, since electrical stimulation of one and the same region is apparently capable of eliciting different responses under different circumstances. Even if the existence of such a center is ultimately confirmed, however, the relationship between it and the social activity known as war is bound to be exceedingly complex. A "fighting neural complex," "war gland," or "aggressive gene" almost certainly will never be discovered, nor need one be postulated. So far nobody has the foggiest idea which structures in the brain are responsible for such typically human qualities as our ability to appreciate the true, the beautiful, the good, and the sacred. Yet few people—least of all the scientists who perform the experiments—have suggested that, because of this, the quest for sanctity, goodness, beauty, and truth does not form part of human nature.

The premise that war can, and often does, prove absolutely fascinating is by no means gainsaid by the fact that not all people fight all of the time, and that some of them have managed to avoid doing so for considerable periods. Most people never visit a museum nor attend a concert in their lives; yet this is not to say that paintings and music are not wonderful things. In war, as in every other field, the thrill is often vicarious. The fact that, in football, for the thousands of persons who roar their approval from the stands or from in front of the TV there are so few actual players does not mean that the game is not enjoyable— quite the contrary. Throughout history, a very large fraction of all games, literature, history, and art created by man owed their existence to the fact that they either imitated war or provided substitutes for it. It is true that, at any one given time and place, most people neither participate in games nor enjoy art. Still, the majority cannot be denied at least the inherent capacity of doing so, for to deny it to them would be to deny it to ourselves also. Furthermore, had war been going on at all times and at all places it would inevitably have become boring. This may be the best explanation as to why every war must ultimately end.

Nor is this in any way contradicted by the existence of countries that have managed to avoid war for comparatively long periods. War not merely serves power, it *is* power; to recall the episode in Swift where the Lilliputians battled each other on Gulliver's outstretched handkerchief, for the small to fight in the presence of the strong is self-defeating and invites ridicule. This consideration may help explain how countries such as Denmark and the Netherlands, which used to wage war with the best, acquired their present pacifism—and also how they may yet abandon that pacifism in the future. The same applies to such bitter enemies as France and Germany, Hungary and Romania, Bulgaria and Yugoslavia, that not so long ago were constantly at each other's throats. Having been gathered under the aegis of much stronger powers, it was probably shame as much as any other factor that caused these countries to halt their squabbles after 1945. However, the world is round. Already today there are abundant signs that in eastern Europe and parts of the Soviet Union at any rate the story has not yet come to an end.

Even Swiss neutrality, that great shining example, is only as old as are trinitarian social structures, and the state that embodies them. The *Eidgenossenschaft* of the disparate Swiss cantons was formed in 1291 under the pressure of war, nor would there have been much point to swearing an *Eid* (oath) of mutual assistance if there had not been a common enemy to fight. For some three centuries after that the people of the mountains had a reputation for bellicosity second to none, so much so that as mercenaries they were the preferred choice of every ruler from the Pope down. The usual explanation for Swiss neutrality— the country's geographical position—cannot account for the change. Clearly in this case neutrality hinges on the existence of frontiers and states as well as the latter's ability to prevent people from crossing the borders. It being the essence of low-intensity conflict that it recognizes neither states nor frontiers, however, the inference is clear. Already there have been cases when French, West German, and Italian terrorists sought refuge on Swiss soil; nor, probably, are terrorist organizations altogether without connections in Switzerland. Should the countries by which the Swiss are surrounded succumb to extensive low-intensity conflict, no doubt the time will come when Swiss people too zestfully join the fray.

All this boils down to saying that, in order to explain the occurrence of war, it is not necessary to postulate the existence of any ulterior objectives other than war itself. This study has had much to say concerning the shifting goals for which war has been fought at different times and places, yet throughout these changes war itself has always been a given. No doubt future generations will resort to various lines of reasoning, some of them so novel as to be almost unimaginable today, in order to justify to themselves and to others the wars that they wage. Meanwhile war's own by no mean negligible attractions will remain intact. No attempt at understanding, planning, and conducting it is likely to succeed if it fails to take those attractions into account; nor will taking them into account do much good unless they are valued, cherished, even loved, for their own sake. Thus, conventional strategic wisdom must be turned upside down. There exists a sense in which war, more than any other human activity, can make sense only to the extent that it is experienced not as a means but as an end. However unpalatable the fact, the real reason why we have wars is that men like fighting, and women like those men who are prepared to fight on their behalf.

To repeat, the true essence of war consists not just of one group killing another but of its members' readiness to be killed in return if necessary. Consequently the only way to bring about perpetual peace would be to somehow eradicate man's willingness, even eagerness, to take risks of every kind up to, and including, death. Whether this eagerness is biologically programmed—whether, to believe with Freud, there exists in the mind of each of us a death wish—this work cannot presume to decide. Even if such a wish does exist, very likely it is neither localized at one particular spot in the brain nor unlinked with other drives. To judge by what psychotherapeutic drugs do to those subjected to them, probably it can be excised only by turning people into zombies: that is, by simultaneously destroying other qualities considered essential to humanity, such as playfulness, curiosity, inventiveness, creativity, even the sheer joy of living. What all these activities have in common is that they involve coping with the unknown. To the extent that coping with the unknown both results in a feeling of power and is a manifestation of it, they themselves may be considered pale imitations of war. In the words of Helmut von Moltke, eternal peace is a dream. Given the price that we would have to pay, perhaps it is not even a beautiful dream.

To say that war involves playing with death is not to equate it with suicide; as the story of Massada proves, suicide is not the beginning of war but its end. Short of tampering with the mind of man, probably the only way to eliminate war is to so increase the power of government as to render its outcome certain in advance. It is conceivable, though most unlikely, that a world-wide, repressive, totalitarian, big-brother type regime will one day attempt to achieve this goal. Probably such a regime could establish itself only in the aftermath of a major nuclear war in which one center of power would somehow manage to eradicate all the rest without itself being eradicated. Nuclear bombardment would have to be followed by extensive police operations conducted, presumably, in a radioactive environment. Once secure in power, the regime would have to rely on a pervasive police apparatus as well as sophisticated technical equipment capable of monitoring everybody all of the time. To prevent the humans in the loop from being outwitted, subverted, or

simply negligent, the technology in question would have to be automated in respect to both operation and maintenance. A completely
automated thought-reading machine—for nothing less would do—
would have to be hooked up with the human brain and capable of
influencing it by chemical or electrical means. Robots would have to
control men, men themselves turned into robots. We find ourselves
caught in a cross between Huxley's *Brave New World* and Orwell's *1984*.
So monstrous is the vision as to make even war look like a blessing.

The third way in which the will to fight, and hence war, might
conceivably be eliminated would be to have women participate in it, not
as auxilliaries or surreptitiously, but as full-fledged, equal partners. This
is not the place to expound on the often imaginary psychological
differences between the sexes, nor on the respective importance of
biological and social factors in governing those differences. Suffice it to
repeat that, with the exception of their disparate roles in the physical
acts of procreation, childbearing, and nursing, nothing has ever been
more characteristic of the relationship between men and women than
men's unwillingness to allow women to take part in war and combat.
Throughout history men have resented having to perform a woman's
role as an insult to their manhood, even to the point where it was
sometimes inflicted as a punishment; had they been forced to fight at the
side of, and against, women, then either the affair would have turned
into mock war—a common amusement in many cultures—or else they
would have put down their arms in disgust. However desirable such an
outcome may be in the eyes of some, it belongs to the realm of phantasy.
One suspects that, should they ever be faced with such a choice, men
might very well give up women before they give up war.

These, of course, are speculations. Their practical significance lies
in the fact that, but for its fighting spirit, no armed force is worth a fig.
Over the last few decades, regular armed forces—including some of the
largest and the best—have repeatedly failed in numerous low-intensity
conflicts where they seemed to hold all the cards. This should have
caused politicians, the military, and their academic advisers to take a
profound new look at the nature of war in our time; however, by and
large no such attempt at reevaluation was made. Held captive by the
accepted strategic framework, time and time again the losers explained
away their defeat by citing mitigating factors. Often they invoked an
alleged stab in the back, blaming the politicians who refused them a free
hand or else the home public which did not give them the support to
which they felt entitled. In other cases they thrust their head in the sand
and argued that they were defeated in a political war, psychological war,

propaganda war, guerrilla war, terrorist war, in short anything but war properly speaking.

As the twentieth century is drawing to its conclusion, it is becoming clearer every day that this line of reasoning will no longer do. If only we are prepared to look, we can see a revolution taking place under our very noses. Just as no Roman citizen was left unaffected by the barbarian invasions, so in vast parts of the world no man, woman, and child alive today will be spared the consequences of the newly-emerging forms of war. Even in the most stable societies, the least they can expect is to have their identity checked and their persons searched at every turn. The nature of the entities by which war is made, the conventions by which it is surrounded, and the ends for which it is fought may change. However, now as ever war itself is alive and well; with the result that, now as ever, such communities as refuse to look facts in the face and fight for their existence will, in all probability, cease to exist.

Postscript: The Shape of Things to Come

We are standing today, not at the end of history but at a historic turning point. Just as Alexander's exploits only reached the Middle Ages as a dim, fantastic tale, so in the future people will probably look back upon the twentieth century as a period of mighty empires, vast armies, and incredible fighting machines that have crumbled into dust. Nor is it even likely that their demise will be regretted, given that each age tends to consider itself the best of all and to grade the past in accordance as it led to, or detracted from, the things that are considered valuable at present.

If no nuclear holocaust takes place, then conventional war appears to be in the final stages of abolishing itself; if one does take place, then it will already have abolished itself. This dilemma does not mean that perpetual peace is on its way, much less that organized violence is coming to an end. As war between states exits through one side of history's revolving door, low-intensity conflict among different organizations will enter through the other. Present-day low-intensity conflict is overwhelmingly confined to the so-called developing world. However, to think this will be so for ever or even for very long is almost certainly a great illusion. Much as cancer destroys the body by passing from one infected organ to the next, so of all forms of war low-intensity conflict is the most contagious. As the last decade of the century dawns, entire regions whose stability appeared assured since 1945—the Indian subcontinent, southeastern Europe, and parts of the Soviet Union—are beginning to go up in flames. So far the effect of these developments on the so-called "First World" has been marginal—but then this world comprises less than one-fifth of humanity. Who can point to a society so isolated, so homogeneous, so rich, and so wallowing in its contentment as to be in principle immune?

The first duty of any social entity is to protect the lives of its members. Either modern states cope with low-intensity conflict, or else they will disappear; the suspicion grows, however, that they are damned if they do and damned if they don't. War being among the most imitative of all human activities, the very process of combating low-intensity conflict will cause both sides to become alike, unless it can be brought to a quick end. Extensive conflict of this nature will cause existing distinctions between government, armed forces, and people to break down. National sovereignties are already being undermined by organizations that refuse to recognize the state's monopoly over armed violence. Armies will be replaced by police-like security forces on the one hand and bands of ruffians on the other, not that the difference is always clear even today. National frontiers, that at present constitute perhaps the greatest single obstacle to combating low-intensity conflict, may be obliterated or else become meaningless as rival organizations chase each other across them. As frontiers go, so will territorial states. All of which is to say that the tail wags the dog by as much as the dog wags the tail. To the extent that war is indeed the continuation of politics, radical shifts in war will inevitably be followed by important changes in politics.

As the old war convention fades away, a new one will no doubt take its place—the waging of war without such a convention being in principle impossible. The coming convention's function will be the same as it has always been: namely, to define just who is allowed to kill whom, for what ends, under what circumstances, and by what means. In addition it will have to provide for *ius in bello* problems such as sanctuaries, parleys, truces, procedures for surrender, and so on, all of which are essential to war's conduct. Much as "natural law" at one time replaced chivalry, so the new convention will be different from the old and go under a different name. Undoubtedly its establishment will be accompanied by many outrages, accidental as well as deliberate. This is not to say that human nature is becoming even more evil than it has always been, nor will all changes necessarily be for the worse. "Civilized" twentieth-century warfare may have forbidden individual soldiers to loot and rape, but went right ahead when it was a question of destroying entire cities from the air. We have no reason to be proud of our humanitarian record. Future ages may well shudder with horror as they remember us.

The demise of conventional war will cause strategy in its traditional, Clausewitzian sense to disappear. So will the most powerful of today's advanced weapons, whose effectiveness is largely a function of the trinitarian environment for which they were designed. To the extent that strategy always involves the building of armed force, however, the principles of doing so will remain the same. This also applies to the threefold obstacles of inflexibility, friction, and uncertainty, given that the first two are inherent in a force of any size and that war without the third is both impossible and unnecessary. Most important of all, the essential principles of strategy will continue to be determined by its mutual, interactive character; that is, the fact that war is a violent contest between two opponents, each governed by an independent will and to some extent free to do as he sees fit. The need to concentrate the greatest possible force and deliver a smashing blow at the decisive point will continue to clash with the need to outwit, mislead, deceive, and surprise the enemy. Victory, as always, will go to the side that best understands how to balance these two contradictory requirements, not just in the abstract but at a specific time, at a specific place, and against a specific enemy.

The goals any social entity sets itself are not arbitrary but at least partly a product of its general belief-system which, in turn, is based on its structure. As the vital warmaking function is taken over by new types of organization, no doubt those organizations will proclaim new myths and define their objectives in radically different ways. As new forms of armed conflict multiply and spread, they will cause the lines between public and private, government and people, military and civilian, to become as blurred as they were before 1648. The point may come where even our present notions of policy and interest—both of which are closely associated with the state—will have to be transformed or replaced by others more appropriate to the new circumstances. None of this is to deny that future societies will follow the example of past ones in fighting for things they consider useful, desirable, and profitable for themselves. It is, however, to say that the nature of those things and the way they are amalgamated with ethical, legal, and religious consider-ations may well differ from ours by as much as ours differ from medieval ones.

In another sense, the question as to what future societies will go to war for is almost irrelevant. It is simply not true that war is solely a means to an end, nor do people necessarily fight in order to attain this objective or that. In fact, the opposite is true: people very often take up one objective or another precisely in order that they may fight. While the usefulness of war as a means for gaining practical ends may well be questioned, its ability to entertain, to inspire, and to fascinate has never been in doubt. War is life written large. Among the things that move between the two poles, war alone both permits and demands the commitment of *all* man's faculties, the highest as well as the lowest. The brutality and the ruthlessness, the courage and the determination, the sheer power that strategy considers necessary for the conduct of armed conflict are at the same time its causes. Literature, art, games, and history all bear eloquent testimony to the same elemental fact. One very important way in which men can attain joy, freedom, happiness, even delirium and ecstasy, is by *not* staying home with wife and family, even to the point where, often enough, they are only too happy to give up their nearest and dearest in favor of—war!

Selected Bibliography

Albert, S., *Bellum iustum: die Theorie des 'Gerechten Krieges' und ihre praktische Bedeutung für die Auswärtigen Auseinandersetzungen Roms in Republikanishen Zeit* (Kallmünz, Lassleben, 1980).
Roman concepts of just war and their practical significance.

Allen, J. W., *A History of Political Thought in the Sixteenth Century* (London, Methuen, 1951).
The birth of the state, among other things.

Anderson, J. K., *Military Practice and Theory in the Age of Xenophon* (Berkeley, Cal., University of California Press, 1970).

Andreski, S., *Military Organization and Society* (Berkeley, Cal., University of California Press, 1968).
Compact work listing various types of armed forces and their relationship to the societies they served.

Andriole, J., ed., *Artificial Intelligence and National Defense* (Washington, D.C., AFCEA International Press, 1987).
How computers have failed to transform warfare.

Angell, N., *The Great Illusion* (London, Heinemann, 1909).
A famous book that argued—just before the greatest conflict in history until then—that war had become *passé* and was about to be replaced by trade.

Ardrey, R., *African Genesis* (London, Fontana, 1961).
A well known "territorial" explanation for the origin of war, that has failed to stand up.

Arendt, H., *On Violence* (New York, Harcourt Brace & World, 1969).
A *tour de force* in which many of the present book's ideas are foreshadowed.

Aristophanes, *Lysystrate* (London, Faber and Faber, 1971).
War as a game for foolish men.

Aristotle, *The Politics* (Harmondsworth, U.K., Penguin Books, 1962).
A *polis* is an association of free men dedicated to living the good life.

Arrian, *The Campaigns of Alexander* (Harmondsworth, U.K., Penguin Books, 1971).

Augustine, St., *Confessions* (Harmondsworth, U.K., Penguin Books, 1961).
——, *The City of God* (London, J. M. Dent, 1945) 2 vols.
Includes the saint's meditations on the circumstances under which just war is possible.

Bachevich, A. J., *The Pentomic Era: the U.S. Army between Korea and Vietnam* (Washington, D.C., National Defense University Press, 1986).
How the U.S Army tried to adapt to nuclear warfare and failed.

Baldick, R., *The Duel, a History of Duelling* (New York, Clarkson, 1965).

230   SELECTED BIBLIOGRAPHY

Barber, R., *The Knight and Chivalry* (Ottawa, N.J., Rowman & Littlefield, 1975).
Good on the history of tournaments, among other things.

Barker, E., *Greek Political Theory* (London, Methuen, 1947).
Splendid literary effort, excellent on the nature of the *polis*.

Barker, J. R. V., *The Tournament in England 1100–1400* (Suffolk, U.K., Boydell Press, 1966).
A comprehensive inquiry into the subject, including also the relationship between tournaments and war.

Barnie, J., *War in Medieval Society, Social Values and the Hundred Years' War 1337–99* (London, Weidenfeld and Nicolson, 1974).

Basinger, J., *The World War II Combat Film* (New York, Columbia University Press, 1986).
The meaning of heroism as interpreted by Hollywood.

Beauvoir, S. de, *The Second Sex* (New York, Knopf, 1953).
Strong on history, but stuffed with strange ideas about the influence of anatomy on the psychology of women.

Best, G., *Honor Among Men and Nations, the Transformation of an Idea* (New York, St. Martin's Press, 1982).

Best, G., *Humanity in Warfare* (New York, Columbia University Press, 1980).
Attempts to mitigate war from the time of the enlightenment on.

Bettelheim, B., *Symbolic Wounds: Puberty Rites and the Envious Male* (London, Collier-Macmillan, 1962).
Are males inferior to females or do they just think so?

Betts, R. K., "Nuclear Weapons and Conventional War," *Journal of Strategic Studies* 11, March 1988, pp. 79–95.
How nuclear weapons have been pushing conventional wars into the periphery.

Binkin, M., and Bach, S. J., *Women and the Military* (Washington, D.C., Brookings, 1977).
A bureaucratically-minded survey of military slots that could be filled by women.

Blekher, F., *The Soviet Woman in the Family and Society* (New York, J. Wiley, 1979).

Bonet, H., *The Tree of Battles* (Liverpool, University of Liverpool Press, 1949).
The most important medieval work on the law of chivalry.

Bouthoul, G., and Carrere, R., *Le defi de la guerre 1740–1974* (Paris, Presses Universitaires de France, 1974).
France's leading "polemologist" sums up his nonstrategic approach to war.

Bowra, C. M., *The Greek Experience* (London, Weidenfeld and Nicolson, 1959).
Heroism in Greek culture.

Boyer, P., *By the Bomb's Early Light* (New York, Pantheon, 1985).
An inventory of early reactions to the atomic bomb; some horrifying, others hillarious, others sad.

Brelich, A., *Guèrre, agóni e cùlti nella Grecia arcàica* (Bonn, Rudolf Habelt, 1961).
An inquiry into the reality of stories about ritual war as fought in ancient Greece.

Bretel, J., *Le tournoi de Chauvency*, M. Debrouille ed., (Paris, Société des belles lettres, 1932).
Firsthand rhymed account of a tournament held in 1285.

Brodie, B., *The Absolute Weapon* (New York, Harcourt, Brace, 1946).

In retrospect, perhaps the most prescient work written on the political effects of nuclear weapons.

———, *War and Politics* (New York, Macmillan, 1973).
For long the best work written on the interaction of war and politics in the nuclear age; rendered out of date by the advent of nontrinitarian warfare.

Brooke-Rose, C., "Woman as a Semiotic Object," in S. Rubin Suleiman ed., *The Female Body in Western Culture* (Cambridge, Mass., Harvard University Press, 1986) pp. 305–16.
The double standard in language.

Brown, D. R., ed., *Women in the Soviet Union* (New York, Teachers College Press, 1968).
How equality in theory has led to exploitation in practice.

Brownmiller, S., *Against Our Will* (New York, Simon and Schuster, 1975).
World history through the keyhole of rape.

Caillois, R., "Le vertige de la guerre," in *Quatre essais de sociologie contemporaine* (Paris, Olivier Perrin, 1951).
War as a celebration of existence.

———, *Man, Play, and Games* (New York, Free Press of Glencoe, 1961).
Games fall into four basic types, and war contains elements of them all.

Caldor, M., *The Baroque Arsenal* (New York, Hill and Wang, 1982).
An anthology of weapons that are too expensive, too fast, too indiscriminate, too big, too unmaneuverable, and too powerful to use.

Callingaert, D., "Nuclear Weapons and the Korean War," *Journal of Strategic Studies* 11, June 1988, pp. 177–202.
If Beijing ever surrendered to nuclear blackmail there are no Chinese sources to prove it.

Carver, M., *War since 1945* (London, Weidenfeld and Nicolson, 1980).
Straight from the horse's mouth: by Britain's ex-chief of the general staff.

Chagnon, N., *The Fierce People* (New York, Holt, Rinehart and Winston, 1968).
An anthropologist's account of life in an Amazonian tribe that was addicted to war.

Chaliand, G., ed., *Guerrilla Strategies: an Historical Anthology from the Long March to Afghanistan* (Berkeley, Ca., University of California Press, 1987).

Churchill, W. S. C., *The River War* (New York, Award Books, 1964).
War as high adventure.

Cicero, M. T., *De Officis* (English trans.; Berkeley, Cal., University of California Press, 1967).

Clancy, T., *Red Storm Rising* (New York, Putnam, 1986).
What World War III will *not* be like.

Clarke, I. F., *Voices Prophesying War* (Oxford, Oxford University Press, 1966).
A survey of imaginary wars and the fun that people had inventing them.

Clarke, M. L., *The Roman Mind: Studies in the History of Thought from Cicero to Marcus Aurelius* (Cambridge, Mass., Cambridge University Press, 1951).

Clausewitz, C. von, *On War* (M. Howard and P. Paret, eds., Princeton, N.J., Princeton University Press, 1976).
The second best work on war ever written.

Clodfelter, M., *The Limits of Air Power* (New York, Free Press, 1989).

How the world's best air force dropped five million tons of bombs on Vietnam, to no avail.

Contamine, J., *War in the Middle Ages* (Oxford, Basil Blackwell, 1984).
A brilliant effort, also on the reasons that made men fight.

Copleston, F. C., *Aquinas* (Harmondsworth, U.K., Penguin Books, 1955).

Cowdrey, H. E. S., "The Peace and the Truce of God in the Eleventh Century," *Past and Present* 46, February 1970, pp. 42–67.
More footnotes than text.

Creveld, M. van, *Fighting Power: German and U.S. Military Performance, 1939–1945* (Westport, Ct., Greenwood Press, 1982).

————, *Technology and War, from 2,000 B.C. to the Present* (New York, Free Press, 1989).

————, "The Origins and Development of Mobilization Warfare," in C. H. McCormick and R. E. Bissell, eds., *Strategic Dimensions of Economic Behavior* (New York, Praeger, 1984), ch. 2.

Davie, M. R., *The Evolution of War* (Port Washington, N. Y., Kennickut Press, 1929).
Good on the military customs of primitive peoples.

Dawson, J. G., ed., *Thomas Aquinas: Selected Political Writings* (Oxford, Oxford University Press, 1948).

Deaux, K., *The Behavior of Women and of Men* (Monterey, Cal., Brooks Cole, 1976).

Demeter, K., *The German Officer Corps in Society and State, 1650–1945* (London, Weidenfeld and Nicolson, 1962).
What it meant to be an officer before professionalism took the place of honor.

Deitchman, S. J., *Military Power and the Advance of Technology* (Boulder, Co., Westview, 1979, rep. 1983).
Better on the characteristics of modern weapons than on what to do with them.

Duby, C., *Guillaume le maréchal ou le meilleur chevalier du monde* (Paris, Fayard, 1984).

————, *The Chivalrous Society* (Berkeley, Cal., University of California Press, 1977).

Duffy, C., *The Army of Frederick the Great* (London, Book Club Edition, 1974).
Well written and excellently illustrated.

Earle, E. M., ed., *Makers of Modern Strategy* (Princeton, N.J., Princeton University Press, 1944).
Still the best work on the development of strategic theory until 1945.

Elkin, H., "Aggressive and Erotic Tendencies in Army Life," *American Journal of Sociology* 51, 1946, pp. 408–13.
How war fosters sex, and vice versa.

Elting, J. R., *Swords Around a Throne: Napoleon's Grande Armée* (New York, Free Press, 1988).
Strong on the spirit of the *Grande Armée*.

Erikson, E., "Womanhood and the Inner Space," in *Identity, Youth and Crisis* (New York, Norton, 1968).
Famous (if nonsensical) chapter on psychological differences between boys and girls.

Euripides, *The Trojan Women* (London, Methuen, 1964).
How the women of the defeated used to be treated.

Fadiman, J., *Mountain Warriors: the pre-Colonial Meru of Mt. Kenya* (Ohio University, Center for International Studies, Papers in International Studies, Africa Series No. 27, 1976).

Feldman, S., *Israeli Nuclear Deterrence: a Strategy for the 1980s* (New York, Columbia University Press, 1982).
Argues that an overt Israeli reliance on nuclear deterrence would stabilize the Middle East.

Ferguson, R. B., ed., *Warfare, Culture, and Environment* (Orlando, Fla., Academic Press, 1984).
A collection of essays on primitive warfare.

———, ed., *War, the Anthropology of Armed Conflict and Aggression* (Garden City, N.Y., Doubleday, 1968).

Fish, L., *The Last Firebase: a Guide to the Vietnam Veterans Memorial* (Shippenburg, Pa., White Mane, 1987).

Flavius, J., *The Jewish War* (Harmondsworth, U.K., Penguin Books, 1959).
The most dramatic blow-by-blow account of a war for existence ever written.

Freedman, L., *The Evolution of Nuclear Strategy* (New York, St. Martin's Press, 1981).
The book to end all books on nuclear strategy.

Freeman, J., ed., *Women: a Feminist Perspective* (Palo Alto, Cal., Mayfield, 1979).
Part four documents the position of women in the labor market under the caption: How real are the gains?

Fried, M. H., *The Evolution of Political Society: an Essay in Political Anthropology* (New York, Random House, 1967).

———, *War, the Anthropology of Armed Conflict and Aggression* (Garden, City, N.Y., Doubleday, 1968).
A collection of essays most of which attempt to explain primitive war in terms of its socio-economic functions.

Froissart, J., *Chronicles* (London, Macmillan, 1930).
The multivolume fourteenth-century account of knightly warfare by a member of the upper classes.

Fuller, J. F. C., *The Last of the Gentlemen's Wars* (London, Faber & Faber, 1934).
How a generation of British soldiers was brought up to believe in war as a sport.

Gabriel R. A., and Savage, P. L., *Crisis in Command: Mismanagement in the Army* (New York, Hill and Wang, 1978).
The book that documented the disintegration of an army.

Gardner, H., *The Mind's New Science: a History of the Cognitive Revolution* (New York, Basic Books, 1985).
An up-to-date, comprehensive survey of research into the mind-body interface.

Garlan, Y., *Recherches de Poliorcétique Grecque* (Athens, École Francaise d'Athens, 1974).
Why Greek cities did not conquer each other's territory.

———, *War in the Ancient World* (London, Chatto and Windus, 1975).
Focuses on social and cultural aspects.

Gat, A., *Clausewitz and the Enlightenment* (Oxford, Oxford University Press, 1989).
The brutal, militaristic, face of Clausewitz reexposed.

Gennep, A. van, *The Rites of Passage* (Chicago, University of Chicago Press, 1960).
The classic work on initiation rites, tests of courage, and the meaning of manhood.

Gilchrist, J. P., *A Brief Display of Ordeals, Trials by Battle, Courts of Chivalry or Honour, and the Decision of Private Quarrels by Single Combat* (London, the author, 1821).
A blow-by-blow account of duels fought in England.

Girard, R., *Violence and the Sacred* (Baltimore, Md., Johns Hopkins University Press, 1977).
The two are by no means as diametrically opposed as appears at first sight.

Glahn, G. von, *The Occupation of Enemy Territory* (Minneapolis, Min., University of Minnesota Press, 1957).
A useful survey of international law as it pertains to this problem.

Gluckman, M., *Custom and Conflict in Africa* (Oxford, Blackwell, 1955).

Goerlitz, C., *History of the German General Staff* (New York, Praeger, 1953).
Tells the story of an institution that used to be the best of its kind.

Golombeck, H., *A History of Chess* (New York, N.Y., Putnam, 1976).

Goltz, C. von der, *The Nation in Arms* (London, W. H. Allen, 1913).
If ever there was a militaristic book, this is it.

Gong, G. W., *The Standard of "Civilization" in International Society* (Oxford, Clarendon Press, 1984).
How Europe exported trinitarian structures and ideas to the rest of the world.

Grant, M., *Gladiators* (London, Weidenfeld and Nicolson, 1967).
Everything you always wanted to know about gladiatorial games and never dared to ask.

Gray, C. S., "War Fighting for Deterrence," *Journal of Strategic Studies* 7, March 1984, pp. 5–28.
A strangelovian essay on how to decapitate the Soviet Union without (hopefully) committing automatic suicide.

Gray, G. J., *The Warriors: Reflections on Men in Battle* (New York, Colophon, 1959).
A perceptive philosopher-soldier thinks about war, battle, love, death, the enemy, and guilt.

Green, P., *Alexander of Macedon* (Harmondsworth, U.K., Penguin Books, 1970).
A portrait of Alexander as a compound of impulsiveness and Machiavellism.

Hackett, J., and others, *The Third World War* (London, Sphere Books, 1978).
World War III as World War II compressed.

Hale, J., "Gunpowder and the Renaissance," in C.H. Carter, ed., *From Renaissance to Counterreformation* (New York, Random House, 1966).

————, "War and Public Opinion in Renaissance Italy," in E. R. Jacob, ed., *Italian Renaissance Studies* (New York, Barnes and Noble, 1960).

Hammond, M., *City-State and World State in Greek and Roman Political Theory until Augustus* (Cambridge, Mass., Harvard University Press, 1951).
Comprehensive treatment of the subject.

Handel, M., ed., *Clausewitz and Modern Strategy* (London, Frank Cass, 1986).

Harper-Bill, C., and Harvey, R., *The Ideals and Practice of Medieval Knighthood* (Suffolk, U.K., Boydell Press, 1987).

Hartigan, R. S., *The Forgotten Victim: a History of the Civilian in War* (Chicago, Precedent, 1982).

———, *Lieber's Code and the Law of War* (Chicago, Precedent, 1983).

Hatto, A. T., "Archery and Chivalry: a Noble Prejudice," *Modern Language Review*, 35, 1940, pp. 40–54.

Heidemann, I., *Der Begriff des Spiels* (Berlin, de Gruyter, 1968).
Follows Schiller and Huizinga in describing play as the only domain where complete freedom is possible.

Herder, J. G., *On Social and Political Culture* (London, Cambridge University Press, 1969).

Herodotus, *The Histories* (Harmondsworth, U.K., Penguin Books, 1954).

Hersh, S. M., *Cover-Up* (New York, Random House, 1972).
The story of My Lai.

Hesse, K., *Der Feldherr-Psychologos* (Berlin, Mittler, 1922).
Yearning for a savior, a post–World War I German officer wrote a superb work on the psychological aspects of military leadership.

Historical Brigade, Office of the Judge Advocate General with the U.S. Forces, ETO, "Statistical Survey–General Courts Martial in the European Theater of Operations", MS 8–3.5 AA, vol. 1, National Archives, Suitland, Md., file No. 204–588 (87).
Who got executed for what reason.

Hobbes, T., *Leviathan* (Oxford, Blackwell, 1946).
Warre as the quintessential human condition.

Holm, J., *Women in the Military* (Novato, Cal., Presidio Press, 1982).

Holmes, R., *Acts of War: the Behavior of Men in Battle* (New York, Free Press, 1985).
Very good on the factors that make men fight; yet shrinks back from the conclusion that those factors also act as the causes of war.

Holt, J.C., and Gillingham, J., eds., *War and Government in the Middle Ages* (Totowa, N.J., Barnes & Noble, 1984).

Homer, *The Illiad* (New York, Doubleday, 1974).
War is for heroes.

———, *The Odyssey* (New York, Harper and Row, 1967).
How one hero was punished for his terrible deeds.

Horne, A., *A Savage War for Peace* (London, Macmillan, 1977).
A massive, if anecdotal, account of how the War in Algeria brought France to the brink of civil war.

Howard, M., ed., *Restraints on War* (Oxford, Oxford University Press, 1979).

Howard, M., *The Causes of War* (Cambridge, Mass., Harvard University Press, 1984).
Contains an excellent short summary of the hardheaded strategic approach.

Howard, M., *War in European History* (Oxford, Oxford University Press, 1976).
Brilliantly articulate short overview with the emphasis on the way war is rooted in society.

Huizinga, J., *Homo Ludens* (Boston, Mass., Beacon ed., 1955).
A great historian reflects on the gamelike elements in war.

———, *The Waning of the Middle Ages* (New York, Doubleday, 1954).

War turned into play as the sign of a declining civilization.

Huntington, S. P., *The Common Defense* (New York, Columbia University Press, 1961).
The standard work on the making of American defense policy.

Huston, N., "The Matrix of War; Mothers and Heroes," in S. Rubin Suleiman ed., *The Female Body in Western Culture* (Cambridge, Mass., Harvard University Press, 1986).
"How long will men make war?—As long as women have children."

Huxley, A., *Brave New World* (London, Chatto and Windus, 1932).
The price of eternal peace.

Inbar, E., "The 'No Choice War' Debate in Israel," *Journal of Strategic Studies* 12, March 1989, pp. 22–37.
How Israel switched from an existential to an instrumental approach to war and was hounded out of Lebanon as a result.

Johnson, J. T., *Just War and the Restraint of War* (Princeton, N.J., Princeton University Press, 1981).

Jolowicz, H. F., *Historical Introduction to the Study of Roman Law* (London, Cambridge University Press, 1952).
Still the best introduction to the subject.

Jomini, A. H., *The Art of War* (Philadelphia, Pa., Lippincott, 1862).
The classic "geometric" approach to strategy.

Juenger, E., *Im Stahlgewittern* (Berlin, Mittler, 1922).
One of the most famous pro-war books ever, written by one who knew it at first hand.

Kahn, H., *On Thermonuclear War* (Princeton, N.J., Princeton University Press, 1960).
Should you want to survive a nuclear war, this book tells you how to do it.

Kalshoven, F., "The Position of Guerrilla Fighters under the Law of War," *Revue du Droit Pénal Militaire et Droit de la Guerre* 11, 1972, pp. 55–90.

Kant, E., *Perpetual Peace, a Philosophical Essay* (New York, Garland ed., 1972).
If only states were democratic there would be no more war.

Kapur, A., *Pakistan's Nuclear Development* (London, Croom Helm, 1987).

Karp, C. M., "The War in Afghanistan," *Foreign Affairs* 64, 5, summer 1986, pp. 1026–47.

Karsten, R., *Blood Revenge, War and Victory Feasts among the Jibaro Indians of Eastern Ecuador* (Washington, D.C., Government Printing Office, 1923).

Kedouri, E., *Nationalism* (London, Hutchinson, 1960).
People are not a nation because they live between the mountain and the river; they live between the mountain and the river because they are a nation.

Keegan, J., *The Face of Battle* (London, Jonathan Cape, 1976).
The battle-pieces are superb, the conclusions perhaps less so.

Keen, M., *Chivalry* (New Haven, Yale University Press, 1984).
Brilliant work on the place of war in medieval culture.

——, *The Law of War in the Late Middle Ages* (London, Routledge, 1965).

Kennan, G. F., *Russia, the Atom, and the West* (New York, Harper and Brothers, 1958).
An American diplomat in Moscow observes Soviet reactions to the American nuclear monopoly.

Kennedy, P. M., "The First World War and the International Power System,"*International Security* 9, 1, summer 1984, pp. 7–40.
An excellent analysis of the strategic origins of the war which completely ignores the reasons why men fought.

Kevles, B., *Females of the Species* Cambridge, Mass., Harvard University Press, 1986).
The position of the female in the animal world.

Kissinger, H., *Nuclear Weapons and Foreign Policy* (New York, Harper and Row, 1957).
An early attempt to set limits and make the world safe for nuclear war.

Knight, W. S. M., *The Life and Works of Hugo Grotius* (London, Sweet & Maxwell, 1925).
Occupies an intermediate position between medieval just war theories and modern ones based on *raison d'etat.*

Koebner, R., *Empire* (London, Cambridge University Press, 1966).
Origin and development of the idea of *Imperium.*

Kohl, W., *French Nuclear Diplomacy* (Princeton, N.J., Princeton University Press, 1971).

Laird, R. F., and Herspring, D. R., eds., *The Soviet Union and Strategic Arms* (Boulder, Co., Westview, 1984).

Laqueur, W., *Guerrilla: a Historical and Critical Study* (London, Weidenfeld and Nicolson, 1977).
Sophisticated and readable, but underestimates the disruptive potential of low intensity war in the modern world.

——, *Terrorism* (London, Weidenfeld and Nicolson, 1977).
Ditto.

Lawson, J., *History of Carolina* (London, Taylor and Baker, 1714).
Contains interesting material on customs connected with North-American Indian warfare.

Leebaert, D., ed., *Soviet Military Thinking* (London, Allen and Unwin, 1981).

Lewis, E., *Medieval Political Ideas* (New York & London, Routledge, 1954).

L'Historie de Guillaume le Maréchal, ed. P. Meyer (Paris, Société de l'Histoire de France, 1901) 3 vols.
A twelfth-century panegyric to a famous knight, written by commission.

Liddell Hart, B.H., *The Ghost of Napoleon* (New Haven, Ct., Yale University Press, 1932).
Clausewitz interpreted as "the Mahdi of Mass."

——, *Strategy* (New York, Praeger, 1967).
The last edition of the twentieth century's most famous work on conventional strategy.

Lin, Chong Pin, *China's Nuclear Weapons Strategy, Tradition within Evolution* (Lexington, Mass., Lexington Books, 1988).
Explains, among other things, why China decided to acquire nuclear weapons.

Livy, Works. (Cambridge, Mass., Harvard University Press, 1953–61) 14 vols.
An extended paean to Roman warfare and essential reading for all its aspects.

Locque, B. de, *Discourses of Warre and Single Combat,* A. Shalvi ed., (Jerusalem, Universities Press, 1968).
Reprint of the 1591 edition.

Lodge, J., ed., *Terrorism: a Challenge to the State* (Oxford, M. Robertsson, 1982).
A country by country survey of terrorism in the EEC and efforts to combat it.

Lorenz, K., *On Aggression* (London, Methuen, 1966).
The twentieth century's best known "ethological" explanation of war.

Loring-Goldman, N., *Female Soldiers—Combatants or Noncombatants?* (Westport, Ct., Greenwood Press, 1982).

Lowman, C., *Displays of Power, Art and War among the Marings of New Guinea* (New York, Museum of Primitive Art, 1973).

Lucian, *A True Story* (Bloomington, Ind., Indiana University Press, 1974).
A tongue-in-cheek description of a world where men prefer warfare to women.

Ludendorff, E., *Der Totale Krieg* (Munich, Ludendorffs Verlag, 1936).

Luttwak, E. N., *Strategy, the Logic of War and Peace* (Cambridge, Mass., Belknap, 1987).
The first chapter was written in heaven.

Luttwak, E. N., and Horowitz, D., *The Israeli Army* (London, Alan Lane, 1975).
Badly in need of updating, but still the best available account, of the period up to 1973 inclusive.

MacDonald, A. C., *Korea, the War before Vietnam* (New York, Free Press, 1986).

Machiavelli, N., *Discourses* London, K. Paul, 1950).

———, *Dell' Arte della Guerra* (Rome, Edizioni Roma, 1936).

———, *The Prince* (Harmondsworth, U.K., Penguin Books, 1961).

Malinowski, B., *Sex, Culture and Myth* (London, Hart-Davis, 1963).
The sexes' role in society as seen by the century's greatest anthropologist.

———, "War and Weapons among the Natives of the Trobriand Islands," *Man* 20, 1920, pp. 5–10.
They played at war.

McElwee, W., *The Art of War from Waterloo to Mons* (London, Weidenfeld and Nicolson, 1974).
The best short work on nineteenth-century warfare.

McNeill, W. H., *The Pursuit of Power: Technology, Armed Force and Society since 1000 A.D.* (New York, Weidenfeld and Nicolson, 1984).

Mead, M., *Male and Female* (Harmondsworth, U.K., Penguin Books, 1950).
A comprehensive treatment of the subject, inspired by Freud and studded with anthropological evidence.

Meinecke, F., *Machiavellism: the Doctrine of Raison d'Etat and its Place in Modern History* (London, Routledge, 1957).

Middlebrook, M., *Task Force: the Falklands War, 1982* (Harmondsworth, U.K., Penguin Books, 1985).
Having finished the book, you still wonder why the British had to fight.

Millet, K., *Sexual Politics* (London, Sphere Books, 1969).
The book that made the feminist revolution.

Milward, A. S., *War, Economy and Society 1939–1945* (Berkeley, Cal., University of California Press, 1977).
Superb on the nonmilitary aspects of mobilization and total war.

Morgan, J. H., *The German War Book* (London, John Murray, 1913).
A translation of the German General Staff's handbook on the laws of war as they then stood.

Moriartry, J. R., *Ritual Combat: a Comparison of the Aztec "War of Flowers" and the Medieval "Melee"* (San Diego, by the author, 1968).

Moskos, C. C., "Female GI's in the Field," in C. C. Moskos, *Soldiers and Sociology* (Washington, D.C., U.S. Government Printing Office, 1989) pp. 33–46.
Based on firsthand observation of mixed companies in training and logistic support missions.

Mosse, G. L., *The Nationalization of the Masses* (New York, Fertig, 1975).
How modern nationalism was made (not born) in order that people should be ready to fight each other.

Murphy, J., and Murphy, F., *Women of the Forest* (New York, Columbia University Press, 1974).
How the "pacification" of a warlike Amazonian tribe caused men to lose their social role.

Murray, H. J. R., *A History of Board Games other than Chess* (Oxford, Clarendon Press, 1952).
A comprehensive catalogue that allows many comparisons between the strategy of games and that of war.

Nietzsche, F., *Human all too Human* (London, Cambridge University Press, 1981).
"A brave army is a convincing argument for the cause in which it fights."

———, *The Will to Power* (New York, Vintage, 1967).
The real cause of war is the will to experience one's power; everything else is merely "epiphenomena."

———, *Thus Spake Zarathustra* (London, Heron, 1957).
"A real man loves two things—danger, and play."

Norbeck, E., "African Rituals of Conflict," *American Anthropologist* 66, 1963, pp. 1254–79.

Nussbaum, A., *Concise History of the Laws of Nations* (New York, Macmillan, 1947).

Nye, J. S., *Nuclear Ethics* (New York, Free Press, 1986).
Balanced and scrupulous, but also vapid; there just isn't any solution.

Oakley, A., *Subject Women: Where Women Stand Today—Politically, Economically, Socially, Educationally* (New York, Pantheon, 1981).

Oakley, R., "International Terrorism," *Foreign Affairs* 65, 3, 1986–87, pp. 611–29.
Gives mixed marks to the Reagan Administration's attempts to deal with the problem.

O'Connel, R. L., "Putting Weapons in Perspective," *Armed Forces and Society* 9, spring 1983, pp. 441–54.
Psychological, social, and anthropological influences on the design and selection of weapons.

Oestreich, G., *Neostoicism and the Origins of the Modern State* (Cambridge, Cambridge University Press, 1982).

Orwell, G., *Nineteen Eighty-Four* (London, Secker and Warburg, 1949).
An end to terrorism—at what price?

Pague de Prate, A. S. Le, *Historie de la Louisiane* (Paris, Leniforme, 1758). 2 vols.
How eighteenth-century Indians made war.

Painter, S., *French Chivalry* (Baltimore, Md., Johns Hopkins University Press, 1940).

Palmer, B., *The 25-Year War: America's Military Role in Vietnam* (New York, Simon and Schuster, 1984).
  Westmoreland's deputy characterizes the U.S. military performance in Vietnam as "satisfactory."

Paret, P., *Clausewitz and the State* (Princeton, N.J., Princeton University Press, 1976).
  Clausewitz presented as a pipe-smoking, slipper-wearing, Western strategist.

Parker, G., *The Army of Flanders and the Spanish Road* (London, Cambridge University Press, 1972).
  The inner workings of a mercenary army explained.

Patton, G., *War as I Knew It* (Boston, Houghton Miflin, 1947).
  How one man can enjoy war.

Phillipson, C., *The International Law and Custom of Ancient Greece and Rome* (London, Macmillan, 1911).
  Still the authoritative work, reprinted in 1979.

Pipes, R., "Why the Soviet Union Thinks it Could Fight and Win a Nuclear War," *Commentary* 64, 1, July 1977, pp. 21–34.
  Why indeed?

Pisan, C. de, *The Fait of Armes & of Chyualerie* (Amsterdam, Theatrum Orbis Terrarum, 1968).

Plato, *Laches* (London, Heinemann, Loeb Classical Library, 1952).
  The question of courage versus military professionalism.

———, *The Laws* (London, Heinemann, Loeb Classical Library, 1953), 2 vols.

———, *The Republic* (Harmondsworth, U.K., Penguin Books, 1955).

Poliakoff, *Combat Sports in the Ancient World: Competition, Violence and Culture* (New Haven, Ct., Yale University Press, 1978).

Polybios, *The Histories* (London, Heinemann, 1922) 6 vols.
  Dry reading, but a first-rate contemporary source on Hellenistic and Roman warfare; in many ways anticipates the modern strategic approach.

Pritchett, W. K., *The Greek State at War* (Berkeley, Ca., University of California Press, 1974-) 3 vols.
  Solid, detailed work on the political, social, cultural, and ideological aspects of Greek war *inter alia*.

Risley, J. S., *The Law of War* (London, Innes, 1897).

Robbins, S., *Auyana, those who Held onto Home* (Seattle, Was., University of Seattle Press, 1982).
  Warfare as practiced by a slash-and-burn, gardening type society of New Guinea.

Rogan, H., *Mixed Company* (New York, Putnam, 1981).
  Documents women's impossible position in an organization from whose principal function—combat—they are excluded.

Rogers, K. M., *The Troublesome Helpmate: a History of Mysogyny in Literature* (Seattle, University of Washington Press, 1966).

Rosalda, M. Z., and Lamphere, L., eds., *Woman, Culture, and Society* (Stanford, Cal., Stanford University Press, 1974).

Ruskin, J., *The Crown of Wild Olive* (London, Basil Wiley, 1878).
  A famous art historian and critic rhapsodizes about the aesthetic value of war.

Russell, F. H., *The Just War in the Middle Ages* (London, Cambridge University Press, 1975).
A brief overview, starting with Augustine.

Sabine, G., *A History of Political Thought* (London, G. Harrap, 1937).
Still very good on everything before 1900.

Schelling, T., *Arms and Influence* (New Haven, Ct., Yale University Press, 1966).
The best work on strategy written since 1945.

Schelling, T., *The Strategy of Conflict* (Cambridge, Mass., Harvard University Press, 1960).
Strategy as a double-sided exercise common to war and games.

Schmitt, C., *The Concept of the Political* (Reading, Mass., Addison-Wesley, 1976).
The monopoly on legitimate violence as the quintessential attribute of the state.

Segal, G., *Defending China* (New York, Oxford University Press, 1985).

Segaller, S., *Invisible Armies, Terrorism into the 1990s* (New York, Harcourt Brace Jovanovitch, 1986).
Many fascinating details on the spread of present-day terrorism and the way states react to it.

Semmel, B., ed., *Marxism and the Science of War* (Oxford, Oxford University Press, 1981).
An anthology of pertinent writings by Marx, Engels, Lenin, Trotsky, Stalin, Mao Tze Dong, Lin Bao, and others.

Service, E. R., *Primitive Social Organization* (New York, Random House, 1962).

Sheehan, N., *A Bright Shining Lie: John Vann and the American Experience in Vietnam* (New York, Random House, 1988).
How the three M's (men, money, machines) proved counterproductive in the war of the strong against the weak.

Silberner, E., *La guerre dans la pensée économique du xvi au xvii siècle* (Paris, Librairie de Recueil Sirey, 1939)
Explains the enlightenment view of war as a game for kings and other useless aristocrats.

Smith, S. B., "Hegel's Views on War, the State and International Relations," *The American Political Science Review* 7, 1983, pp. 624–32.
War as the factor that creates nations and helps to keep them going.

Speer, A., *Inside the Third Reich* (New York, Macmillan, 1970).
Total war as seen by one of its principal architects.

Spinney, F., *Defense Facts of Life* (Boulder, Co., Westview, 1986).
How not even the richest power on earth can afford to buy and maintain modern weapons.

Sterling, C., *The Terror Network* (New York, Berkley Books, 1982).

Summers, H., *On Strategy: A Critical Analysis of the Vietnam War* (Novato, Cal., Presidio Press, 1982).
An American officer blames the politicians for the army's failure in Vietnam.

Sun Tzu, *The Art of War* (Oxford, Oxford University Press, 1963).
The best work on war ever written.

Tacitus, *Germania* (Middletown, Conn., American Philological Association, 1935).

Interesting for the role of war and wargames among early Germanic tribes.

Taylor, F. W., *The Principles of Scientific Management* (New York, Harper and Row, 1911).
A famous engineer explains his recipe for achieving efficiency.

The Song of Roland (Harmondsworth, U.K., Penguin Books, 1937).
Absolutely essential for understanding medieval attitudes to war and heroism.

Thucydides, *History of the Peloponnesisn War* (Harmondsworth, U.K., Penguin Books, 1954).
A grand panorama of every aspect of Greek politics and warfare.

Tiger, L., *Men in Groups* (London, Nelson, 1969).
Had men not made war, of what use would they be?

Tölle-Kastenbein, R., *Pfeil und Bogen im Antiken Griechenland* (Bochum, Duris, 1980).

Tsipis, K., *Arsenal: Understanding Weapons in the Nuclear Age* (New York, Simon and Schuster, 1983).
An up-to-date survey of nuclear weapons, by a real expert.

Turney-High, J. H., *Primitive War, its Practice and Concepts* (Columbia, S.C., University of South Carolina Press, 1971).
Probably the best single work on the subject; argues that the essence of war is organization and that tribal societies have not discovered it.

Ullmann, W., *A History of Political Thought: the Middle Ages* (Harmondsworth, U.K., Penguin Books, 1965).

——, *The Individual and Society in the Middle Ages* (London, Methuen, 1967).

——, *Law and Politics in the Middle Ages* (Ithaca, N.Y., Cornell University Press, 1975).
All these works are concerned with the way medieval "politics" were rooted in law.

Vagts, A., *A History of Militarism* (New York, Norton, 1937).
Rightly denounces the trappings of militarism as obstacles to military efficiency, yet overlooks their importance for military morale.

Vattel, E., *The Law of Nations* (Philadelphia, Pa., Johnson, 1852).
The classic eighteenth-century work setting out the legal theory of trinitarian warfare.

Veblen, Th., *The Theory of the Leisure Class* (New York, Macmillan, 1899).
How the vocation of the upper class—be it war or anything else—becomes a social ideal.

Vernant, J. P., ed., *Problèmes de la guerre en Grèce ancienne* (Paris, Mouton, 1968).
Includes essays on the limitation of war and the treatment of the defeated.

Walzer, M., *Just and Unjust Wars: a Moral Argument with Historical Illustrations* (New York, Basic Books, 1977).
A Vietnam-inspired inquiry into the relationship between war and justice in the modern age.

Waltz, K. N., *The Spread of Nuclear Weapons: More May be Better* (Adelphi Papers No. 171, London, International Institute of Strategic Studies, 1981).
Though the thesis is thoroughly un-American, it may have greater merit than originally thought.

Wavell, A., *Soldiers and Soldiering* (London, Jonathan Cape, 1953).
A British Fieldmarshal reflects on the things that make men fight and endure.

Weiler, J., *Der Agon im Mythos, zur Einstellung der Griechen zur Wettkampf* (Darmstadt, Wissenschaftliche Buchgesellschaft, 1974).
The relationship between war and sport in the ancient world.

Westmoreland, W. C., *A Soldier Reports* (New York, Doubleday, 1976).
Considering the reputation Westmoreland has acquired in the eyes of many, his memoires are surprisingly solid and informative.

Wilson, A., *The Bomb and the Computer* (London, Barnie and Rockliff, 1968).

Wright, C., "Feudalism and the Hundred Years' War," in E. Leach, S. N. Mukherjee and J. Ward, eds., *Feudalism: Comparative Studies* (Sydney, Sydney Association for Studies in Society and Culture, 1985).
Good on the economic basis of late feudal warfare and, by analogy, modern low-intensity conflicts between irregular forces.

Wright, Q., *A Study of War* (Chicago, University of Chicago Press, 1941).

Index